P9-DMX-075

THE RIVERSIDE HISTORY
OF THE
UNITED STATES

WILLIAM E. DODD, EDITOR

THE NEW NATION

BY

FREDERIC L. PAXSON

PROFESSOR OF HISTORY
UNIVERSITY OF WISCONSIN

BOSTON AND NEW YORK
HOUGHTON MIFFLIN COMPANY
The Riverside Press Cambridge

PREFACE

A NEW nation has appeared within the United States since the Civil War, but it has been only accidentally connected with that catastrophe. The Constitution emerged from the confusion of strife and reconstruction substantially unchanged, but the economic development of the United States in the sixties and seventies gave birth to a society that was, by 1885, already national in its activities and necessities. In many ways the history of the United States since the Civil War has to do with the struggle between this national fact and the old legal system that was based upon state autonomy and federalism; and the future depends upon the discovery of a means to readjust the mechanics of government, as well as its content, to the needs of life. This book attempts to narrate the facts of the last half-century and to show them in their relations to the larger truths of national development.

FREDERIC L. PAXSON.

CONTENTS

MAPS AND CHARTS

THE NEW NATION

THE NEW NATION

CHAPTER I

THE CIVIL WAR

THE military successes of the United States in
its Civil War maintained the Union, but entailed
readjustments in politics, finance, and business that
shifted the direction of public affairs for many years.
In the eyes of contemporaries these changes were
obscured by the vivid scenes of the battlefield, whose
intense impressions were not forgotten for a generation. It seemed as though the war were everything, as though the Republican party had preserved
the nation, as though the nation itself had arisen
with new plumage from the stress and struggle of
its crisis. The realities of history, however, which
are ever different from the facts seen by the partici-
pant, are in this period further from the tradition of
the survivor than in any other stage of the development of the United States. As the Civil War is
viewed from the years that followed it, the actu-
alities that must be faced are the facts that the
dominant party saved neither the nation nor itself
except by changing its identity; that economic and
industrial progress continued through the war with
unabated speed, and that out of the needs of a new
economic life arose the new nation.

The Republican party, whose older spokesmen had been trained as Whigs or Democrats, had by 1861 seasoned its younger leaders in two national campaigns. It had lost the first flush of the new enthusiasm which gave it birth as a party opposed to the extension of slavery. The signs of the times had been so clear between 1856 and 1860 that many politicians had turned their coats less from a moral principle than from a desire to win. When Lincoln took up the organization of his Administration, these clamored for their rewards. There was nothing in the political ethics of the sixties that discountenanced the use of the spoils of office, and Lincoln himself, though he resented the drain of office-seeking upon his time, appears not to have seen that the spoils system was at variance with the fundamentals of good government.

It was a Republican partisan administration that bore the first brunt of the Civil War, but the struggle was still young when Lincoln realized that the Union could not stand on the legs of any single party. To develop a general Union sentiment became an early aim of his policy and is a key to his period. He was forced to consider and reconcile the claims of all shades of Republican opinion, from that of the most violent abolitionist to that of the mere unionist. In the Democracy, opinion ranged from that of the strong war Democrat to that of the Copperhead whose real sympathies were with the Confederacy.

To conciliate a working majority of the voters of the Union States, a majority which must embrace

many Union Democrats, Lincoln steadily loosened
the partisan bonds. The congressional elections of
1862 showed that he was still far from success. His
overtures to the Democrats of the border States fell
into line with his general scheme. His tolerance of
McClellan and his support of Stanton, both of whom
by sympathy and training were Democrats, reveal
the comprehensive power of his endurance. As the
election of 1864 approached to test the success of
his generalship, he had to fight not only for a majority in the general canvass but for the nomination
by his own party.

There were many men in 1864 who believed that
the war was a mistake and that Lincoln was a
failure. The peace Democrats denounced him as a
military dictator; to the radical Republicans he was
spineless and irresolute. Within his own Cabinet
there was dissension that would have unnerved a less
steady man. Chase, the Secretary of the Treasury,
wanted to be President, and had allowed his friends
to intrigue in his behalf, yet had not withdrawn
from the counsels of his rival. At various times he
had threatened to resign, but Lincoln had shut his
eyes to this infidelity and had coaxed him back.
Not until after the President had been renominated
did he accept the resignation of Chase, and even
then he was willing to make the latter Chief Justice
of the Supreme Court.

Chase, in the Cabinet and in touch with dissatisfied Republicans outside, was a menace to impartial
administration. Less distressing, but noisier than he,
was John C. Frémont, the first nominee of the

party, who had sulked in the midst of admiring
friends since Lincoln had removed him from important military service in 1861. About him the extreme abolitionists were gathered, and in his favor
there was held a convention in May, 1864. But this
dissenting movement collapsed upon itself before
the elections in November.

The Republicans went into convention at Baltimore, on June 7, 1864. The candidacy of Chase
had faded, that of Frémont was already unimportant, and the renomination of Lincoln was assured.
But the party carefully concealed its name and, cater-
ing to loyalists of whatever brand, it called itself
" Union," and invited to its support all men to
whom the successful prosecution of the war was the
first great duty. It was a Union party in fact as
well as name. Delegations of Democrats came to it
from the border States, and from one of these the
convention picked a loyal Democrat for the Vice-
Presidency. With Lincoln and Andrew Johnson on
its ticket, with a platform silent upon the protective
tariff, and with an organization so imperfect that no
roll of delegates could be made until the convention
had been called to order, the Administration party
of 1864 was far from being the same organization that
had, in 1856, voiced its protest against the Kansas-
Nebraska Bill.

The excesses of the Democrats aided Lincoln almost as much as the efforts of the party which nominated him. A convention at Chicago, in August,
presided over by Governor Seymour, of New York,
and under the dominance of Clement L. Vallandig-

ham, did not need to denounce the war as a failure in order to disappoint the Union Democrats. Not even the nomination of McClellan, nor his repudiation of the platform, could undo the result of such leadership. It was far from certain which ticket would receive the greater vote in November, but it was clear that union against disunion was the issue, and that men would vote according to their hopes and fears. The former were in the ascendant when the polls were opened, for Sherman had gained a decisive victory in his occupation of Atlanta, while Farragut had gained another at Mobile Bay. On the strength of these successes the Union ticket carried every State but Delaware, Kentucky, and New Jersey.

Chase, who left the Treasury during the presidential campaign, had by that time finished the work which carried the financial burdens of the Civil War and provided party texts for another generation. He had come to his task without special fitness, but had speedily mastered the essentials of war finance. In his reports he outlined the policy which Congress followed, more or less closely. Taxes ought to be increased, he urged, to meet all the costs of civil administration, interest on the debt, and sinking fund for the same. These were current burdens which the country ought not to try to escape. But the extra cost of the war, which was to be regarded as a permanent investment by the Union for its own defense, might fairly be made a charge upon posterity. To meet these he urged the creation of a sufficient bonded debt.

The Thirty-seventh Congress (1861–63) had been

more ready to borrow than to tax. In all its experience until 1861 the United States had met no
crisis in which large revenues had been required. In
the thirty preceding years its total annual receipts
had ranged from $20,000,000 to $81,000,000, while
in the fiscal year in which the war began the total
had reached $83,000,000, of which $41,000,000
were loans rather than revenue. Since the panic of
1857 the Treasury had faced a deficit at the end of
each year, and had been compelled not only to spend
its accumulated surplus on current needs, but to
borrow heavily. The tariff duties, collected at the
custom-houses, were, as they always had been, the
mainstay of the revenue. But these had not met
the needs of the three lean years before the war.

Had there been no war, the disordered finances of
the United States might, in 1861, have called for
corrective measures and new taxes, and these could
not have become effective before 1862 or 1863. As
it was, loans were resorted to for first-aid. In 1862
they alone were more than six times as great as the
total receipts of 1861; in 1865 they were nearly
three times as great as in 1862. Taxes were authorized more reluctantly than loans, they became profitable more slowly, and did not, until the last year
of war, reveal the fiscal capacities of the United
States.

The favorite national tax of the United States had
always been the tariff. Supplemented by miscellaneous items which included no internal revenue after
1849, and no direct tax after 1839, it carried most
of the financial burdens. Whether parties preferred

it high or low, or levied it for protection or for revenue, they had continued to cherish it as a fiscal device, and had acquired no experience with alternate sources of supply. Like the army of the United States, which in time of war had to break in its volunteer levies before it could win victories, the Treasury and Congress had to learn how to tax before they could bring the taxable resources of the United States to supplement the loans.

The tariff was revised and increased several times between 1861 and 1865, and yielded its greatest return, $102,000,000, in 1864. The result was due to both the swelling volume of imports and the higher rates. Like all panics, that of 1857 had lessened the buying capacity of the American people. In hard times luxuries were sacrificed and treasury receipts were thereby greatly curtailed. A return to normal conditions of business would have been visible by 1861 had not war obscured it. Steadily through the war a prosperous North and West bought more foreign goods regardless of the price.

The rate of tariff was based upon the probable revenue, the protective principle, and the tax burdens already imposed upon American manufacturers. Not until 1863 were the internal or direct taxes noticeable, but in 1864 these passed the tariff as a source of revenue, with a total of $116,000,000. In 1866 this total was swollen to $211,000,000. Like the tariff, the income, excise, and direct taxes were often revised and raised, and many of the tariff increases were dependent upon them. When the American manufacturer, who already declared that he could stay in business only because the tariff protected him from European competition, found himself burdened with a tax on his income and with others upon his commercial transactions and his output, he complained bitterly of the disadvantage at which he was placed. To equalize his burdens, the import rates were repeatedly raised against the foreigner. By the end of the war, the tariff exceeded anything known in American experience, and was fixed less with the intention of raising revenue than of enabling the American producer to pay his internal tax. Less than $85,000,000 were collected from the customs in 1865; while $211,000,000 came from internal sources.

By taxing and borrowing the United States accumulated $88,000,000 in 1861, $589,000,000 in 1862, $888,000,000 in 1863, $1,408,000,000 in 1864, and $1,826,000,000 in 1865. The Treasury, unimportant in the world's affairs before 1861, suddenly became one of the greatest dealers in credit. Its debt of $2,808,000,000, outstanding in October, 1865, affected the interests and solidity of international finance, and indicated, as well, resources of which even boastful Americans had been unaware in 1861. One item in the debt, however, was a menace to the security of the whole, which was but little stronger than its weakest part.

The physical currency in which the debt was to be created and the expenses paid was as difficult to find in 1861 as the wealth which it measured. After Jackson destroyed the second Bank of the United States there had been no national currency but coin, and too little of that. Gold and silver had been coined at the mint, and the former had given the standard to the dollar. In intrinsic worth the gold dollar, as defined in 1834 at the ratio of sixteen to one, was slightly inferior to its silver associate, and by the law of human nature, which induces men to hold the better and pass the cheaper money, the value of the gold coin had become the measure of exchange.

The coined money did not circulate generally. It was devoted to a part of the business of government, and to the needs of the banks which provided the actual circulating medium. Scattered over all the States, hundreds of state and private banks issued their own notes to serve as money. At best, and in theory, these were exchangeable for gold at par; at worst, they were a total loss; yet as they were, variant and depreciated since the panic of 1857, they were the money of the people when the Civil War began. Before the end of 1861 the banks gave up the pretense of redeeming their notes in coin. The United States Treasury suspended the payment of specie early in 1862, and thereafter for seventeen years the paper money in circulation depended for its value on the hope that it would some day be redeemed.

The needs of the Treasury, in the crisis of suspension, induced Congress to authorize the emission of $450,000,000 of legal-tender paper money. These notes, soon known as the "greenbacks," became the measure of the difference between standard money and coin. Issued at par, they sank in value and fluctuated until in the darkest days of 1864 a dollar in gold could be exchanged for $2.85 in greenbacks. Yet they were called dollars, and the creditor was forced to accept them in payment of his debts. They were themselves a forced loan, borrowed by compulsion from the people, and constituting $433,000,000 in the total debts of the United States in 1865.

The greenback element in the national debt threatened the integrity of the whole. Should redemption take place at par, and at once, the credit of the United States could not fail to be strengthened. But should the greenbacks be allowed to remain below par, should more of them be issued, or should the United States avail itself of its technical privilege to pay off part of the bonded debt in "lawful money" manufactured by the printing-press, the weakest item in the total might easily depress the whole.

The future of American politics after 1865 was largely determined by the methods through which the revenue had been increased and by the fate of the greenbacks, but more important for the immediate future than either of these was the great fact that in five years the United States had been able to incur its net debt of $2,808,000,000, and had raised in addition more than $700,000,000 through taxation. It was a prosperous Union that emerged from the Civil War, and every region but the South was strong in its conscious wealth.

The whole of the United States had shared in the unusual growth in the period following the Mexican War, in which the new railroads were tying the Mississippi Valley to the seaboard. The census of 1860 reported an increase of 36 per cent in total population in ten years, somewhat unevenly divided, since the Confederate area had increased but 25 per cent, as compared with 39 per cent in the North and West, yet large enough everywhere to keep up the traditions of a growing population. The growth continued in the next decade, despite the Civil War. It is not to be expected that it should have touched the record of the fifties, for 2,500,000 men were drawn from production for at least three years — the three years in which most of them would have grown to manhood and married, had there been no war. The South, desolated by war, and with nearly every able-bodied white man in the ranks, stood still, with under 9 per cent increase. But the whole country grew in population from 31,443,321 to 38,558,371 (22 per cent), while the North and West, in spite of war, grew 27 per cent, — more than the South had done in its most brilliant decade.

How far the North and West would have gone had they not been hampered by the depression after 1857 cannot be stated. These regions had suffered most from the panic, since in them railroads and banks, factories and cities, and all the agents of a complex industrial organization had been most active. The industrial disturbance had disarranged for the time the elaborate Northern system. The simpler South, with its staple crops, its rural population, and its few railways, had suffered less. Southerners before the war had seen in their immunity from the effects of panic a proof of their superiority over

other social orders; they had misread the times and
prophesied the disintegration of the industrial organization of the North.

The South seceded before the rest of the United
States emerged from the panic period. In the next
four years the treasury receipts show the resources
of the loyal States. Industry, recovered from its depression, went ahead unnoticed in the noise of war,
yet little impeded by the fact of war.

Communication by rail brought the most significant
of the single changes into the Northern States. Before the panic of 1857 the trunk-line railways had
completed their net of tracks between the Mississippi
and tidewater. Nearly ten thousand miles had been
built in the Old Northwest alone in the ten preceding years. But the effect of this on business, certain
to come in any event, was not seen until secession
closed the Mississippi to the agricultural exports of
the Northwest. For a part of 1861 and 1862 traffic
piled up along the young railroads extending from
St. Louis and Chicago to Buffalo, Pittsburg, New
York, and Philadelphia. But before 1863 these lines,
notably the New York Central, the Erie, and the
Pennsylvania, had adapted themselves to the trade
which the South had thrust upon them; and never
since secession has New Orleans regained her place
as the great outlet of the Mississippi Valley.

The fundamental change in the direction of its
trade added to the prosperity of the North. In the
additions to the transportation system, made to ac-
commodate the new business, new railroads were
less prominent than second tracks, bridges, tunnels,

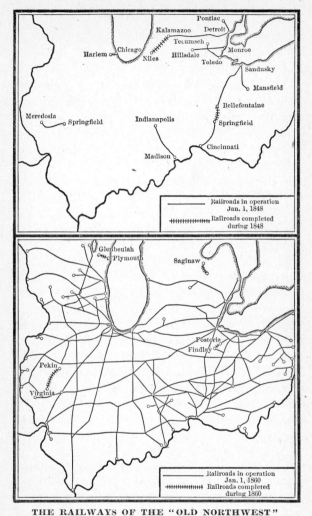

THE RAILWAYS OF THE "OLD NORTHWEST"

Showing the development between 1848 and 1860, upon which the Civil War prosperity of the region was based

and terminal facilities. The experimental years of railroading had passed before most of the lines learned the importance of city terminals. The growth of the cities and the rising price of land made the attainment of these more difficult than they need have been, while city governments and their officials learned that illicit profits could be made out of the necessities of the railroads. The great lines, active in the development of their plants, and consolidating during the sixties to get the benefits of unified management, added to the bustle in the cities in the North.

The United States was an agricultural country until the beginning of manufacturing and the revolution in communication made it profitable to concentrate people and capital in the cities. Between 1850 and 1880 the number of cities with a population of 50,000 more than doubled. The actual construction of the houses, the water and lighting systems, and the sewers for these communities gave employment to labor. As cities grew, their more generous distances brought in the street-car companies, whose occupation of the public streets added to the temptations and opportunities of the officials of government. The swelling manufactures increased the city groups and gave them work.

The country life itself began to change. The typical farming families, developed by pioneer conditions, had remained the social unit for several generations, but these felt the lure of the cities which drew their boys and girls into the factories. Domestic manufactures could not compete in quality, appearance, or price with the output of the new factories. The farmer began to give up his slaughtering and butter-making, as he had already abandoned his spinning and weaving, and devoted himself more exclusively to raising crops. Here, too, the mechanical improvements touched his life. Agricultural machinery was coming into general use, while the new railroads carried off his produce to the great markets which the rising cities created.

The number of employees of American factories increased more than half between 1860 and 1870, while the capital invested and the goods turned out were more than doubled. The United States was for the first time looking to a day when all the ordinary necessities of life could be made within its limits. At Chicago, St. Louis, New York, Boston, Philadelphia, and a host of cities in the interior, men were not disturbed by the war in their attempt to exploit the abundant resources of the continent. The manufacture of food began to shift from the household to the city factory, to the advantage of the cities lying near the great fresh areas of farm lands. The flour mills of the Northwest, the meat-packing establishments at Chicago and elsewhere, the distilleries of central Illinois, utilized the agricultural staples and transformed them for export. The presence of factories forced upon the city governments, East and West, already embarrassed by the pains of rapid growth, the problems of police power and good government. Charters written for semi-rural villages were inadequate when the villages became cities.

Clothing, no less than food, passed into the factory,

thanks to Elias Howe and his sewing-machine and the shoe machinery of McKay. Before the war the influences of this change were visible in the increasing demand for cotton. Now came the great growth of the textile regions of the East, around Fall River and Philadelphia, and of the shoe factories in the Lynn district.

The use and manufacture of machines gave new stimulus to those regions where coal and iron, placed conveniently with reference to transportation, had fixed the location of smelters and rolling-mills. In the middle of the sixties Henry Bessemer's commercial process for the manufacture of steel marks the beginning of a revolution in the construction of railroads and bridges, as well as in public and private architecture. Pittsburg became the heart of the steel industry, and the young men who controlled it fixed their hands upon the commercial future of the United States. The newest of industries, the trade in petroleum and its oils, reached fifteen millions in Pittsburg alone in 1864.

The trunk-line railways with their spurs and branches adjusted themselves early in the war to the new direction of business currents. They then began to carry the new inhabitants into the cities, the new manufactures to their markets, and to press upon iron, coal, and timber for their own supplies. Men of business laid the foundations of huge fortunes in supplying the new and growing demands. The stock company, with negotiable shares and bonds, made it possible for the small investor to share in the larger commercial profits and losses.

The growth and elaboration of companies and commerce were projected upon a legal system that was most accustomed to small enterprises and local trade. Not only had the corporations to establish customs and precedents among themselves, but courts, legislatures, and city councils had to face the need for an amplification of American law. The speed with which the new life swept upon the country, the inexperience of both business men and jurists, the public ignorance of the extent to which the revolution was to go, and the cross-purposes inevitable when States tried to regulate the affairs of corporations larger than themselves, make it unnecessary to search further for the key to the confusing half-century that followed the Civil War.

The rapid changes in manufacturing, transportation, urban life, and business law that came with the prosperity of the early sixties gave to these years an appearance of materialism that has misled many observers. None of the developments received full contemporary notice, for war filled the front pages of the newspapers. The men who directed them were not under scrutiny, and could hardly fail to bring into business and speculation that main canon of war time that the end is everything and that it justifies the means. But though war was not the sole American occupation between 1861 and 1865, and though a new industrial revolution was begun, material things often gave way in the American mind to altruistic concepts and the service of the ideal.

Congress endowed the agricultural colleges in the early years of the war, and the state universities, though thinned by the enlistment of their boys, established themselves. The creation of new universities, the endowment of older foundations, and the beginning of an education that should fit not only for law, medicine, and theology, but for business, agriculture, engineering, and teaching, all bear testimony to the real interests of American democracy. The ideal was as yet far removed from the fact, and the intellectual leaders of the United States were yet to pass through a period of black pessimism, but the people were still firm in their faith that education is the mainstay of popular government, and gave their full devotion to both.

The four years of the Civil War carried the United States over a period of social and economic transition and left it well started on the new course. They enlarged and expanded the activities of government, hastening that day when there should exist a public conviction that government is a matter of technical expertness and must be run in a scientific manner for the common good. They raised the problems of taxation and currency to a new importance, and impressed their significance upon the men who directed the industries of the country. In their prosperity they made it possible to save the Union ; and at their close a Union party, uncertain of its strength and its personnel, faced the problems of a united country which included an industrial North, a desolated South, and a vanishing frontier.

BIBLIOGRAPHICAL NOTE

For further references upon the Civil War period, consult William E. Dodd, *Expansion and Conflict* (in this series), and F. L. Paxson, *The Civil War* (1911). The best and most exhaustive narrative is J. F. Rhodes, *History of the United States from the Compromise of 1850 to the Final Restoration of Home Rule at the South in 1877* (7 vols., 1892–1906), and this may be supplemented to advantage by E. D. Fite, *Social and Industrial Conditions in the North during the Civil War* (1910). There is a convenient account of the election of 1864, with platforms and tables of votes, in E. Stanwood, *A History of the Presidency* (1898) and there are many valuable documents in E. McPherson's annual *Political Manual*. The biographies of W. H. Seward, by F. Bancroft, and Jay Cooke, by E. P. Oberholtzer, are among the best of the period. There are no better summaries of finances than D. R. Dewey's *Financial History of the United States* (1903, etc.) ; W. C. Mitchell's *History of the Greenbacks* (1903) ; and J. A. Woodburn's *Thaddeus Stevens* (1913). In the *Annual Cyclopædia* (published by D. Appleton & Co., 1861–1902) are useful and accurate accounts of current affairs. E. L. Godkin began to publish the *Nation* in New York in the summer of 1865, and H. V. Poore issued the first volume of his annual *Manual of the Railroads of the United States*, in 1868.

CHAPTER II

THE WEST AND THE GREENBACKS

THE activity of the North and the East between 1861 and 1865 was imitated and magnified among the youthful communities that made up the western border and ranged in age from a few weeks to thirty years. These had been mostly agricultural in 1857. Iowa, Minnesota, Wisconsin, and Kansas had been the frontier before the Civil War. In place of these, now grown to be populous and more or less sedate, a new group appeared farther west, within what had been believed to be the " American Desert." By 1868 Congress completed the subdivision of the last lands between the Missouri River and the Pacific, since which date only one new political division has appeared in the United States.

The last frontier, that developed after 1857, was novel as well as new. It was made up of mining-camps. Everywhere in the Rocky Mountains prospectors staked out claims and introduced their free-and-easy life. Before 1857 the group of Mormons around the Great Salt Lake was the only considerable settlement between eastern Kansas and California. Now came in quick succession the rush to Pike's Peak and Colorado Territory (1861), the rush from California to the Carson Valley and Nevada Territory (1861), and the creation of the agricultural territory of Dakota (1861) for the up-river Missouri country, where in a few more years were revealed the riches of the Black Hills. In 1863 the mines of the lower Colorado River gave excuse for Arizona Territory. Those of the northern Continental Divide were grouped in Idaho in the same year, and divided in 1864 when Montana was created. Wyoming, the last of the subdivisions, was the product of mines and railroads in 1868. Oklahoma was not named for twenty years more, but had existed in its final shape since the passage of the Kansas-Nebraska Bill in 1854.

The legitimate influence of these mining-camps upon the United States was great. It was no new thing for Congress to solve its national problems on the initiative of the West. Since the passage of the Ordinance of 1787 this had been a frequent occurrence, and the history of the public lands had always been directed by Western demands. In 1862 the agricultural West, whose capacity to cultivate land had been magnified by the new reaper of McCormick, had obtained its Homestead Act, by which land titles were conveyed to the farmer who cleared the land and used it. Thomas H. Benton had fought for this through a long lifetime. He died too soon to see the full apotheosis of the squatter, who gradually developed, in point of law, from the criminal stealing the public land to the public-spirited pioneer in whose interest a wise Congress ought to shape its laws. Under the influence of this new Homestead Law, aided by the Preëmption Law, which remained in force, land titles were established in the Mountain States as rapidly as the Indians could be removed.

The frontier mining territories were loud in demanding that Congress should give them more land, remove the Indians, extend police protection, and give them mails and railroads. The miner disliked the isolation which his speculations brought upon him, and Congress unfolded new powers to remove it for him. In 1858 it organized the great overland mail that ran coaches to California in less than twenty-five days. The pony express provided faster service in 1860–61. And after private money had built the telegraph line to the Pacific, both Congress and the West took up the subject of a continental railway.

In the summer of 1862 a group of railroad companies was authorized to build a track from the Missouri River (which had already been reached at St. Joseph by a railway from the East) to California. As modified by law in 1864 the contract provided for extensive government aid in the speculation: twenty sections of land for every mile of track, and a loan of United States bonds at the rate of at least $16,000 per mile. But the West had little capital, and the prosperous East had better investments at home, so that money could hardly be got into this scheme on any terms. The Western promoters were driven to shifty extremes before they overcame the Eastern belief that no continental railroad could pay. Not until 1866 was the construction work begun in earnest.

Between 1866 and 1869 the building of the Union

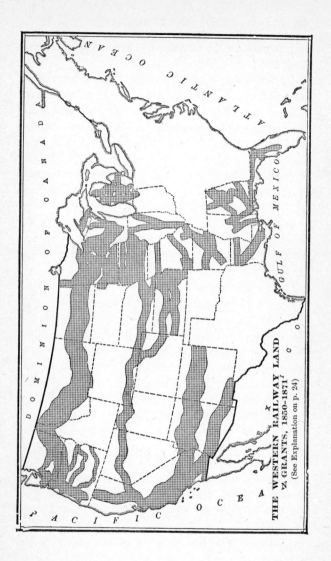

THE WESTERN RAILWAY LAND
GRANTS, 1850-1871
(See Explanation on p. 24)

Explanation of the map of

THE WESTERN RAILWAY LAND GRANTS, 1850–1871

(This map is based upon the one in Donaldson, Public Domain, 948, and includes certain wagon-road lands.)

There never were any public lands in the State of Texas. Oklahoma lay within the Indian Country in which no lands were available for grants between 1850 and 1871.

The railway land grants, authorized between 1850 and 1871 lay within the areas shaded, and consisted, in all cases, of alternate sections on each side of the track. The sections retained by the United States were, however, withdrawn from entry upon filing of the railway survey, and remained withdrawn until the railway allotment had been made. Regions thus impeded in their development often became centers of hostility toward the railroads.

Pacific was the most picturesque enterprise in America. Across the great plains, the desert, and the mountains, from Council Bluffs to Sacramento, it was pushed. In the West, Stanford and his group of California visionaries carried the burden. The eastern end brought out no single great promoter. Both ends fought the problem of timber and stone and railroad iron, but most of all of labor. Stanford finally imported the Chinese coolie for the job. Civil War veterans and new immigrants did most of the work on the eastern end. And along the eastern stretches the Indian tribes of the plains watched the work with jealous eyes. The Pawnee, the Sioux, the Arapaho, and the Cheyenne saw in the new road the end of a tribal life based upon wild game.

Severe Indian outbreaks accompanied the construction of the railroad, as the tribes made their last stand in Wyoming, Colorado, and the Indian Territory. Before the line was done, the tribes of the plains were under control in two great concentration camps, in South Dakota and Indian Territory, and the worst of the Indian fighting in the West was over.

In the spring of 1869 the railroad was finished and a spectacular celebration was held near Ogden, in Utah Territory. The finishing stroke was everywhere regarded as national, since not only had Congress given aid, but the union of the oceans was an object of national ambition. With the completion, the problem shifted from the exciting risks of construction and finance to the prosaic duties of paying the bills, and with the shift came a natural falling-off in enthusiasm.

The Union Pacific was the longest railroad of the sixties, and aroused the greatest interest. In an economic way it is merely typical of the speculative expansion of the North that began early in the Civil War and continued increasingly thereafter. The United States was engaged in a period of hopeful growth such as has followed every panic. After a few years of depression, stagnation, and enforced economy, business had revived about 1861. Confidence had increased, loans had been made more freely, and capital had taken up again its search for profitable investment. In the newer regions, where permanent improvements were least numerous, the field for exploitation had been great. The climax of exploitation was reached throughout the West.

As had been true at all the stages of the westward movement, the West was heavily in debt, and upon a forced balance would generally have shown an excess of liabilities over assets. Borrowed money paid much of the cost of emigration. During the first year the pioneer often raised no crops and lived upon his savings or his borrowings. He and his local merchant and his bank and his new railroad had borrowed all they could, while the creditor, living necessarily in the older communities where saving had created a surplus for investment, lived in the East, or even in Europe. The necessary conditions of settlement and development had prepared the way for a new sectional alignment of business interests, those of the Far West and the Northwest taking their tone from the interests of a debtor class, while those of the East represented those of the creditor. The possible cleavage was revealed as real when the United States Treasury Department, in its work toward financial reconstruction, approached the subject of the greenbacks.

The legal-tender greenbacks, which were in circulation to the extent of $433,000,000 in 1865, constituted not only a part of the debt of the war, but the foundation of the currency in circulation. Throughout most of the war they were supplemented by the notes of state banks, local token-money, and fractional currency, or "shinplasters," of the United States. Coin ceased to circulate in 1862 and was used only by those whose contracts obliged them to pay in gold or silver. In 1863 Secretary Chase inaugurated a system of national banks, to circulate a uniform currency, secured by United States bonds, but these did not become a factor in business until the state bank notes had been taxed out of existence in 1865. After this time national banks were formed in large numbers, replacing the uncertain notes of the state banks with their own notes, which were quite as good as greenbacks. But all paper money was below par in 1865, and gold remained out of circulation, at a premium, until the end of 1878.

The depreciation of the greenbacks reflected a popular doubt as to the outcome of the Civil War. They entailed hardship upon all who received them as dollars, since their purchasing value was below the standard of one hundred cents in gold. When the Government, desperate in war time, forced its creditors to accept them at par, it did an injustice which it regarded as real, though necessary. The speedy restoration of the greenbacks to par received the immediate attention of the Treasury upon the return of peace.

Hugh McCulloch, of Indiana, who became Secretary of the Treasury in 1865, was a banker of long experience and success. He proposed, if allowed, to reduce the whole war debt, including the greenbacks, to long-term bonds bearing a low rate of interest, and to create a sinking fund which should redeem them as they fell due. This involved the withdrawal from circulation of the greenbacks, and the destruction of that amount of the money used in business. Congress authorized it, however, and McCulloch canceled greenbacks from month to month until he had reduced the total to $356,000,000 in February, 1868.

The withdrawal of the legal tenders had not been long under way before protests began to come in upon the Treasury and Congress from the West. Bad as the depreciated currency was, it was the only currency available for the active business of the country. If the greenbacks should go there would be nothing to take their place until coin should finally emerge from hiding. The reduction of the volume of money in a time of increasing business would enforce upon each dollar an enlarged activity and a greater market value. The price of money rising, the price of all commodities measured in money would necessarily fall, and in a period of falling prices the West thought it saw financial catastrophe. There was enough real truth in the contention that resumption meant a fall in prices for the Treasury to be compelled to make the difficult choice between this evil and the other evil of a depreciated currency forced upon the people.

The creditor East regarded the possible increase in the purchasing value of the dollar with entire complacency. Its selfish interests harmonized with sound theories of finance. But in the debtor West the process had so different an aspect that the financial obligations of the United States were obscured by the local interest.

The great "boom" of the West began after the depreciation had commenced. Most of the Western debts, whether on the farm of the settler, the stock of the merchant, or the bonds of the industrial corporation, had been created in legal-tender dollars of the value of the depreciated greenbacks. Any appreciation which might come to the greenbacks must increase the content-value of the debt. If "dollars," borrowed when they were worth sixty cents in gold, were to be repaid in "dollars" worth eighty or more cents in gold, the debtor was repaying one third more than he had received, and no appeal to the importance of public credit could make him forget his loss. He resented not only the decrease in the actual amount of money, but the appreciated value of the remainder.

McCulloch, trained in finance, was ready to sacrifice the debtor for the sake of national solvency, — and, indeed, one or the other had to yield. But Congress felt the pressure, which was strong from all the West, and most strong from the Northwest, be-

tween Pittsburg and Chicago, whose industry had
been reorganized during the years of war. In February, 1868, the retirement of more greenbacks was
forbidden by law, the amount then in circulation
being $356,000,000. The inflation which war had
brought about was legalized in time of peace, and the
Supreme Court ultimately ruled [1] that the issue of
legal tenders, in either war or peace, is at the free
discretion of Congress.

Like every other West, the West of 1868 was in
debt; like every other debtor community, it was
liable to yield to theories of inflation, and was prone
to look to politics for redress of grievances. The
farmers of Massachusetts and Connecticut had followed Shays for this purpose in 1786; Ohio and
Kentucky had attacked the second Bank of the
United States when it forced their banks to pay
their debts; and now the Northwest listened to politicians who told them that more greenbacks would
cure their ills.

The advocates of the Greenback movement urged
that the legal tenders be retained as the foundation
of the currency, and that all bonds and interest pay-
able in "lawful money" be paid in paper. By thus
increasing the volume of greenbacks in circulation
they hoped to avoid a fall in prices or an increased
pressure on the debtor. Wherever men were heavily
in debt, they accepted this doctrine. George H. Pendleton, of Ohio, became its most prominent spokesman, though it received the support of men as far
apart as Thaddeus Stevens and B. F. Butler, and on it

[1] In the cases of Knox vs. Lee and Juilliard vs. Greenman.

as an issue Pendleton sought to obtain for himself the Democratic nomination for the presidency in 1868.

The aspirations of Pendleton, when his friends brought his "Ohio Idea" to the national convention, in Tammany Hall, New York, on July 4, were opposed by the similar desires of Chief Justice Chase, who still wanted the Presidency, and Horatio Seymour, the Democratic war Governor of New York. In its leader, commenting on the convention, *Harper's Weekly* asserted that "The Democratic Convention of 1864 declared the war a failure. The loyal people scorned the words and fought on to an unconditional victory. The Democratic Convention of 1868 declares that the war debt shall be repudiated. And their words will be equally spurned by the same honorable people." Pendleton failed to secure the nomination, which went to Seymour, on the twenty-second ballot, with Francis P. Blair, Jr., for the Vice-Presidency, but the "Ohio idea" was embodied in the platform of the party, although Seymour distinctly disavowed it.

Pledged to what the East commonly regarded as repudiation, the Democratic party was severely handicapped at the beginning of the campaign. Not only could their opponents reproach Seymour as a Copperhead, but they could profess to be frightened by Wade Hampton and the "hundred other rebel officers who sat in the Convention." Already including "treason," and disloyalty, the indictment was amended to include dishonor, by the Republicans, who scarcely needed the strong popularity of Grant to carry them into office.

The Republican party was compelled to disguise itself as "Union" in 1864, and it paid for the disguise during the next four years. Upon the death of Lincoln, the Tennessee Democrat, Andrew Johnson, took the oath of office. The bond which kept Democrats and Republicans together as Unionists had dissolved with the surrender of Lee, so that Johnson was enabled to follow his natural bent as a strict constructionist. His policies had carried him far away from the radical Republicans before Congress convened for its session of 1865-66, and led to a positive breach with that body in 1866.

The quarrel between Johnson and the Republican leaders was occasioned by his views upon the rights of the Southern States, conquered in war and held within the military grasp of the United States. It was his belief, as it had been Lincoln's, that these States were still States and were in the Union, even though in a temporarily deranged condition. As President, entrusted with force to be used in executing the laws, he regarded himself as sole judge of the time when force should no longer be needed. And in this spirit he offered pardon to many leaders of the Confederacy in May, 1865. He followed amnesty with provisional governments, and proclaimed rules according to which the conquered States should revise their constitutions and reëstablish orderly and loyal governments. He had reorganized the last of the eleven States before Congress could interfere with him.

The difference between Johnson and his Republican associates lay in the character of the restored

electorates in the South. The whole white population had, in most States, been implicated in secession. There was no Union faction in the South that
remained loyal throughout the war. Pardoned and
restored to a full share in the Government, these
Southern leaders would come back into Congress as
Democrats, and with increased strength. The Thirteenth Amendment abolished slavery, and raised the
representation of the negroes in the South from the
old three-fifths ratio to par. Every State would come
back with more Representatives than it had had before the war, and with the aid of Northern Democrats it was not unlikely that a control of Congress
might be obtained.

To Northern Republicans it was unreasonable
that the conquered South should be rewarded instead
of punished, and that any theory of reconstruction
should risk bringing into power the party that
Union men, headed by Lincoln, had defeated in
1864. Politicians, interested in the spoils of office,
were enraged at the thought of losing them. Disinterested Northerners, who had sacrificed much to
save the Union, believed it unsafe at once to hand
it over to a combination of peace Democrats and
former " rebels." Yet this was Johnson's plan, and
Congress, with radical Republicans in control, set
about to prevent it.

Although Johnson, as President, controlled the
patronage, Congress possessed the power, if not the
moral right, to limit him in its use. No appointment
could be made without the consent of the Senate,
which was Republican. In 1867 Congress enacted

that no removal should be made without the same consent, in a Tenure-of-Office Bill that brought the dispute to a climax. More important than this power of concurrence was the exclusive right of each house to judge of "the elections, returns, and qualifications" of its own members. So long as the Southern Senators and Representatives were out of Congress no power could get them in without the consent of either house. Violent advisers of the President argued that a Congress excluding the members of eleven States by prearrangement was a "rump," and without authority, but they failed to influence either the conduct of the majority or the acts of Johnson.

In the Thirty-ninth Congress, which sat in 1865 and 1866, it was the problem of the leaders, Charles Sumner in the Senate and Thaddeus Stevens in the House, to hold the party together and to block the designs of the President. In the House, the heavy Republican majority made this easy. In the Senate the majority was slighter, and could be kept at two thirds only by unseating a Democratic Senator from New Jersey, after which event both houses were able to defy Johnson and to pass measures over his veto. The vetoes began when Johnson refused his consent to the Freedmen's Bureau and the Civil Rights Bills. These and all other important acts of reconstruction were forced upon the President by the two-thirds vote.

The split, so far as founded upon honest divergence in legal theory, was embarrassing. It was made disgraceful by the violence of the radical Republicans and the intemperate retorts of Johnson. In 1866

Congress sent the Fourteenth Amendment to the States for ratification. In 1867 it passed its bills for actual reconstruction under the control of the army of the United States, and defied Johnson to interfere by refusing to allow him to remove officials from office.

Johnson carried himself through the partisan struggle with ability and success. His language was often extreme, but he enforced the acts which Congress passed as vigorously as if they had been his own. So far as any theory of the Constitution met the facts of reconstruction, his has the advantage, but in a situation not foreseen by the Constitution force outranked logic, and the radical Republicans with two-thirds in each house possessed the force. There was no lapse in the President's diligence and no flaw in his official character which his enemies could use. They began to talk of impeachment in 1866, but could find no basis for it.

The Tenure-of-Office Act furnished the pretext for impeachment. Advised by his Attorney-General that it was unconstitutional, Johnson dismissed the Secretary of War, Edwin M. Stanton, for whose protection the law had been passed. In removing Stanton he broke with Grant, commanding the army, over a question of veracity, and gave to Congress its chance. In February, 1868, the House of Representatives voted to impeach him.

The trial of Andrew Johnson before the Senate dragged through April and May. The articles of impeachment were long and detailed in their description of the unquestioned bad manners of the President, but the only specific violation of law cited was in the case of Stanton, and here it could be urged both that the law was unconstitutional and that it was so loosely drawn that it did not really cover this case. In brief, it was the policy of Johnson that was on trial, and it was finally impossible to persuade two-thirds of the Senators that this constituted a high crime or a misdemeanor. The President was acquitted in the middle of May, while the Republican party turned to the more hopeful work of electing his successor.

In the fight over Johnson party lines had been strengthened and defined so that no Unionist, not in sympathy with congressional reconstruction, could hope for the nomination. No other issue equaled this in strength. The greenback issue was condemned in a plank that denounced "all forms of repudiation as a national crime," but ran second to the basis of reconstruction. No other candidate than Ulysses S. Grant was considered at the Chicago Convention.

Few men have emerged from deserved obscurity to deserved prominence as rapidly as General Grant. In 1861 he was a retired army officer, and a failure. In 1863, as the victor at Fort Donelson and at Vicksburg, he loomed up in national proportions. In the hammering of 1864 and 1865 it was his persistence and moral courage that won the day. In 1868, as commander of the army, and fortunate in his quarrel with Johnson, he was the coveted candidate of both parties, for he had no politics. Held by his associations to the Republican leaders, he was nominated at Chicago on the first ballot, with

Schuyler Colfax, of Indiana, as his Vice-President.

The nomination of Grant occurred as the impeachment trial was drawing to a close. Before Congress adjourned it readmitted several of the Southern States that had been restored under the control of Republican majorities. Tennessee was already back; the new States were North Carolina, South Carolina, Georgia, Florida, Alabama, Louisiana, and Arkansas. Only three States remained under provisional control when Grant was elected in November and seated in the following March. As he took the oath of office there were few, North, South, or West, who did not rejoice in his election ; he had defeated the Greenback pretension, which endeared him to the East; the West remembered that he had been born and bred in the Mississippi Valley; and to the South he presented the clean hands of the regular army officer, and the welcome promise of his letter of acceptance, "Let us have peace."

BIBLIOGRAPHICAL NOTE

For general accounts of the Far West in this period consult K. Coman, *Economic Beginnings of the Far West* (2 vols., 1912), and F. L. Paxson, *The Last American Frontier* (1910). These should be supplemented by E. L. Bogart, *Economic History of the United States* (1907), K. Coman, *Industrial History of the United States* (2d ed., 1910), W. A. Scott, *The Repudiation of State Debts* (1893), and W. C. Mitchell, *History of the Greenbacks*. The more valuable memoirs include H. McCulloch, *Men and Measures of Half a Century* (1888), and J. G. Blaine, *Twenty Years of Congress* (2 vols., 1884). A brilliant analysis of the financial interests of the debtor sections is M. S. Wildman, *Money Inflation in the United States* (1905). Rhodes continues to furnish a comprehensive narrative, and is paralleled by the shorter W. A. Dunning, *Reconstruction, Political and Economic, 1865–1877* (in *The American Nation*, vol. 22, 1907). A detailed account of impeachment politics is in D. M. DeWitt, *Impeachment and Trial of Andrew Johnson* (1903), and in J. A. Woodburn, *The Life of Thaddeus Stevens* (1913). J. P. Davis, *The Union Pacific Railway* (1894), is the standard account of the early movement for a continental railroad. S. L. Clemens (Mark Twain) presents a vivid picture of frontier life in *Roughing It* (1872), while A. B. Paine, *Mark Twain* (3 vols., 1912), contains much material of general historical interest for this period.

CHAPTER III

THE eight Southern States whose votes were cast in 1868 were far different from the States of the same names in 1860, and were, like the three still outside the Union, largely under the control of radical Republicans. Restoration, after a fashion, they had received, but it had been accompanied by a revolution in society, in politics, and in economic life. "Reconstruction" is an inappropriate name for what took place.

Many efforts have been made to show the price paid by the South for its attempt at independence, but these have always failed to be exact. No scheme of accounting can uncover all the costs. It is a sufficient suggestion as to the total that a million men, at the prime of life, were diverted from ordinary production for about three years. Not only did the South lose the products of their labor, but it lost many of them, while its houses, barns, and other permanent improvements wore out, were burned, or went to pieces from lack of care. Its slave property was destroyed. Poverty was universal within the region of the Confederacy when Johnson issued his amnesty proclamation and the troops came home.

The most immediate problems before the Southern planter in the spring of 1865 were his dilapidated buildings, his spring crops, and his labor supply. Without money or credit, he needed all the stiffness of a proud caste to hold off bankruptcy. The daughter of a prominent Mississippi planter told later how her father, at seventy years, did the family washing to keep his daughters from the tub. A society whose men and women took this view of housework (for the daughters let their father have his way) had much to learn before it could reëstablish itself. Yet this same stubbornness carried the South through the twenty trying years after the war.

The system of slave labor was gone, but the negroes were still the chief reliance for labor. It appears from the scanty records that are available that the planters expected to reopen the plantations using the freedmen as hired laborers. In 1865 and 1866 they tried this, only to find that the negro had got beyond control and would not work. Supervision had become hateful to him. A vagrant life appealed to his desire for change. At best, he was unintelligent and indolent. In a few years it became clear that the old type of plantation had vanished, and that the substitute was far from satisfactory.

Failing at hiring the negro for wages, the planter tried to rent to him a part of the estate. But since the tenant was penniless the landlord had to find much or all of the tools and stock, and too often had to see the crops deserted while the negro went riding around the county on his mule, full of his new independence. The census records show the decline of the plantation as the labor system changed. In 1860 the average American farm contained 199 acres, while those of the eleven seceding States ranged in average from 245 in Arkansas, to 430 in Georgia, and 591 in Texas. All were far above the national average, for the economics of the plantation system impelled the owner ever to increase his holdings. In 1870, and again in 1880, the reports show a rapid decline. The average for the whole country went down from 199 to 134 acres in the twenty years, as intensive agriculture advanced, but the South declined more rapidly than the whole, and in 1880, in all but two States, the average farm was less than half its size before the Civil War.

The vagrant, shiftless freedman was a social problem as well as economic. To fix his new status was the effort of the legislatures that convened in 1865, under the control of those who had qualified as loyal in Johnson's scheme. In several States laws were passed relating to contracts, apprenticeship, and vagrancy, under which the negro was to be held to regular work and the employer was given the right to punish him. The laws represented the opinion of the white citizens that special provisions were needed to control and regulate the negro population now that the personal bond of the owner for the good behavior of his slaves was canceled. To the North, still excited and nervous in 1865, the laws appeared to embody an overt attempt to restore the essentials of slavery. They served to embitter Congress toward Johnson's plans, and to convince Republicans that the professed loyalty of former Confederates was hypocritical, — that these must not be permitted to return at once to federal office or to Congress.

It was not until the summer of 1867 that Congress substituted governments of its own design for those which Johnson had erected by proclamation. These, meanwhile, had proceeded to revise their constitutions and to adopt the Thirteenth Amendment, which was proclaimed as part of the Constitution in December, 1865. The direct hand of Congress was shown in the strengthening of the Freedmen's Bureau in the spring of 1866, and the passage of the Fourteenth Amendment in the following summer.

The Freedmen's Bureau had its excuse in the poverty and ignorance of the negroes who crowded about the invading armies. Toward the end of the war it was authorized to administer abandoned property, and to aid the freedmen in farming upon the same. It did wide charitable and educational work in easing the abrupt change from slavery to freedom, and would have been dissolved a year after the return of peace had not Congress maintained it to offset the tendencies of Johnson's administration. Hereafter the agents of the Bureau were thrown into politics until 1872.

The permanent government of the conquered South by the army was repugnant to even radical Northerners, yet the white inhabitants were Democratic almost to the last man, and if restored to civil rights would control their States. The only means of developing a Southern Republican party that might keep the South " loyal " was the enfranchisement of the freedman, for which purpose the Fourteenth Amendment was submitted. The agents of the Bureau were expected not only to feed and

clothe the negroes, but to impress upon them the fact
that they owed their freedom to the Republicans.
Some spread the belief that the Democrats desired
to restore slavery. Many built up personal machines.
The responsibility upon these white directors of the
negro vote was great, and was too often betrayed.
Generally not natives, and with no stake in the
Southern community, they lined their own pockets
and earned the unkindly name of " carpet-baggers."
The Territories had always known something of this
type of ruler, but the States, hitherto, had known
bad government only when they made it themselves.

The Reconstruction Acts of 1867 ordered the
President to divide the South into five military districts, whose commanders should supersede all the
state officers whom Johnson had restored. With
troops behind them, these commanders were, first,
to enroll on the voting list all males over twenty-one.
The negroes, before the adoption of the Fourteenth
Amendment, were thus given by Congress the right
to vote in their respective States, and were included
in the lists. Excluded from the lists were the leaders of every Southern community, those whites who
had held important office in the Confederacy ; and
none was to be enrolled, white or black, until he had
taken an ironclad and offensive oath of allegiance.

Based upon the list of voters thus made up, state
conventions were to be summoned to revise the constitutions. In every case they must modify the laws
to admit the status of the freedmen, must ratify the
Fourteenth Amendment with its guaranty of civil
rights, and must extend the right of suffrage to the

blacks. When all these things had been done, with army officers constantly in supervision, the resulting constitutions were to be submitted to Congress for final approval or rejection.

No constitutional theory ever met all the problems of reconstruction. The war had been fought on the basis that no State can get out of the Union. If this was true, then all the States were still States, and it was a reasonable presidential function to restore order and withdraw the troops. The unreasonable result of this theory was the immediate restoration of an enlarged influence to those very men who had tried to break the Union, at a moment when the greenback movement threatened the foundations of public faith. Yet Congress, by pretending to readmit or restore States, denied that they were still States, and by implication conceded the principle for which the Confederacy had contended: that the members of the Union could get outside it. The power of Congress to seat or unseat members, however, placed it beyond all control. Every effort to get the courts to interfere broke down, when the suits were directed against the President (Mississippi *vs.* Andrew Johnson), or the Secretary of War (Georgia *vs.* Stanton). A personal suit that promised some relief (*Ex parte* McCardle) was evaded by a sudden amendment of the law relating to appeals. The situation was unpremeditated, and the Constitution made no provision for its facts. In the end, reconstruction must be judged by its results rather than by its legality. If it brought peace, restored prosperity, safeguarded the Union, and created no new grievances of its own, it was good, whatever the Constitution.

Johnson enforced the Reconstruction Acts with care, and the Southern conventions, meeting in the autumn of 1867, sat into the following winter. In five of the States the roll of electors showed a majority of negroes, and in none were conservatives able to control the election of delegates. The old leaders were still disfranchised, and many of them could not believe that the North would permit the radicals to subject them to the control of illiterate negroes. The resulting conventions contained many negroes and were dominated by white Republicans, carpet-baggers, or scalawags as the case might be. An active part in directing them was taken by the officers of the Freedmen's Bureau, while the freedmen were consolidated by the secret ritual of the Union League. Only Tennessee escaped the ordeal, she having ratified the Fourteenth Amendment so promptly that Congress could not evade admitting her in 1866.

An analysis of the conventions of 1867 reveals the extent of the political revolution which Congress intended to thrust upon the South, whose industrial revolution was now well advanced. Planters had begun already to break up their estates and entrust small holdings to cash renters, or share tenants, known as "croppers." Their financial burdens were heavy, but with intelligent government and reasonable commercial credits from the North, the problems of labor and capital might be met. But the men who must control the economic future of the South were excluded from the Government as traitors. Their places were filled by Northern adventurers and by negroes. The Mississippi convention included seventeen negroes, and was called the "black and tan." Inexperience and incompetence were in control, leading to extravagance and dishonesty, but the conventions were generally superior to the legislatures which followed them.

Framing new constitutions, most of the States had met the demands of Congress by the summer of 1868, with the respectable portion of the South looking on in desperate silence. The war had left no grievances equal to those now being suffered. Seven of the new constitutions were adopted in time for the radicals to give to their States votes in the election of 1868. Alabama, making the eighth, was allowed to vote under a constitution which Congress had forced upon her after it had failed of ratification by the people. Only Georgia and Louisiana, of these eight, did not give their votes to Grant. Only Virginia, Mississippi, and Texas remained without the pale when Grant was inaugurated in 1869.

The completion of reconstruction in its formal sense was reached during Grant's first Congress. Mississippi completed her process in February, 1870. She had in 1868 voted down the reconstruction constitution, taking courage in the leadership of a conservative governor, Humphreys. When he was removed, and replaced by a Northern governor, the conservatives lost heart and ratified the constitution that they had rejected. Their delay cost the State one more humiliation, since in the interval the Fifteenth

Amendment had been submitted by Congress and made a condition of readmission for the recalcitrant States. A Republican legislature, the first fruit of reconstruction, accepted this and sent to Washington as the new Mississippi Senators the Northern military governor, Ames, and a negro preacher named Revels.

Virginia was readmitted in January, 1870. Her original loyal government under Pierpont, which Lincoln had respected, had been supplanted by a military régime, having lost its last chance for recognition when it rejected the Fourteenth Amendment in 1867. Under congressional direction a negro-radical convention made a new constitution which was forced upon the people in January, 1870. Texas, too, was in her final stage of restoration in 1870, and like Virginia and Mississippi was readmitted upon conditions that had become more onerous since the passage of the Reconstruction Acts in 1867.

Eleven States, all the old Confederacy, had been restored by the spring of 1870 ; but one, Georgia, was ejected after restoration, and thus became the last item in congressional reconstruction. In 1868 Georgia had ratified her new constitution and moved her capital from its ante-bellum location at Milledgeville to the new town growing upon the ashes of Atlanta. She had ratified the Fourteenth Amendment, but her first legislature had so poorly read the meaning of Congress that it expelled every negro whom the radicals had elected to membership. Congress had thereupon declined to seat the Georgia delegation at Washington, and had renewed the probationary period until the legislature, humbled and browbeaten, had undone the expulsion, whereupon Georgia received her final recognition.

The arbitrary acts of Congress, passed by the radicals over the unvarying vetoes of Johnson, find little sanction in the Constitution, but it is to be expected that the laws should suffer in a time of war. Congress held off the day of restoration until it saw in the South what its majority believed to be loyal governments. Its majority could not believe that any party but its own was loyal, and was thus led to a policy much more debatable than that of actual reconstruction. Step by step it moved. The abolition of slavery, in the Thirteenth Amendment (effective December 18, 1865), was expected by all and accepted without a fight. The next amendment, inspired by a fear that the freedmen would be oppressed and by a hope that they might be converted into a political ally of the Republicans, was submitted to the States before the Reconstruction Acts were passed, and was proclaimed as part of the Constitution July 28, 1868. Only compulsion upon the Southern States procured its ratification. It left negro suffrage optional with the States, but threatened them with a reduction in representation in Congress if they refrained from granting it. In the Southern States Congress had already planted a negro electorate by law. The Fifteenth Amendment forbade the denial of the right to vote on grounds of race, color, or previous condition of servitude, and was not submitted to the States until after the inauguration of General Grant. A fear that the South would disfranchise the freedmen, pay the price, and revert to Democratic control seems to have been the prime motive in its adoption. When it was proclaimed, March 30, 1870, the radical Republicans had done everything in their power to save themselves, and had inflicted on the conquered States, in malice, ignorance, or mistaken philanthropy, a condition that in the North, with its trifling number of negroes, was tolerated with reluctance.

The South was in name completely restored in 1870, but neither restoration nor reconstruction was in fact far advanced. In the latter process it was yet clearing away the wreckage of the institution of slavery, breaking up the plantations, devising new systems of tenure and wage, rebuilding the material equipment that the war had left desolate. The former process was only commenced. It was unthinkable that an American community should permit itself to remain subject to the absolute control of its least respected members, yet this was the aim of white disfranchisement and negro suffrage. Law or no law, the restoration of the South was not complete until its government was back in the control of its responsible white population.

Almost without exception, until 1870, the Southern State Governments were what Congress had chosen to make them. Their Senators and Representatives in Congress were Republican, commonly of the carpet-bag variety. Their governors, administrative officers, and legislatures were Republican, too. Rarely were they persons of property or standing in their communities, and often, as their records show, they were both black and illiterate. Had all possessed good intentions they could hardly have hoped to meet the local needs, which called for a wise revision of law in order that the community might recover and live. That their work should be accompanied by error and waste was inevitable.

From the contemporary accounts of travelers in the South, from public documents, from the growing body of Southern biography and reminiscence, it is easy to gather a mass of detail upon the extravagance of the Reconstruction Governments. Printing bills and salary lists rose without a corresponding increase in service done. When expenditures exceeded the revenues, loans were created carelessly and recklessly. For negroes, only a few months out of the cotton-field, there was an irresistible attraction in the plush carpets, the mahogany desks, and the imported cuspidors that the taxpayers might be forced to provide for the comfort of their servants. A free and continuous lunch, with ample food and drink, was set up in one of the capitols. Gratuitous waste was the least of the burdens inflicted upon the South.

It is unreasonable to lay all the corruption of the Reconstruction Governments to the account of the congressional policy. The period of the Civil War was one of abuse of power by local officials everywhere. It took a Tweed in New York to drive a Northern public to revolt, and a Nast to focus public attention upon the crime. In other States, where rogues were less brutal in their methods, or prosecutors less acute, the evil ran, not unnoticed but unchecked. In the South the same phenomena were resented with greater vigor than in the North because the crimes were more openly and clumsily committed, and because they were the work of "outsiders."

Deliberate theft of public money was so common as to occasion no surprise. In no State were books so kept that the modern student can be sure he knows where all the money went. Graft in contracts, fraud in the administration of schools and negro-relief schemes, sale of charters and votes, illegal issues of bonds, improvident loans to railroads, combined to enrich the office-holder and to increase the volume of public debts. A long series of repudiations of these debts injured Southern credit for many years. South Carolina occasioned the most vivid description of the orgy in a book entitled *The Prostrate State*, by a Maine abolitionist and Republican, named Pike; but several other States would have furnished similar materials to a similar historian.

So far as law was concerned, the South was helpless in those regions in which the negroes approached a majority. The military garrisons which Congress kept on duty saw to it that the freedmen were protected, yet were unable in the long run to control the white population. It is a vexed question whether negro violence or white was the first to appear, but by 1867 events had begun to point the way to the elimination of negro control by force or fraud. By law it could not be destroyed unless the whites struggled and argued for negro votes, treating the negroes as citizens and equals, which was generally as impossible as an acceptance of their control.

The Ku-Klux Klan was a secret movement, with slight organization, that appeared earliest in Tennessee, but spread to nearly every crossroads in the South. It began in the hazing of negroes and carpetbaggers who were insolent or offensive to their neighbors. Its members rode by night, in mask, with improvised pomp and ritual, and played as much upon the imagination of their victims as upon their bodies. Frequently it revenged private grievances and went to extremes of violence or murder. From hazing it was an easy step to intimidation at election time, the Ku-Klux Klan proving to be an efficient means of reducing the negro vote. It was so efficient, indeed, that Grant asked and Congress voted, in 1871, special powers for the policing of the South. In this summer a committee of Congress visited Southern centers and accumulated a great mass of testimony from which a picture of both the Ku-Klux Klan outrages and the workings of reconstruction may easily be drawn. The reign of terror subsided by 1872, but it had done much to dissuade the negro from using his new right, and had started the movement for home rule in the South.

That the normal politics of the South was Democratic is shown by the votes of the border States, where a population of freedmen had to be assimilated and Congress could not interfere. Delaware, Maryland, and Kentucky voted against Grant in 1868, although all the restored Confederate States but two voted for him. In Georgia the Democrats swallowed their pride, electioneered among the negroes, and elected a conservative State Government in 1870.

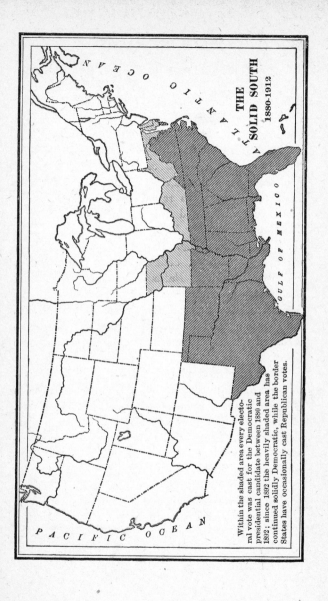

THE
SOLID SOUTH
1880-1912

Within the shaded area every electoral vote was cast for the Democratic presidential candidate between 1880 and 1892; since 1892 the heavily shaded area has continued solidly Democratic, while the border States have occasionally cast Republican votes.

Tennessee escaped negro domination from the start. Virginia, late to be readmitted, had consolidated her white population as she watched the troubles in South Carolina and Mississippi, and never elected a radical administration. In North Carolina, after a fight that approached a civil war, a Democratic State Government was chosen in 1870. The rest of the Confederate States followed as opportunity offered; after 1872 the process was rapid, and after 1876 there was no Republican administration in the old South. The Republican party, itself, almost disappeared from the South at this time. A bare organization, largely manned by negroes, endured to enjoy the offices which a Republican National Administration could bestow, and to contribute pliant delegations to the national conventions of the party. But the South had become solid in the sense that its votes were recorded almost automatically for the Democratic ticket.

Force and fraud played a large part in the restoration of white control, but it could not have been effective without some connivance from the North. Before 1872 the keenness of Northern radicalism was blunted. Thoughtful Republicans began to examine their work and criticize it. " We can never reconstruct the South," wrote Lowell, " except through its own leading men, nor ever hope to have them on our side till we make it for their interest and compatible with their honor to be so." A social order which needed the constant support of troops lost the confidence of political independents. These, as the presidential campaign of 1872 drew near, openly expressed their hostility to reconstruction as carried out by Grant, and threatened to prevent his reëlection.

The first term of Grant ended unsatisfactorily. His appointments to office were marked by favoritism and incapacity. He appointed the only really inferior man who has ever represented the United States in London, — one who thought it not incompatible with his high office to publish a treatise on draw-poker, and to appear as bellwether in a mining prospectus. Grant's personal intimates included shifty financiers. Corruption and misgovernment at the South were held against him, though Congress was properly to blame for them. Only in his stand for honest finance, his effort to improve the Indian service, and his conclusion of the disputes with Great Britain, could his supporters take great pride.

The settlement with England was his greatest achievement. Since the summer of 1862, when the Alabama had evaded the British officials and had gone to sea, the American Minister in London had continued to press for damages. The Alabama claims were based on the assertion that the law of neutrals required Great Britain to prevent any hostile vessel from starting, in her waters, upon a cruise against the United States. In the face of official rebuff and popular sneers Charles Francis Adams formulated the claims. His successor, Reverdy Johnson, reached a sort of settlement which the Senate declined to ratify, and which Sumner denounced. It was Sumner's contention that the Civil War was prolonged by British aid and that a demand for national dam-

ages (perhaps $2,000,000,000, or Canada, by way
of substitute) ought to be advanced. So tense did
the international situation become in 1869 and 1870
that friends of peace were frightened. Boundaries,
fisheries, and general claims aggravated the situation, which was given into the hands of a Joint High
Commission, hastily summoned to meet in Washington in 1870. The resulting Treaty of Washington,
and the successful arbitrations which followed it,
eliminated Sumner's extreme contention but vindicated the main American claims and founded Anglo-
American relations on a more secure basis than they
had ever known. It was Grant's great triumph, but
it was a political danger as well, for the negotiator
in charge, Charles Francis Adams, loomed up as the
possible presidential candidate of the Republican
dissenters.

The Liberal Republicans included the enemies of
Grant as well as dissatisfied reformers of all sorts.
Carl Schurz, the great German-American independent, was their leader. Horace Greeley, whose *Tribune* had done much to make the Republican party
possible, gave them his support. Charles Francis
Adams was not indifferent to them. Salmon P. Chase
wanted their nomination. Young newspaper men, like
Whitelaw Reid and Henry Watterson, tried to control them. And the new group of civil service reformers, disappointed in Grant, hoped that the new
party would take a step toward better government.
At Cincinnati, in May, 1872, they met in mass convention, and nominated Horace Greeley and Gratz
Brown. Their platform denounced Republican re-

construction, urged the return to self-government in the South, and advocated civil service reform, specie payments, and maintenance of public credit. The schism became more threatening when the Democrats saw a chance through fusion, and nominated the same candidates at Baltimore in July.

No quainter political figure has appeared in America than Horace Greeley, thus transferred from his editorial office to the stump. Long used to the freedom of the press, he had advocated many things in his lifetime, had examined and exploited unpopular social reforms, had contradicted himself and retraced his tracks repeatedly. The biting cartoons of Nast exploited all these; but no contrast was so absurd as that which brought to the great denouncer of slavery and the South the support of the party of the South.

The Republican Convention renominated Grant at Philadelphia without opposition, refused Colfax a second term, and picked Henry Wilson for Vice-President. Its platform, as in 1868, was retrospective, taking pride in its great achievements and assuming full credit for the war, reconstruction, and financial honor. It offered its ticket to all the States for the first time since 1860, and elected Grant with ease. The inharmonious Democrat-Liberal-Republican alliance increased the Republican majority, but the returns from the South confirmed the suspicion that home rule was in sight.

Restored completely to themselves, four years later, the Southern Governments ceased to play much part in national affairs and continued the economic rebuilding of their region. It was thirty

CHAPTER IV

THE PANIC OF 1873

" Are not all the great communities of the Western World growing more corrupt as they grow in wealth?" asked a critical and thoughtful journalist, Edwin L. Godkin, in 1868, as he considered the relations of business and politics. He answered himself in the affirmative and found comrades in his pessimism throughout that intellectual class in whose achievements America has taken conscious pride. For at least ten years they despaired of the return of honesty. James Russell Lowell, decorated with the D.C.L. of Oxford, and honored everywhere in the world of letters, was filled with doubt and dismay as late as 1876, at " the degradation of the moral tone. Is it, or is it not," he asked, " a result of democracy? Is ours a 'government of the people by the people for the people,' or . . . for the benefit of knaves at the cost of fools?"

It was not without reason that serious men were fearful in the years in which military heroes dominated in politics, and in which commerce struggled with its revolution. Had they foreseen the course of the next generation, noted the progress of new ideas in government, the extension of philanthropy and social relief, and the passion for education that swept the country, they need not have despaired. Godkin, himself, could not have made a living from his *Nation*, with its high ideals, its criticism, and its despondency, in a land that was wholly rotten. The young college presidents of the period could not have found a livelihood in a country that was not fundamentally sound. At Harvard, Charles William Eliot broke down the old technique of culture and enlarged its range; at Michigan, James Burrill Angell proved it possible to maintain sound, scholarly, and non-political education, in a public institution supported by taxation; in a new university a private benefactor, Johns Hopkins, gave to Daniel Coit Gilman a chance to show that creative scholarship can flourish in a democracy. But the essential soundness of the Republic was as much obscured in 1868 as its wealth had been in 1861, and for the present the objects on the surface, brought there by violent convulsion, represented its less creditable part.

The years of Grant's Presidency were filled with unsightly episodes, that were scandalous then and have been discouraging always. In his first year of office, Jay Gould and James Fisk, tempted by the premium on gold, tried to corner the market, and Grant's public association with the speculators brought upon him fair reproach. Tweed, exposed and jailed after a long fight, revealed the close alliance between crooked politics and business in the cities, and became a national disgrace. Less prominent than these but far from proper were Schenck and Frémont. The latter was arrested in France, charged with promoting a railroad on the strength of land grants that did not exist. He had been close to the old Republican organization, and the figurehead of the radicals in 1864, so that his notoriety was great. Schenck, while Minister in London, posed as director of a mining company, and borrowed from the promoters of the scheme the money with which he bought his shares. When the company proved insolvent, and perhaps fraudulent, Grant was forced to recall him. Critics who saw dishonesty or low ethical standards in these men were ready to see in the carnival of the Reconstruction Governments wholesale proofs of decadence.

During the campaign of 1872 yet another item was added to the unpleasant list. Letters were made public showing how Congressmen had taken pay, or its equivalent, from men behind the Union Pacific Railroad. The scandal of the Crédit Mobilier touched men in all walks of life, beginning with Schuyler Colfax, Vice-President of the United States, including Blaine, Allison, and Garfield, Wilson and Dawes, and other men who no longer held office. Some of these denied the charges and proved their innocence. But none entirely escaped the suspicion that their sense of official propriety was low, and their list sampled the Republican party at all its levels. One of the victims, Colfax, talked freely in 1870 of gifts received — a carriage from a Congressman and horses from an express company.

In 1872 the notorious Butler aimed at the governorship of Massachusetts. He failed to get the Republican nomination, but the strength of his candidacy showed the uncritical devotion of many voters to success. He resumed his seat in Congress, unabashed, and put through an act properly increasing the salaries of Washington officials, but applying also to the men who voted for it and to the session just ending. Its makers went home to explain their part in the " salary grab" to their constituents, and many never returned to Congress.

Other improprieties of the first Administration of Grant came to light in his second term. His Secretary of War, Belknap, confessed to the sale of offices. In the Treasury Department were uncovered the whiskey frauds which tainted even Grant's private secretary. And the Speaker of the House, Blaine, was shown to have urged a railroad company to recognize his official aid, promising not to be a " deadhead in the enterprise " in its future service.

There is no better illustration of the commercial ethics of the sixties than may be found in the letters of Jay Cooke, philanthropist and financier. With a lively and sincere piety, and an unrestrained generosity, he at once extended hospitalities to the political leaders of the day, carried their private speculations on his books, and performed official services to the Government. It was impossible to tell where his public service ended and his private emolument began, but there was nothing in his life of which he was ashamed. A friend of General Grant, and liberal patron of his children, Cooke was actually entertaining the President at his country home just outside of Philadelphia when the failure of his banking house precipitated the panic of 1873.

There had been financial uneasiness abroad and in the United States for several months, but few had anticipated the collapse of credit that followed the suspension of Jay Cooke and Company, September 18, 1873. If this house failed, none could be regarded as safe. Jay Cooke had established his reputation during the Civil War through his ability to find a market for United States bonds. After the war he had carried his activity and prestige into railways. In 1869 he had become the financial agent of the Northern Pacific, and customers, encouraged by their good bargains in the past, continued to invest through him as he directed. His personal followers, numerous and confident, had been taught to believe his credit as sound as that of the Government whose bonds he had handled. When he collapsed, overloaded with Northern Pacific securities, in which his confidence was enthusiastic, the panic was so acute that the New York Stock Exchange closed its doors for ten days, to prevent the ruinous prices that forced sales might have created. Thirty or more banking houses were drawn down by the crash within forty-eight hours. Others followed in all the business centers, while trade stood still through the paralysis of its banking agents.

The distribution of the panic throughout the United States followed the usual course. In the first crisis, banking houses broke down, unable to meet the runs of their depositors or their original obligations. The depositors next, unable to secure their own funds or to obtain their usual loans, were driven to insolvency. After the failure of banks came that of railroads, the wholesale houses, and the factories. As these last defaulted, the loss was spread over their employees, their contractors, and their creditors. Confidence was everywhere destroyed. Investments were lost, or lessened, or put off indefinitely in their payments. After a few days the acute crisis was over, but the resulting depression brought stagnation to business. Industries marked time, at best; expansions were out of the question; new enterprises were not heard of. From 1873 until 1879 the United States was engaged in recovery from the injury which the panic had done and from the weakness which it had revealed.

The panic, followed by five years of economic prostration, was only occasioned by the failure of Cooke. Its real causes lie throughout the period of Civil War expansion. Never had the daily necessities of the United States equaled its production, and the resulting surplus, available for permanent improvements, was larger than ever in the sixties because of the growing use of machinery. Funds for investment, produced at home and increased through the strong foreign credit of the United States, tempted and aided the speculative development of the North and West. Yearly greater sums were sunk in municipal improvements that brought in no return, or in railroads that were slow in paying, or in errors that were a dead loss. The loss from the Civil War was an added charge upon the surplus. Great fires in Boston and Chicago consumed more of it. By 1870 the United States was using surplus at a rate that threatened soon to exhaust it. When the limit should be reached, new enterprises must necessarily cease, and all that were not wisely planned must fall, dragging down others in their ruins. For months before the failure of Jay Cooke, business had been dangerously near this margin. His failure, caused by his inability to find a market for Northern Pacific, merely precipitated the inevitable crash.

The faulty currency, outstanding since the war, and adding to the business uncertainty, now aggravated the panic when it broke. The greenbacks were slowly rising in value. They profited by the growing credit of the United States, and received a special increase because of the development of business. After 1865 business transactions grew in number and volume more rapidly than the amount of available money, and this, driven to greater activity in circulation, rose in value from the increased demand. As the purchasing value of the dollar increased, prices, measured by the greenbacks, necessarily fell, while the equivalent of every debt that had to be paid in a specified number of dollars as steadily rose. Indeed, so great was the increase of production from the new farms, reached by the new railroads, and supplying raw materials for the new factory processes, that prices fell, even when stated in terms of gold. In a period of falling prices and appreciating currency, the gap between the poor and the rich was widened. The debtor carried a growing burden while the creditor harvested an unearned increase. Persons who lived on fixed salary or income profited by the fluctuations, but commercial transactions were made more difficult for the debtor.

The organized Greenback movement had figured in politics during the campaign of 1868, and made a special appeal to the debtor section during the hard times after 1873. The Republican Congress had, in 1869, sealed the professions of the party's platform by passing a resolution "to strengthen the public credit," in which it declared "that the faith of the United States is solemnly pledged to the payment in coin or its equivalent," of the greenbacks, and that the United States would not take advantage of its creditors by paying off its "lawful-money" bonds in depreciated paper. All debts created before the war or during its early years had lost through depreciation, just as the later debts had gained through the reverse.

Despite this pledge, advocates of greenback inflation, with Butler among their leaders, became more numerous in both parties after the panic, and an attempt was made to have Congress reverse itself. Grant's Secretary of the Treasury gave a new construction to the law by reissuing during the critical days of the panic some $26,000,000 of greenbacks that had been called in by McCulloch. He raised the total outstanding to $382,000,000, and Congress in 1874 passed a law increasing the amount to $400,000,000, in an act named by its opponents the "Inflation Bill." To the surprise of many, Grant sharply vetoed the act, adhering to his views of 1869 on the evils of an irredeemable paper currency. During the next winter John Sherman, Senator from Ohio, induced Congress to take a step in fulfillment of the guaranty which Grant had saved. On January 14, 1875, it was provided that the Treasury should resume the payment of specie on demand on January 1, 1879.

Ultimately Congress was saved from the act of repudiation which the Greenbackers urged upon it, but while the movement flourished it added another to the catalogue of troubles with which men like Godkin and Lowell were distressed. Easterners, in general, had as little understanding of the West as they had had of the race problem in the South. They were disposed to attribute to inherent dishonesty the inflation movement, and to ignore the real economic grievance upon which it was founded. The suspicions directed against the ethical standards of the West were increased by the Granger movement, to which the panic gave volume and importance.

Among the social phenomena of 1873–74 was the sudden emergence in the Northwest of a semi-secret, ritualistic society, calling itself the "Patrons of Husbandry," but popularly known as the "Grange." It was founded locally upon the soil, in farmers' clubs, or granges, at whose meetings the men talked politics, while their wives prepared a picnic supper and the children played outdoors. It had had a nominal existence since 1867, but during the panic it unexpectedly met a new need and grew rapidly, creating 1000 or more local granges a month, until at its maximum in 1874 it embraced perhaps 20,000 granges and 1,600,000 persons. In theory the granges were grouped by States, which latter were consolidated in the National Grange; in fact, the movement was almost entirely confined to the region north of the Ohio River, and even to the district northwest of Chicago.

Such a movement as the Grange, revealing a com-

mon purpose over a wide area and in a great number
of citizens, could not but affect party allegiance and
the conduct of party leaders. Simultaneously with
its development the legislatures of the Northwest —
Illinois, Wisconsin, and Iowa — became restive under
existing conditions, and assumed an attitude which
became characteristic of the Grange, — one of hostility to railroads and their management. With the
approval of the people, these States passed, between
1871 and 1874, a series of regulative acts respecting
the railways, which were known at the start as the
"Granger Laws," and which became a permanent
contribution to American government.

To Eastern opinion the Greenback movement had
been barefaced repudiation ; the Granger movement
seemed to be confiscation ; for every law provided
a means by which public authority should fix the
charge imposed by the railroad upon its customer.
Both movements need to be studied in their local
environment, which at least explains the Western
zeal in clamoring for the greenbacks, and shows that
in the Granger movement the West saw farther than
it knew.

The Civil War period marks a new era in the history of American railways. Prior to the panic of
1837, the few lines that were built were local. Few
could foresee that the railway would ever be more
than an adjunct to the turnpike and canal in bringing the city centers closer to their environs. In the
revival of industry after the panic of 1837, the
mileage increased progressively, and before the next
panic checked business in 1857 the tidewater region

was well provided, and the Alleghanies had been crossed by several trunk lines whose heads extended to the Lakes and to the Mississippi. But in these years the change was of degree rather than of kind. The lines were built to supplement existing routes, like the Erie Canal, the Lakes, the Ohio River, or the Mississippi. They connected communities already well developed and prosperous, and in undertaking new enterprises promoters had figured upon capturing the profits of existing trade.

In the new epoch of the sixties there were only new fields to conquer. The great enterprises were forced to speculate upon the development of the public domain and to find their profits in the business of communities to which they themselves gave birth. Natural waterways and roads extended little west of Chicago. The new fields were entered by the railroads without prospect of any competition but that of other railroads. The resulting communities, born and developed between 1857 and 1873, were peculiarly the creatures of, and dependent on, the railway lines.

This inevitable dependence on railways colored the history of Wisconsin, Iowa, and Minnesota, and, to a lesser degree, of all the West. While men were yet prosperous and sanguine and without adequate railway service, they offered high inducements to promoters of railways. Once the roads were built and the communities began to pay for them and to maintain them, the dependence was realized and anti-railway agitation began. The fact that they were commonly built on money borrowed from the East threw debtors and creditors into sectional classes injurious to both.

The antagonism to railways was increased because these yet regarded their trade as private, to be conducted in secrecy, with transportation to be sold at the best rates that could be got from the individual customer. The big shipper got the wholesale rate; the small shipper paid the maximum. Favoritism, discrimination, rebates, were the life of railway trade, and railway managers objected to them only because they endangered profits, not because they felt any obligation to maintain uniformity in charges.

In a community as dependent on the railways as the Northwest was, the iniquity of discriminatory or extortionate rates was soon seen. The East, with rival routes and less dependence on staple interests, saw it less clearly. The charges were paid grumblingly in good times; in bad times, when the rising greenbacks squeezed the debtor West and the panic of 1873 stopped business everywhere, the farmers soon made common cause. They seized upon the skeleton organization of the grange and gave it life. In 1874 their organized discontent compelled attention.

The Granger Laws were an attempt to establish a new legal doctrine that railways are quasi-public because of the nature of the service which they render and the privileges they enjoy. This principle was overlaid in many cases by the human desire to punish the railroads as the cause of economic distress, but it was visible in all the laws. It is an old rule of the common law that the ferryman, the baker,

and the innkeeper are subject to public control, and
railways were now classified with these. In Wisconsin, the " Potter " Law established a schedule with
classified rates, superseding all rate-cards of railroads in that State. Illinois created a railroad and
warehouse commission with power to fix rates and
annul warehouse charters. In Iowa the maximum
rates were fixed by law.

The railroads failed to realize at once what the
new laws meant. They denounced them as confisca-
tory, and attacked them in court as wrong in theory
and bad in application. Even admitting the principle
of regulation, the laws were so crudely shaped as to
be nearly unworkable. Farmer legislators, chosen on
the issue of opposition to railways, were not likely
to show either fairness or scientific knowledge. Coming at the same time with the panic of 1873, it is
impossible to measure the precise effect of any of
these laws, and all were modified before many years.
But the railroads' objection lay beneath the detail,
and the fundamental fight turned on two points —
the right of public authority to regulate a rate at all,
and whether state regulation was compatible with
the power of Congress over interstate commerce.

By 1876 the appeals of the railroads against the
constitutionality of these Granger Laws had gone
through the highest state courts to the Supreme
Court of the United States. In the spring of 1877
that body handed down a definitive decision in the
case of Munn *vs.* the State of Illinois in which it
recognized that the " controlling fact is the power to
regulate at all." It held that when the institutions

in question (in this case warehouses) established themselves, they did so "from the beginning subject to the power of the body politic to require them to conform to such regulations as might be established by the proper authorities for the common good." It upheld the rate laws, declared that they were not an infringement upon the powers of Congress, and thus gave formal sanction to a new doctrine in American law.

The legal consequences of the "Granger Cases" extended through the ensuing generation. The need for public intervention grew steadily stronger, and as time went on it became clear that this control could not be administered by orators or spoilsmen, but called for scientific training and permanence of policy. It was one of many influences working to reshape American administrative practice.

The Granger movement had close relations with the panic of 1873, although it must anyway have appeared in the Northwest at no remote date. As a political force it soon died out, leaving the principle of regulation as its memorial. With the gradual recurrence of prosperity the Northwest found new interests, and as early as 1877, when the decisions were made, the passion had subsided.

It was, however, a gloomy United States that faced the end of its first century of independence, in 1876. Pessimism was widely spread among the best educated in the East. Public life was everywhere discredited by the conduct of high officials. The South was in the midst of its struggle for home rule, which it could win only through wholesale force and

fraud. The West was discouraged over finance and
still depressed by the panic. Yet Philadelphia went
ahead to celebrate the centennial as though it were
ending the century as hopefully as it had begun.

The Exposition at Philadelphia this year was a
revelation to the United States. Though far sur-
passed by later "world's fairs," it displayed the
wide resources of the United States and brought
home the difference between American and European
civilization. The foreign exhibits first had a chasten-
ing influence upon American exuberance, and then
stimulated the development of higher artistic standards. In ingenuity the American mind held its own
against all competition. But few Americans had traveled, the cheap processes of illustration were yet
unknown, and in the resulting ignorance the United
States had been left to its assumption of a superiority unjustified by the facts. From the centennial
year may be dated the closer approach of American
standards to those of the better classes of Europe.

In the summer of 1876 the thirty-eighth State,
Colorado, was added to the Union. It had been seventeen years since the miners thronged the Kansas
and Nebraska plains, bound for "Pike's Peak or
Bust!" In the interval the mining camps had become permanent communities. Authorized in 1864
to form a State, they had declined to accept the
responsibility and had lingered for many years with
only a handful of inhabitants. Now and then entirely
isolated from the United States by Indian wars, they
had prayed for the continental railroad, only to be
disappointed when the Union Pacific went through

CHAPTER V

THE HAYES ADMINISTRATION

THE reëlection of Grant in 1872 was almost automatic. No new issue had forced itself into politics to stir up the old party fires or light new ones. The old issues had begun to lose their force. Men ceased to respond when told that the Union was in danger; they questioned or ignored the statement. Many of them contradicted it and voted for Greeley in 1872, but they were impelled to this by repulsion from Republican practice rather than by attraction to Democratic promise. Yet, on the whole, the habit of voting the Union or Republican ticket retained its hold on so many in the North that Grant's second term was insured, and it was even possible that a Republican successor might profit by the same political inertia.

The second term (1873–77) added no strength to Grant or to his party. Throughout its course, administrative scandals continued to come to light, striking at times dangerously near the President, but failing to injure him other than in his repute for judgment. The period was one of financial depression and discouragement. The best intellect of the United States was directed into business, the professions, and educational administration. Politics was generally left to the men who had already controlled it, and these

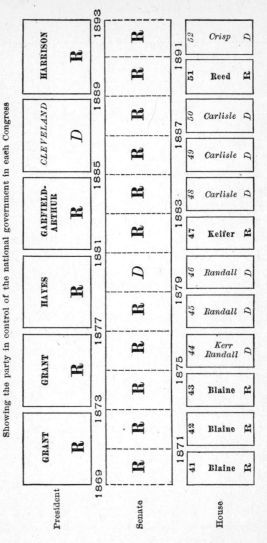

THE POLITICAL SITUATION AT WASHINGTON, 1869–1917

Showing the party in control of the national government in each Congress

President	GRANT	GRANT	HAYES	GARFIELD-ARTHUR	CLEVELAND	HARRISON
	R	R	R	R	D	R
	1869	1873	1877	1881	1885	1889	1893

Senate	R	R	R	R	R	R	R	R	R	R	R	R
	D	D
	1869	1871	1873	1875	1877	1879	1881	1883	1885	1887	1889	1891	1893

| House | 41 Blaine R | 42 Blaine R | 43 Blaine R | 44 Kerr Randall D | 45 Randall D | 46 Randall D | 47 Keifer R | 48 Carlisle D | 49 Carlisle D | 50 Carlisle D | 51 Reed R | 52 Crisp D |
| | 1869 | 1871 | 1873 | 1875 | 1877 | 1879 | 1881 | 1883 | 1885 | 1887 | 1889 | 1891 |

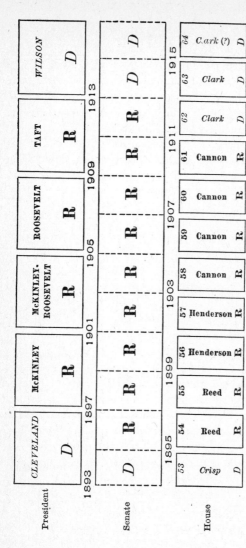

President										
1893	CLEVELAND *D*	1897	McKINLEY *R*	1901	McKINLEY-ROOSEVELT *R*	1905	ROOSEVELT *R*	1909	TAFT *R*	1913	WILSON *D*	1915

Senate: *D* | R | R | R | R | R | R | *D* | *D*

House (by Congress number):

| 53 Crisp *D* | 54 Reed R | 55 Reed R | 56 Henderson R | 57 Henderson R | 58 Cannon R | 59 Cannon R | 60 Cannon R | 61 Cannon R | 62 Clark *D* | 63 Clark *D* | 64 Clark (?) *D* |

During only three of the ten Congresses between 1875 and 1895 did either party control the national government. The Democrats were in possession only once, in the 53d Congress. The Republicans controlled the 47th Congress by manipulation of senators, and the 51st by Reed's drastic rules. Most of the partisan legislation of twenty years was enacted during these three Congresses.

were the men who had risen into prominence in the
period of the Civil War.

A new and not a better type was brought into
American politics by the Civil War. Notwithstanding the bad manners and excesses of ante-bellum
politics, the leaders had been men of defined policy,
only occasionally reaching high office through trickery
or personal appeal. Now came the presence of an intense issue which smoothed out other differences,
magnified a single policy,— the saving of the Union,
— and gave opportunity to a new type of intense,
patriotic, narrow mind. Men of this type dominated
in the reconstruction days. As the sixties advanced,
their number was recruited by men who had won
prominence and popularity on the battlefield, who
used military fame as a step into politics, and who
came into public life with qualifications adapted to
an issue that was closed.

Few of the leaders of the period 1861 to 1876 ever
grew into an understanding of problems other than
those of the Civil War. The most eminent of them
were gone before the latter year. Lincoln was dead ;
Grant had had two terms; Stevens was gone; Sumner
had been driven from party honor before his death ;
Chase had died Chief Justice, but unhappy. With
these men living, lesser men had remained obscure.
As they dropped out, a host of minor leaders,
trained to a disproportionate view of the war and
ignorant of other things, controlled affairs.

About these men the scandals of the Grant Administrations clustered, and their standards came to be
those of the Republican party organization. They

represented a dead issue, which they had never directed when it was alive, and were chosen by voters whose choice had become automatic. In their hands office tended to become a thing to be enjoyed for its own sake, not a trust to be fulfilled.

If the Republican organization was drifting into the control of second-rate men who misrepresented the rank and file, the status of the opposition was no better. At the South the Democratic party was openly founded on force and fraud. In the deliberate judgment of the white population of the South, negro control was intolerable and worse than any variety of political corruption that might be necessary to prevent it. The leaders of the party in this section had borne so important a part in the Confederacy that it was hopeless to think of them for national leaders, while they could meet the Northern charge of fraud only by the assertion of a greater alternate evil, which their opponents would not recognize as such. The South could be counted on for Democratic votes, but not as yet for leaders.

In the North and West the Democratic party was still weakened by its past. Its leaders of the early sixties, where they had not joined the Union party, were Copperheads, and were as little available as ex-Confederates. One of them, Seymour, whose loyalty, though he was in opposition to Lincoln, is above question, had been nominated and defeated in 1868. So few had been available in 1872 that the party had been reduced to the indorsement of Horace Greeley. Even the scandals of the Republican administration could not avail the Democrats unless a leader could be

found free from the taint of treason and copperheadism and strong enough to hold the party North and
South.

In the paucity of leaders during Grant's second
Administration the Democrats turned to New York
where a reform governor was producing actual results
and restoring the prestige of his party. Like other
Democrats of his day, Samuel J. Tilden had few
events in his life during the sixties to which he could
"point with pride" in the certain assurance that
his fellow citizens would recognize and reward them.
He had been a civilian and a lawyer. He had not
broken with his party on its "war a failure" issue
in 1864. He had acted harmoniously with Tammany
Hall while it began its scheme of plunder, in New York
City. But he had turned upon that organization and
by prosecuting the Tweed Ring had made its real
nature clear. Within the party he had led the demand to turn the rascals out, and had been elected
Governor of New York on this record in 1874. As
Governor he had proved that public corruption was
non-partisan and had exposed fraud among both parties so effectively that he was clearly the most available candidate when the Democratic Convention met
in St. Louis in 1876.

The only competitors of Tilden for the Democratic nomination were "favorite sons." Thomas A.
Hendricks, a Greenbacker, was offered by Indiana
and pushed on the supposition that this doubtful
State could not be carried otherwise. Pennsylvania
presented the hero of Gettysburg, General Winfield
Scott Hancock, through whom it was hoped to bring

to the Democratic ticket the aid of a good war record. The other candidates received local and scattering votes, and altogether they postponed the nomination for only one ballot. On the first ballot Tilden started with more than half the votes; on the second he had nearly forty more than the necessary two thirds. Hendricks got the Vice-Presidency, and the party entered the campaign upon a program of reform.

The Republicans had completed their nominations some weeks before the Democrats met, and having no unquestioned leader had been forced to adjust the claims of several minor men. Six different men received as many as fifty votes on one ballot or another, but only three factions in the party stood out clearly. The Administration group had sounded the public on a third term for Grant, and receiving scanty support had brought forward Conkling, a shrewd New York leader, and Morton, war Governor of Indiana. The out-and-out reformers were for Bristow, who had made a striking reputation as Secretary of the Treasury, over the frauds of the Whiskey Ring. Between the two groups was the largest single faction, which stood for James G. Blaine from first to last.

The political fortunes of James G. Blaine prove the difficulty with which a politician brought up in the Civil War period retained his leadership in the next era. Blaine had been a loyal and radical Republican through the war. Gifted with personal charms of high order, he had built up a political following which his unswerving orthodoxy and his service as Speaker of the House of Representatives served to widen. Never a rich man, he had felt forced to add to his salary by speculations and earnings on the side. In these he had come into contact with railroad promoters and had not seen the line beyond which a public man must not go, even in the sixties. His indiscretions had imperiled his reputation at the time of the Crédit Mobilier scandal. They became common property when an old associate forced him to the defensive on the eve of the convention of 1876. In the dramatic scene in the House of Representatives when Blaine read the humiliating "Mulligan" letters that he had written years before, tried to explain them, and denounced his enemies, he convinced his friends of his innocence, and evidenced to all his courage and assurance. But his critics, reading the letters in detail, were confirmed in their belief that if his official conduct was not criminal, it was at least improper, and that no man with a blunted sense of propriety ought to be President.

Despite all opposition, Blaine might have won the nomination had not a sunstroke raised a question as to his physical availability. He led for six ballots in the convention, and only on the seventh could his opponents agree upon the favorite son of Ohio, General Rutherford B. Hayes, who added to military distinction a good record as Governor of his State.

Neither Hayes nor Tilden represented a political issue. Each had been nominated because of availability, and each party contained many voters on each side of every question before the public. Even the appeal to loyalty and Union, which had worked in three campaigns, failed to stir the States. Blaine, expert in the appeal, had revived it over the proposition to extend pardon and amnesty to Jefferson Davis, but his frantic efforts, as he waved the "bloody shirt," evoked no general enthusiasm. The war and reconstruction were over, but the old parties had not learned it.

There was doubt throughout the canvass as to the nature of the issue, and when the votes were counted there was equal doubt as to which of the candidates had been elected. Tilden had received a popular plurality over Hayes of about 250,000 votes, but it was not certain that these carried with them a majority of the electoral college. Of the 369 electoral votes, Tilden and Hendricks had, without question, 184; while Hayes and Wheeler were equally secure in 166. The remaining 19 (Florida, Louisiana, and South Carolina) were claimed by both parties, and it appeared that both claims were founded on widespread fraud. Unless all these 19 votes could be secured, Hayes was defeated, and to obtain them the Republican party set to work.

For weeks between the election and the counting of the electoral votes the United States debated angrily over the result. The Constitution required that when Congress should meet in joint session to hear the returns, the Vice-President should preside, and should open the certificates from the several States; and that the votes should then be counted. It was silent as to the body which should do the counting, or should determine which of two doubtful returns to count. Since the outcome of the election would turn upon the answer to this question, it was necessary to find some solution before March 4, 1877.

Failing to find in the Constitution a rule for determining cases such as this, Congress made its own, and created an Electoral Commission to which the doubtful cases were to be submitted. This body, fifteen in number, five each from Senate, House, and Supreme Court, failed, as historians have since failed, to convince the United States that the claims of either Republican or Democratic electors were sound. Honest men still differ in their beliefs. The members came out of the Commission as they went in, firm in the acceptance of their parties' claims, and since eight of the fifteen members were Republican, the result was a decision giving none of the nineteen contests to Tilden, and making possible the inauguration of Rutherford B. Hayes.

There was bitter partisanship shown over the contest, and the Democrats, with a real majority of popular votes, maintained that they had been robbed of the Presidency. Excepting this, there was no issue that clearly separated the followers of Hayes from those of Tilden when the former took the oath of office. There was likewise, unhappily for Hayes, no common bond by which the President could hold his own party together and make a successful administration.

Like three of his predecessors, John Adams, John Quincy Adams, and Martin Van Buren, Hayes was carried into office by the weight of a well-organized machine, rather than by his own hold upon the people. Like all of them he fought faction as a consequence, and every new step in administration forced upon him increased his embarrassment in conducting the Government. At the start, he alienated many Republicans by his policy toward the South.

Before the election Hayes had reached the conclusion that coercion in the South must be abandoned. The people must be left in control of their own institutions, and if they mishandled them must take the consequences. This meant that the last of the States, in which only the army garrisons had kept the Republicans in office, must revert to the control of the Democrats. It also meant an attack upon the President by those who still believed the South a menace, and those who cherished it as a political issue, — the "sentimentalists controlled by knaves," in Godkin's language. Hayes acted upon his conviction as soon as he took office, withdrew the troops, and turned over to the South her own problems. Political reconstruction, as shaped by Congress, had broken down in every part, and it remained to be seen whether the constitutional reconstruction, as embodied in the amendments, would be more permanently effective.

In addition to taking their issue from them, Hayes deprived the politicians of their plunder. The personal conduct of his household added nothing to his popularity in Washington, for his wife served no wines and gave to the White House the atmosphere of the standard middle-class American family. His official family struck a blow at the political use of offices.

Although many of the Liberal Republicans of 1872 were still dissatisfied and saw no prospect of a change of heart for their party, most of them had voted for Hayes, and one of them was taken into the new Cabinet. Carl Schurz became Secretary of the Interior, bringing into office for the first time an active desire to reform the civil service. Congress had made a timid experiment in civil service reform early in the seventies, but had soon wearied of it. Schurz announced that his subordinates would be chosen on merit, and acted upon the announcement.

The storm broke at once upon the Secretary over the issue of the patronage, and soon reached the President. The offices were not only valued assets of Senators and Representatives, who held control over their followers through them, but had come to be regarded as the cement that held the national party organization together. In the absence of an issue, the binding force of the offices had an enlarged importance. But Hayes generally backed up Schurz in the fight. The Indian Bureau, in particular, profited by the new policy. Two serious outbreaks had recently occurred as the result of bad administration. In one, Custer had been led to his destruction; in the other Chief Joseph and the Nez Percés had worried the regular army through a long campaign. The Democratic House of Representatives had in this very period been striking at the army appropriations in order to shape Grant's Southern policy. It had enabled Nast to draw, in one of his biting cartoons, a picture of the savage, the Ku-Klux, and the Congressman shaking hands over a common policy.

Schurz and his Indian Commissioner foresaw the changes needed, now that the range Indians had all been consolidated on reserves, and took this time to reorganize the service.

Hayes refused to give over all the offices as spoils, and removed some officials for pernicious political activity. The most important removal was that of Chester A. Arthur, Collector of the Port of New York, whose enraged friends, Conkling among them, became the center of the attack on the titular head of the party. Sneering at the sincerity of the new policy, Conkling cynically declared that "when Doctor Johnson said that patriotism was the last refuge of a scoundrel, he ignored the enormous possibilities of the word reform." But because Hayes did not in every case follow an ideal that no other President had even set, he lost the support of the reformers who soon denounced him nearly as fiercely as did the "Stalwarts."

Even if Hayes had been able to keep a united party behind him, his Administration could scarcely have been marked by constructive legislation. His party had lost control of the House of Representatives in the election of 1874. The Forty-fifth Congress, chosen with Hayes in 1876, and the Forty-sixth, in 1878, were Democratic, and delighted to embarrass the Administration. Dissatisfied Republicans saw the deadlock and laid it upon the shoulders of the President. The Democratic Congress checked Administration measures, and managed to advance opposition measures of its own. Twice Hayes had to summon special sessions because of the failure of appropriation bills, and in his first winter the opposition endangered those policies of finance to which the Republican party had become pledged.

The Greenback agitation, rising about 1868 and stimulated by the panic of 1873, had not subsided when Hayes became President. It had lost much of its force, but there continued throughout the West, in both parties, a spirit that encouraged inflation of every sort. In Congress there were repeated efforts to repeal the Resumption Act of 1875, which the Democratic platform had denounced the next year. And when a sudden increase in the production of silver reduced its price, a silver inflation movement was placed beside the Greenback movement.

The United States had used almost no silver coin between 1834 and 1862 because the coinage ratio, sixteen to one, undervalued silver and made it wasteful to coin it. No specie was used as currency between 1862 and 1879, and the relative market prices of bullion remained close to their usual average until the year of panic. During the seventies the price of silver fell as new mines were opened in the West. The ratio rose above sixteen to one, and silver, from being undervalued at that ratio, came to be overvalued. It would now have paid owners of silver bullion to coin it into dollars at the legal rate, but Congress had in 1873, after a generation of disuse of silver, dropped the silver dollar from the list of standard coins. As silver fell in value, mine-owners asked for a renewal of coinage, and inflationists joined them, hoping for more money of any kind. During the winter of 1878 a free silver coinage bill, passed by the Democratic House under the guidance of Richard P. Bland, of Missouri, was under consideration in the Republican Senate.

John Sherman, the defender of gold resumption, was no longer in the Senate to fight this Bland Act. He had become Hayes's Secretary of the Treasury, and in this capacity was working toward resumption and upholding Hayes in his war on the spoilsmen. In his place, Allison, of Iowa, forced an amendment to the Bland Bill, taking away its free-coinage character and substituting a requirement to buy a specified amount of silver bullion each month — from $2,000,000 to $4,000,000 worth — and coin it. Thus amended, the House concurred in the act, which Hayes vetoed in February, 1878. It became a law over his veto.

The Administration was embarrassed in its financial policy, but not defeated. The Resumption Bill withstood attacks and, as the day for the resumption of specie payment approached, the price of greenbacks reflected the growing credit of the United States. It reached par two weeks before the appointed day. When that day arrived, Wednesday, January 1, 1879, John Sherman had the satisfaction of seeing the change to a coin basis effected without a shock. More gold was turned into the Treasury for exchange with greenbacks than greenbacks for redemption in gold. It appeared that Horace Greeley had been right when he had maintained that "the way to resume is to resume," — that few would want gold if they could get it.

The adherence of Hayes to the gold standard and

resumption drove from his side another body of Republicans. He had now lost the reformers and the spoilsmen, the radical Republicans and the inflationists, and no one hoped or believed that he would recall his pledge for a single term and be renominated in 1880 to succeed himself. The disintegration of his party was as complete as the collapse of its issues. On no subject, between 1876 and 1880, was it possible to bring before the public a distinctive party issue. The uncertainties of the campaign of 1876 were increased during the next four years.

Both parties had ceased to represent either policies or the people. The office-holders were in no sense the leaders of their communities. Industry, social life, education, and religion had parted company with politics since the decline of the Union issue, and unless a new political alignment could be found there was a prospect of continued rivalry for offices alone. Yet men were beginning to realize that a new period of growth had begun during the Hayes Administration, and that American institutions, formulated before the Civil War, had ceased to meet industrial needs.

BIBLIOGRAPHICAL NOTE

J. F. Rhodes terminates his great history with the election of 1876, and although he has promised sometime to continue it, he has as yet published only a few scattered essays upon the later period. A. M. Gibson, *A Political Crime* (1885), is a contemporary and partisan account of the electoral contest ; P. L. Haworth, *The Hayes-Tilden Disputed Presidential Election* (1906), is a recent work of critical scholarship ; E. Stanwood may be relied upon for platforms, tables of votes, and other formal details, in his *History of the Presidency*. *The Writings and Speeches of S. J. Tilden* (2 vols., ed. by J. Bigelow, 1885) are useful, as are the Blaine books: J. G. Blaine, *Twenty Years of Congress*, E. Stanwood, *James Gillespie Blaine* (1905, in American Statesmen Series); G. Hamilton (pseud. for M. A. Dodge), *James G. Blaine* (1895, a domestic biography) ; and the spicy *Letters of Mrs. James G. Blaine* (edited by H. S. B. Beale, 2 vols., 1908). Other useful biographies or memoirs exist for R. P. Bland, Roscoe Conkling, Robert G. Ingersoll, O. H. Platt, T. C. Platt, John Sherman, and Carl Schurz, etc., while the most important work on the period is *Rutherford Birchard Hayes*, by C. R. Williams (1914), in which voluminous manuscript sources have been used.

CHAPTER VI

BUSINESS AND POLITICS

A GREAT commercial revival, affecting the whole United States, began during the Administration of Hayes. Ingersoll had predicted it, in defining his candidate in 1876, when he declared: " The Republicans of the United States demand a man who knows that prosperity and resumption, when they come, must come together ; that when they come, they will come hand in hand through the golden harvest-fields ; hand in hand by the whirling spindles and the turning wheels ; hand in hand past the open furnace doors ; hand in hand by the flaming forges ; hand in hand by the chimneys filled with eager fire, greeted and grasped by the countless sons of toil." In every section and in every occupation commerce revived during 1878 and 1879. Manufactures began to invade the South ; mining-booms gave new life to the camps of the Far West ; the wheat-lands of the Northwest, reached by the " Granger " railroads and cultivated by great power machines, produced a new type of bonanza farming ; in the Southwest and on the plains great droves of cattle produced a new type of cattle king ; and the factory towns of the East began again to grow. Connecting the various sections, the railroads played a new part, and built more miles of track in the next ten years than in any decade before or since. The whole country awoke as from an anæsthetic, tested its muscles to find that they were stronger than ever, and set to work again.

The silent evidence of the United States Treasury testifies to the prosperity of the next ten years. The average expenditures of the United States from 1850 to 1860 were under $60,000,000; they ranged between 1880 to 1890 from $244,000,000 to $297,000,000 without exhausting the supply. Yearly, despite the heavy drains upon it, a surplus accumulated to the embarrassment of the Government and the demoralization of Congress. The aggregate accumulation for ten years was over $1,000,000,000.

The disbursements of the United States were growing at a higher rate than its population, though this was keeping up the traditions of a new country. From 31,443,321 inhabitants, with which the nation faced the Civil War in 1860, it had grown to 38,558,371 in 1870, and it was now, in 1880, 50,155,783. In mobility and activity it had increased even more rapidly than this, for it was served by nearly three times as many miles of railway (87,000) in 1880 as when the war broke out. Along the old frontier the percentage figures for population and railway mileage were highest, but everywhere a larger population was moving more actively, and studying itself more intently than ever before. It was also generating more internal friction than ever. In the silver mines at Leadville in 1878 had occurred one of the great forerunners of economic clash. This had been preceded in 1877 by the railway strikes of Pennsylvania and the East. In California, Dennis

Kearney and the Irish were driving the Chinese from society in the interest of "America for Americans." The murders by the "Molly Maguires" had brought condign punishment upon the lawless in the anthracite region; and throughout the East men were vaguely conscious of a secret society that called itself the Knights of Labor.

Complexity, class interest, and the problems at once of labor and of capital, thrust themselves upon a society that had occupied its continent and used most of its free land. The Centennial had revived the study of American history from patriotic reasons. An intense interest in self-analysis now kept this alive, as Henry Adams, James Schouler, and John Bach McMaster devoted themselves to a scrutiny of historic facts, as colleges began to create chairs of American history, as James Ford Rhodes retired from his office to his study to write the history of his own times. In the next few years associations for the study of political economy, political science, sociology, and history multiplied the testimonies to the existence of a new nation.

It was many years before the study of history and institutions reached the eighties and began to place events in their true proportion. Then it appeared that there was in fact a fundamental economic problem and that the political issues of the decade faced it from various angles.

The United States had nearly reached its greatest capacity in production by 1880, and was no longer able to consume its output. Through its first century there had been a rough plenty everywhere, —enough food, enough work, and free land, — so that the industrious citizen need never go hungry, although he was rarely able to acquire great wealth. Men had worked with their own hands and with the labor of their beasts of burden, as men had ever worked. Their land had appeared, indeed, to be the land of opportunity. Population had doubled itself in a short generation, and America had called upon the oppressed of Europe to aid in reclaiming the plains and forests. With all the labor and opportunity, there had rarely been either an overproduction or a lack of work.

The industrial revolution changed the nature of American society in many directions. Through an improved system of communication, whose results were first visible between 1857 and 1873, it had broadened the realm to be exploited, brought the rich plains of the West into agricultural competition with the Middle West and the East, and enabled an increased production of staples by lessening freights and widening the area of choice. As the result of rapid communication grain, cotton, and food animals increased more rapidly than population. The use of manures and a more careful agriculture on the smaller farms — and all the farms were growing smaller — further swelled the productivity of the individual farmer.

Machinery increased the capacity of the laborer as transportation widened his choice of home. The factories, as they were reorganized in the new period of prosperity, found that invention had lessened the need for labor and increased the product. Machine tools in agriculture, in iron and steel, in textiles, in shoemaking, rendered the course of manufacture nearly automatic, and when steam neared its limit in dexterity active minds could see electricity holding out a new promise.

In 1880 population and the capacity to consume American products were growing less rapidly than the power to produce. The United States was finding every year greater difficulty in selling all its output. It was possible to foresee the day when overproduction might be a menace unless there should be some reorganization of society to meet the new problem. Pending the arrival of that reorganization, prices fell.

A study of the prices of standard commodities shows that there was a constant, moderate decline after the Civil War. During the war nominal prices, expressed in depreciated greenbacks, rose far above the normal, but when corrected to a gold basis they show little change. At the end of the war, however, the steady decline set in; by 1880 it was perceptible, and by 1890 it had come to be generally admitted. It continued until 1900, when the larger production of gold and an extended use of bank credits and checks, increased the volume and mobility of currency and started a general rise in prices. Inflationists believed, in the eighties, that the falling prices were due to an appreciation of gold, and demanded more money because they so believed; but overproduction appears to give a better explanation of the decline than gold appreciation. In the falling prices may be seen a proof of the enlarged production and a justification of serious study of remedial measures.

Solutions, intended to restore good prices and to correct social evils, became numerous as the eighties advanced. Tariff reformers claimed that the tariff was a vexatious interference with proper freedom of trade, without which a foreign market for American surplus could not be obtained. The protected manufacturers retorted that only through a higher tariff could manufactures be developed and an enlarged consuming population of factory workers be created at home. A Western economist brushed both these aside and found the key to the situation in the disappearance of free land, and urged a single tax upon land as a panacea. United labor found the cause to be unrestricted immigration. Too much government, with its extravagance and corruption, was a cause in the mind of extreme theoretical democrats. Too little government was equally responsible for the discords, in the eyes of growing groups of socialists and communists.

Before 1890 the United States was involved in an elaborate discussion of its troubles and their causes, but in 1880 the period had only just begun and its trend was not clear to the political leaders who were yet quarreling over the spoils of office. Hayes was ending his term in disfavor, and was passing into the jurisdiction of the historians, which was much more kindly disposed toward him than was that of his contemporaries. He had gone into office without being the leader of his party and without having a single definitive issue. He had alienated one faction after another; while in Congress, in which both houses were never Republican, it was never possible to pass

constructive laws. The fight for the next nomination
began soon after his inauguration.

Grant and Blaine were the most probable candidates for the Republican nomination as the spring of
1880 advanced. For the former there was a feeling of
affection among the senatorial crowd, headed by Roscoe Conkling, who had been so severely disciplined
by Hayes. The refusal of the President to allow the
officials of the United States to engage too actively
in politics had brought about the dismissal of Arthur
and Cornell from their posts, and a prolonged quarrel
with the Senate. Hayes had won here, but the defeated leaders turned upon his Southern policy, demanded a "strong" candidate who would really keep
the South in check, and called for Grant as the only
strong man who could lead his party. Grant was willing in 1880 as he would have been in 1876. Upon
his return from his trip around the world his candidacy was pressed and had strong support among Civil
War veterans and men who were displeased with
Hayes.

Blaine, too, was still a candidate, drawing his
strength from men of the same type as those who stood
for Grant. He might have secured the nomination had
he not been opposed by the Secretary of the Treasury,
John Sherman, whose friends thought his distinguished service in the cause of hard money entitled
him to a reward. A special element in Sherman's
strength was a group of pliant negro delegates, from
the Southern wing of the party, which was brought
to Chicago under close guard, fed and entertained in
a suite at the Palmer House, and voted in a block as

Sherman's managers directed. None of these three, Grant, Blaine, and Sherman, could please the reform element, that found its choice in Senator George F. Edmunds of Vermont.

The convention at Chicago was marked by the fight of Conkling to secure unity and the nomination for Grant, and by the stubbornness with which the opposing delegates held out against a third term and for their own candidates. In the end the deadlock was broken when the followers of Blaine and Sherman shifted to the latter's floor manager, James A. Garfield, and gave him the nomination on the thirty-sixth ballot. The Vice-Presidency was thrown to the Conkling men, falling upon Chester A. Arthur, who accepted it against the desires of his leader. The platform was a "code of memories" as it had been in 1876 and 1872, congratulating the party on its successes of the past and having no clear vision of the future.

The Democratic party in 1880 was without leader or issue, as it had been since 1860. Tilden, who might have been renominated and run on the charge that he was counted out in 1876, was sick. He was unwilling to run unless the demand were more spontaneous than it appeared to be. In its perplexity the party turned to a military hero who called himself a Democrat and had been passed over in 1876. General Winfield Scott Hancock had never been in active politics, but was now nominated over a long list of local candidates. William H. English, of Indiana, who was known to have money, and was believed to be ready to use it in the campaign, was the vice-presidential candidate.

The canvass of 1880 was fought during a prosperous summer on issues that were largely personal. As Sherman said of Ohio in 1879, so he might have said of the country in 1880, that "the revival of industries and peace and happiness was a shrewd political trick of the Republicans to carry" the United States. Following their practice for three campaigns, the old line speakers dwelt upon the conditions in the South. An Indiana rhyme "for young Democrats" ran : —

> "Sing a song of shotguns,
>   Pocket full of knives,
> Four-and-twenty black men,
>   Running for their lives ;
> When the polls are open
>   Shut the nigger's mouth,
> Is n't that a bully way
>   To make a solid South ? "

But the audiences were unresponsive. An old political reporter remembers being in the national headquarters late in the campaign, and hearing Blaine, who had been stumping for Garfield, say, "You want to fold up the bloody shirt and lay it away. It 's of no use to us. You want to shift the main issue to protection." Not until the campaign was nearly over did a real issue emerge.

The protective tariff had not played a large part in any campaign since 1860. In 1868 and 1872 both parties had looked forward to the reduction of revenue to a peace basis, adopting mild planks to that effect. In 1876 the topic had been more prominent in the platforms, but not in the canvass. In 1880 Hancock was questioned on the tariff during one of his speeches. The question was probably unpremeditated, but it took the candidate unaware, for as an officer in the regular army he had never given the matter thought. His evasive answer, that the tariff was a local issue only, gave an opening to his opponents, who forced the tariff to a prominent place in the few remaining days before election. They made much of Hancock's ignorance, and perhaps by this maneuver offset the disadvantage done to Garfield by a forged letter, which purported to show him as a friend of cheap labor and Chinese immigration. Garfield and Arthur were elected by a small plurality over Hancock. No one received a popular majority, for a third candidate, named Weaver, headed a Greenback-Labor ticket and polled 308,000 votes.

General James A. Garfield would have become Senator from Ohio in 1881 had not his election transferred him to the Presidency. The fifty years of his life covered a career that was typically American. The son of a New England emigrant, he was born in the Connecticut Reserve in Ohio. He worked his way from the farm through the log school to college. His service on the towpath of the Ohio Canal, in the course of his education, became a strong adjunct to his popularity among the common people. He taught Latin and Greek after leaving college, studied law, worked into politics, and went to the front upon the call for troops. He left the war a major-general to enter Congress, in 1863, where he sat until his election to the Senate in 1880. He was the friend of John Sherman and had been the manager of his campaign. Like his friend, and like most Ohio Republicans, he believed that the tariff was one of

the bases of prosperity in his State. In his campaign
a young Cleveland merchant named Hanna raised
funds among the local manufacturers on the plea
that Republican success and their interests would go
hand in hand. In his inaugural address, however,
Garfield said nothing of the new issue which was
threatening to enter politics, but dwelt upon the supremacy of law, the status of the South, hard money,
religious freedom, and the civil service.

The Republican party had been left broken and
in hostile camps by President Hayes; Garfield tried
in his Cabinet to change this and " to have a party
behind him." The State Department went to his
rival and ally, Blaine, whose personal following was
larger than that of any other American politician.
The independent Republicans, who had seceded in
1872 and had muttered ever since, were pleased by
the elevation of Wayne MacVeagh, a Pennsylvania
lawyer, to the post of Attorney-General. A friend of
Conkling, who had made a striking record in the
New York Post-Office through two terms, Thomas
L. James, became Postmaster-General. The sensi-
bilities of the West, always jealous of the East in
matters of finance, were appeased by the selection of
William L. Windom, of Minnesota, as Secretary of
the Treasury, for "any Eastern man would be accused
of being an agent or tool of the ' money kings' and
' gold-bugs' of New York and Europe." The Cabinet as a whole was received with favor, but the harmony which its members promised was soon disturbed.

The appointment of Blaine as Secretary of State,
which Garfield had determined upon a few days after

his election, was a blow to Roscoe Conkling. Hayes had struck at Conkling in removing Arthur and Cornell. Now when Garfield decided to please himself in the New York collectorship, Conkling saw in the act the hand of Blaine. He fell back upon the practice of senatorial courtesy, and held up the confirmation of the appointment. When he found himself unable to coerce the President, he broke with him as he had broken with Hayes, and this time he and his colleague from New York, Thomas Collier Platt, resigned their seats and appealed to the New York Legislature, then in session. The move was not without promise. Cornell was now Governor of New York. Arthur, with the prestige of the Vice-Presidency, left his chair in the Senate to work for the reëlection and triumphant return of Conkling and Platt, on the doctrine that the appointments of a President must be personally acceptable to the Senators from the State concerned. But the New York Legislature failed to give the martyrs their vindication, and permitted them to remain in private life. Their friends, the "Stalwarts," ceased to support Garfield.

James, who was not enough a follower of Conkling to emulate him, remained in the Post-Office, where he had already found wholesale corruption. It had been the practice of the Post-Office to classify the mail routes according to their method of transportation, and to mark those running by stage or rider by a star on the general list. These had come to be known as the "star routes." The contracts for the star routes were flexible in order to meet the shifting needs of the Western population that lived away from railways and depended upon the stage-coach. When the business of any route justified a better service than it was receiving, the Department was at liberty to increase the service, hasten speed, and raise the pay without a re-letting of the contract. During the latter seventies the growth of settlement throughout the remoter West had justified a large increase in star-route costs, but James discovered not only legitimate increase but collusive fraud. The official in charge, in collusion with former Congressmen who " knew the ropes," and with the mail contractors, had awarded original contracts to low bidders who had no intention of fulfilling their bids. After the letting of contracts the compensation had been increased without investigation or reference to actual needs.

The unearned profits had been shared by the promoters and the dishonest officials, and some of it had gone into the Republican campaign fund. A former Senator, Dorsey by name, who was indicted for fraud in 1882, had been Secretary of the Republican National Committee in 1880, and had been hurried to Indiana to save that State. He did this so effectively that his friends gave him a dinner, which Arthur attended, and at which the allusions to his methods in Indiana were but loosely veiled. Brady, the official in the Post-Office, had collected the usual assessments on federal office-holders for Garfield's campaign fund. When he and others were threatened with criminal prosecution they produced letters by which they hoped to prove that Garfield was cognizant of and had approved their financial methods. How far they might have succeeded in blackening the President and stopping his prosecutions must remain unknown, for he was shot on July 2, 1881, while on his way to a college celebration, and died on September 19.

The murderer of Garfield declared to the policeman who arrested him, "I am a Stalwart and want Arthur for President." It was soon learned that he was a disappointed candidate for office, and irresponsible Washington gossip soon had it that Garfield's friends wanted him to hang, while Arthur's thought he was only insane. The murderer's sister, in an incoherent book based on his story, asserted, "Yes, the 'Star-Route' business killed Garfield! The claim, 'The Stalwarts are my friends,' hung Guiteau!" He was perhaps insane, and was certainly irresponsible, but his crime, coming simultaneously with the notoriety of the star-route frauds and the demands of Conkling, emphasized the pettiness of factions and the need for a reform in the civil service.

The illness of Garfield dragged on through eleven weeks in the summer of 1881, with bulletins one day up and the next down. The strain told on every one in the Administration. The prospect of Arthur's succession called attention to the fact that the Vice-President is rarely nominated for fitness, but is chosen at the end of a hot convention, in carelessness, or to placate a losing side. It led soon to the passage of an adequate Presidential Succession Act. The death of Garfield threw the control to the Republican faction that disliked him most.

Blaine, the head of Garfield's Cabinet, was most directly affected by the catastrophe. He had stepped from the Senate into the State Department at Garfield's request. While he was a receptive candidate for the Presidency this post suited his needs and gratified his taste. He loved business and liked to associate with men. He had a diplomatic vision that led him to formulate a more constructive policy than most Secretaries have had.

With England, Blaine found negotiations upon the Isthmian Canal pending, having been taken up by Hayes. His attitude in his notes of 1881 failed to meet the approval of Great Britain, and ignored obligations that the United States had long before accepted. But it pointed to an American canal and was part of his larger scheme. His America was inclusive of both continents, and drew him to hope for larger trade relations in the Western Hemisphere. With the approval of Garfield he had started to mediate in South America, in a destructive war between Chile and Peru. He had on foot, when Garfield died, a scheme for a congress of the American States in the interest of a greater friendliness among them. The invitations for this gathering had just been issued when Arthur reorganized his Cabinet, brought F. T. Frelinghuysen in as Secretary of State, and let Blaine out. There was no public office ready for him at this time, so he retired to private life and the historical research upon which his *Twenty Years of Congress* was founded. Jefferson Davis had just brought out his *Rise and Fall of the Confederate Government*, while the Yorktown centenary, like the centennial of independence, had stimulated the market for historical works.

BIBLIOGRAPHICAL NOTE

The United States Census of 1880 is more elaborate and reliable than its predecessor of 1870, and may be supplemented to advantage by H. V. Poor, *Manual of the Railroads of the United States for 1880*, which contains a good sketch of railroad construction, and by R. P. Porter, *The West from the Census of 1880* (1882). E. E. Sparks, *National Development* (in *The American Nation*, vol. 23, 1907), is a useful survey of the years 1877 to 1885, and contains a good bibliographical chapter. The bibliographies in Channing, Hart, and Turner's *Guide to the Study and Reading of American History* (1912) are specially valuable for the years 1876 to 1912. E. B. Andrews, *The United States in Our Own Time* (1903), is discursive and entertaining. Special phases of material development may be reached through D. R. Dewey, *Financial History of the United States ;* T. V. Powderly, *Thirty Years of Labor* (1889); H. George, *Progress and Poverty* (1879 ; and often reprinted), and the Aldrich Report on Prices (52d Congress, 2d session, Senate Report, No. 1394). Many interesting details are to be found in W. C. Hudson, *Random Recollections of an Old Political Reporter* (1911) ; and J. F. Rhodes has touched upon this period in his essays, among which are "A Review of President Hayes's Administration in the Light of Thirty Years" (*Century Magazine*, October, 1909) ; "The Railroad Riots of 1877" (*Scribner's Magazine*, July, 1911) ; and "The National Republican Conventions of 1880 and 1884 " (*Scribner's Magazine*, September, 1911). Among the economic journals started in the eighties, and containing a wealth of scholarly detail for contemporary history, are the *Quarterly Journal of Economics* and the *Political Science Quarterly*.

CHAPTER VII

THE NEW ISSUES

GARFIELD died before he met his first Congress, the Forty-seventh, which was elected with him in 1880, but he lived long enough to foresee the first chance to do party business that had appeared since 1875. When Grant lost the lower house at the election of 1874, the Democrats gained control of that body and Michael C. Kerr, of Indiana, supplanted Blaine as Speaker. On Kerr's death in 1876, Samuel J. Randall, of Pennsylvania, took the place, and was continued in it through the next two Congresses, in the latter of which, the Forty-sixth, his party controlled the Senate too. It had been impossible to produce an agreement between the Senate, the House, and the President on important new matters. They could not always agree even on appropriations, and all Republicans felt with Mrs. Blaine when she wrote, after the election of 1880, "Do you take in that the House is Republican, and the Senate a tie, which gives the casting vote to the Republican V.P.? Oh, how good it is to win and to be on the strong side!"

When the new Congress organized, Randall ceased to be Speaker and became leader of the minority, while J. Warren Keifer, of Ohio, took his place, with a small Republican majority behind him. In the

Senate the predictions of Mrs. Blaine were fulfilled, although the accident which made a President of Arthur left the Senate without a Vice-President. In the even division of the Senate, the two independent members controlled the whole. Judge David Davis, transferred " from the Supreme Bench to the Fence," became the presiding officer, and generally voted with the Republicans, though elected as a Democrat. Mahone, of Virginia, an Irishman and an ex-Confederate, called himself a " Readjuster," and voted with the Administration. These two men made it possible to carry party measures through Congress.

Shortly after Congress met in 1881, Arthur reorganized his Cabinet, allowing the friends of Garfield to resign and putting his own Stalwart friends in their places. The new Secretary of State, Frelinghuysen, took up Blaine's policies and mangled them. He adhered to the general view of an American canal, as Blaine had done. He pushed the influence of the United States in Europe as far as he could, keeping Lowell, in England, busy in behalf of Irish-Americans whose lust for Home Rule got them into trouble with the British police. But he dropped the South American policy, recalled the invitations to the Pan-American Congress, and kept hands off the Chilean war. Blaine protested in vain against this humiliating reversal.

The decision of Arthur to take counsel from the Stalwarts aroused fears among others of the party that his would be the administration of a spoilsman. His first message, however, somewhat allayed these fears, for it dwelt at length upon the unsatis-

factory status of the civil service, and the need for
a merit system that should govern removals and appointments. He promised his support to measures
even more thoroughgoing than the reformers had
asked, and, in January, 1883, signed the "magna
carta" of civil service reform.

The use of public offices for party purposes had
been regarded as a scandal by independents of both
parties for four administrations. The long list of
breaches of trust, revealed in the seventies, had
made reformers feel that incompetence and spoils
endangered the life of the nation. As late as 1880,
they had heard a delegate in the Republican Convention, when asked to vote for a civil service plank,
exclaim indignantly: "Mr. President, Texas has had
quite enough of the civil service . . . We are not
here, sir, for the purpose of providing offices for the
Democracy. . . . After we have won the race, as we
will, we will give those who are entitled to positions
office. What are we up here for?" And they had
become used to the silent or outspoken resistance
to their demands from men in "practical" politics.

The history of the civil servants of the United
States falls into three periods: Before 1829, 1829–
65, and 1865–83. In the first period they were commonly treated as permanent officials. Rarely had
they been removed for partisan purposes, although it
had been the wail of Jefferson that "few die, and
none resign." Appointments had often been given
as the reward for past services, but none had felt a
need for a general proscription of officials upon the
entry of a new President.

Andrew Jackson brought a new practice into use in 1829. His election followed a political revolution, in which it was believed by his supporters that the National Republican party had become corrupt. It was a matter of faith and pledge to turn the incumbents out of office. Hungry patriots crowded round the jobs, while Jackson's advisers included men who in New York and Pennsylvania had already learned how to use the offices as retainers for future service. Advocacy of the Democratic principle of rotation in office was in practice easily converted into the maintenance of the maxim that "to the victors belong the spoils."

Every President after Jackson used the offices for partisan purposes, and few objected to the practice on theoretical grounds. The simplicity of the National Government made the habit less destructive than it otherwise would have been. The spoils system did not enter the army or navy, the only extensive technical departments of the United States. In other branches of the Government a large majority of the officials were unskilled penmen, whose places could easily be filled with others as little skilled as themselves. Always a few clerks who knew the business were saved to guide the recruits, and the departments were generally working again before a President met his first Congress.

Lincoln was not different from his predecessors in the use of offices. He permitted the most complete sweep that had yet been made, being forced to an unusually high percentage of new appointments by the necessity of removing Southerners. In his hands the patronage became an additional weapon for the Union, upholding the leaders in Congress, and striking at the backsliders. In the election of 1864 the Union party carried all the branches of the Government, and it had a vision of four years of complete control of the offices when the death of Lincoln brought a Tennessee Democrat into the White House.

The discussion of civil service reform, on theoretical grounds, began about 1865, when the evil of removals for party purposes was shown to the Senate. Johnson was trying to use the patronage for his own ends, in opposition to the will of the radicals in Congress. Reformers who maintained the iniquity of this custom now found temporary converts among the Republicans. They got a committee appointed on the civil service in 1866, and President Grant announced his conversion to the principle early in his Administration.

In 1871 Congress tried the experiment of a modest appropriation ($25,000) for a reform of the civil service, and Grant placed the test in the hands of George William Curtis, a leader of the new reform. The commission breasted the whole current of politics, found that Grant would not support it in critical cases, and was abandoned by Congress after a short trial. The demand, however, increased, receiving the support of the independents who were Liberal Republicans in 1872, and who thereafter constituted a menace to party regularity. Schurz, Godkin, and Curtis were their admitted leaders. In 1872 and 1876 they persuaded the great parties to put general pledges for civil service reform into their platforms. Schurz, as Secretary of the Interior under Hayes, put their ideal partly into practice. In 1881 they were a well-recognized body of advocates, with a definite doctrine of non-partisan efficiency, which few politicians denied in principle or liked in fact.

Public attention was focused upon the civil service by the events of 1881. The fight between Garfield and Conkling raised not only the question of the relative rights of President and Senate in appointments, but that of the use of offices for the support of political machines. The frauds uncovered in postal administration by the star-route investigations could hardly have occurred in a department administered by experienced and competent officials. The murder of Garfield by a disappointed office-seeker gave additional emphasis to the need for reform, and these things coming together made possible the passage of a civil service act earlier than its advocates expected.

President Arthur recommended the reform in 1881, and his party, chastened by the fall election of 1882, took up a law in the session of 1882-83. Eaton, one of the leading reformers, and first chairman of the Civil Service Commission, wrote the bill which Congress passed with little real debate. Men who hated the measure knew the unwisdom of opposing it. A board of three commissioners was created in 1883 to classify the civil servants, prepare rules and lists, and conduct examinations. The classified service, removed from politics, began with 13,780 officers in 1884; by 1896 it contained 87,044; by

1911, 227,657. It grew most actively toward the end of each administration, as outgoing Presidents transferred to it the offices that they had filled. Its best recommendation was to be found in the opposition of politicians toward it.

Arthur did better than the reformers had hoped in urging and administering the Civil Service Act. He prosecuted the star-route trials, even among his Stalwart friends.

In 1882 Congress, with Arthur's approval, took up a revision of the tariff. Neither of the great parties had, in 1882, received a clear mandate touching the tariff, although it was true that most Republicans were content with the system in its general outlines, while a considerable number of Democrats were listening to tariff reform and asking for a tariff for revenue only. It had been eighteen years since the last general revision had taken place, and in that period unforeseen conditions had developed, whose tendency was at once to point the need for a readjustment of schedules and to create a class of citizens whose profits would be touched thereby. The course of financial reconstruction between 1865 and 1875 had raised the rate of actual protection beyond the expectations of its advocates.

In 1865 the revenues of the United States, amounting to $322,000,000, and far exceeding the needs of the Treasury in time of peace, came chiefly from the tariff and the internal revenue. The two taxes were dependent upon each other. Each increase in the latter had forced an increase in the former, lest special burdens should be laid upon American manufacture. The ideal of protection had never been lacking, nor had special interests failed to look out for themselves, but the dominant spirit in the war taxes was revenue.

When Congress undertook to reduce the revenue to a peace basis, it found that every approach to the tariff aroused classes of interested manufacturers, while every attack upon the internal revenue was welcomed by the public. As a result, following the line of least resistance, most of the internal taxes were removed by 1870, leaving the tariff rates where they had been, and higher than any protectionist had asked. A large part of the tariff rate had been intended to equalize the internal revenue tax ; the removal of the latter created to that extent an incidental protection, which was unexpected but was none the less acceptable. Some few details of the tariff were modified by special acts, and there was a flat reduction of ten per cent in 1872. But the panic of 1873 reduced the revenues and frightened Congress, in 1875, into restoring the ten per cent. In 1882 the rates of 1865 remained substantially unchanged, leaving the protected industries in the enjoyment of an incidental protection never intended for them and created only by accident in the general reduction of revenue.

Spasmodic attacks were made upon the tariff system throughout the seventies, but since few defended it on principle they failed to affect the public. The tariff was not a political issue. Opposition to it was confined to members of the Democratic party, in search for weapons to turn against the Republicans, and to theorists and economists who had little connection with politics. There were free-trade clubs after 1868, though few ever wanted to establish real free trade. All that the free-trader commonly desired was a mitigation of protection and the establishment of reasonable rates. Godkin, Schurz, Sumner of Yale, David A. Wells, Edward Atkinson, and Henry D. Lloyd taught the tariff-for-revenue theory wherever they could find listeners. Wells wrote on "The Creed of Free Trade," in the *Atlantic Monthly* in 1875, and was sure he had found the issue of 1876. But in neither this nor the next campaign did the parties face the issue. In 1880 the tariff figured only as a means of embarrassing Hancock, while Garfield did not even mention it in his inaugural.

The forces that compelled a revision of the tariff in 1882–83 had to do with revenue and expenditures. Following the new prosperity the receipts increased beyond the ability of Congress to spend them. There was a small surplus in 1879. In 1880 it was $68,000,000; in 1881, $101,000,000; in 1882, $145,000,000; in 1883, $132,000,000. The surplus was a constant incentive to extravagance and deranged the currency. If it was allowed to remain in the Treasury, its millions were withheld from circulation, and contraction was the result; if it was applied to the purchase or redemption of bonds, the national bank currency was contracted, for this was founded upon bonds owned by the banks; and it could not be spent without the invention of new channels. The temptation to increase pension payments was strengthened, while public works multiplied without reason.

The waste of money on public works induced

Arthur to advertise the need for a reduction of the revenue. The annual River and Harbor Bill had consumed $3,900,000 in 1870, and $8,900,000 in 1880. In 1882 the bill was swollen to over $18,000,000 by greed and log-rolling. Arthur vetoed it as unreasonable and unconstitutional in August, 1882. It passed over his veto, but the defeat of his party in the following November was construed as a vindication of the President. The Republicans lost control of the House of Representatives, Democratic governors were elected in Massachusetts and Pennsylvania, in New York, Connecticut, New Jersey, and Indiana, and critics began to ask if this was the beginning of the end of the party. The certainty that party bills could not be passed in the next Congress, with the control divided, stimulated the Republicans to act while they could. The Civil Service Act was passed early in 1883, and on the same day the House took up the consideration of a new tariff.

Arthur, in 1881, had urged that the revenues be reduced and the tariff be revised, and Congress had created a commission to investigate the needed changes, in May, 1882. This committee was in session throughout the following summer, sitting in manufacturing centers all over the East and hearing testimony from all varieties of manufacturers. It had been organized on a conservative basis, containing members familiar with the needs of sheep-raisers and wool manufacturers, and iron and sugar, as well as experts on administration. Its enemies thought that it was pledged to protection at the start. The commission expressed a belief that the country desired to adhere to the general idea of protection, but it early learned the force of the demand for revision and reduction, and sent into the House, in December, 1882, a project for a bill intended to reduce the tariff at least twenty per cent. The bill based on this was reported from the Committee on Ways and Means on January 16, 1883, and was debated until February 20, and then abandoned in the House for a bill which had passed the Senate.

The Senate Bill was in the form of an amendment to an Internal Revenue Bill already before that house. It was passed on February 20 under the leadership of the young Senator from Rhode Island, Nelson W. Aldrich, and was sent to conference by the House a week later. In conference a new bill was substituted for the Senate Bill. This was hurried through both houses in time to receive the signature of Arthur on March 3, 1883.

The tariff of 1883 failed to meet the demand for a revision. Its debates show the difficulties attendant upon the construction of any tariff. Congress was divided upon the theory of protection, both parties including high protectionists as well as tariff-for-revenue men. The revenue-producing side of the tariff increased the complexities, since every change in a rate might affect the standing of the Treasury. In addition to the economic and the fiscal needs, quite serious enough, there was the tireless influence of the lobby of manufacturers, pressing for single rates which should aid this business or that. Few Congressmen were sufficiently detached in interests to be entirely dispassionate as they framed the schedules. Many did not even try to disguise their desire to promote local interests. Neither party had a mandate on the tariff in 1882, but when the act had become a law it was clear that most of the Republican leaders voted cheerfully for all the protection they could get, that the intent to reduce the revenue had failed, and that what little hope of revision remained was in the opposition party. "The kaleidoscope has been turned a hair's breadth," said the *Nation;* "and the colors transposed a little, but the component parts are the same." It was deliberate bad faith throughout, urged a Democratic leader, and "finished this magnificent shaft [of the tariff policy] which they had been for years erecting, and crowned it with the last stone by repealing the internal tax on playing cards and putting a twenty per cent tax upon the Bible."

Throughout the tariff debate no argument had been used more steadily than that of the protectionists that protection to labor was their aim. The degradation of "pauper labor" in Europe was contrasted repeatedly with that prosperity that was typical of America. The insistence upon the argument revealed the desire to conciliate a class that was being noticed in American society for the first time.

The great labor problem before the Civil War had been that of getting enough laborers and meeting the competition which the abundant free lands of the West had offered. Labor organizations and strikes had been so unusual that public opinion had not yet come to regard them as normal features of society. But the manufacturing development of the

POPULATION AND IMMIGRATION, 1850-1910

(Table and Diagram based upon Thirteenth Census, 1910, Population,
Vol. 1, pp. 129, 130.)

	Total Population.	Foreign and Mixed Parentage.	Foreign Born.
1910 . .	91,972,266	18,897,837	13,345,545
1900 . .	75,994,575	15,646,017	10,213,817
1890 . .	62,947,714	11,503,675	9,121,867
1880 . .	50,155,783	8,274,867	6,559,679
1870 . .	39,818,449	5,324,268	5,493,712
1860 . .	31,443,321		4,096,753
1850 . .	23,191,876		2,240,535

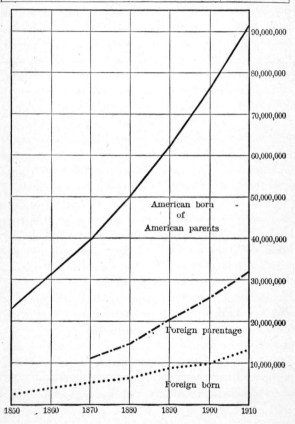

sixties in iron and steel, in textiles, and in other machine industries, threw workmen together in increasing number, taught them their interests as a class, and set the scene for an outbreak of strikes when the shops shut down or reduced wages in the depression of the seventies. About 1877 these strikes shocked society by their violence. Neither had the public been educated to the strike itself, nor the labor leaders to that moderation, without which public sympathy cannot be retained or strikes won. A feeling adverse to organized labor swept the country and endangered the existence of the labor movement.

The Knights of Labor received the heaviest weight of disfavor. This was an industrial union, founded in 1869, embracing labor of all trades, and held together by a secret organization. Dismissal so often followed admitted membership in a union that secrecy was defensible, but secrecy mystified and frightened the public. The policy of secrecy was abandoned in 1882, after the excesses of the " Molly Maguires" had brought discredit upon all organized labor. Under the leadership of Grand Master Workman Powderly the Knights carried on an open and aggressive campaign of education for labor and inspection laws throughout the Union. The American Federation of Labor, founded in 1881 and reorganized in 1886, aided in this general work, and with the Knights helped to reconcile the public to the principle of unionism.

State bureaus of labor appeared in many States as the result of the general agitation. An eight-hour law, for federal employees, had been gained in 1868, while in 1884 a Commissioner of Labor was created in the Department of the Interior. Arthur was urged to give the post to Powderly, but selected instead an economist less actively identified with the propaganda, Carroll D. Wright, under whose direction the Bureau grew steadily in importance. Its reports became quarries for statistical information on the labor problem, and its success justified its incorporation in the new Department of Commerce and Labor in 1903.

The "Army of the Discontented," as Powderly called the workers, demanded education and protective laws, and turned their attention to competition about 1882. The cutting of wages by peasant laborers, newly arrived in America, was a grievance as soon as labor became class-conscious. Opposition to this became virulent in the Far West, where the foreigner was also a Mongolian. The Chinese of the Pacific Slope, more frugal and industrious than Americans, were harried in the early eighties, and violence was done them in many quarters. Garfield had been weakened in 1880 by a forged letter seeming to show that he favored the introduction of more Chinese. So numerous were the persecutors that Congress responded to the demand for a Chinese Exclusion Bill, in spite of the Treaty of 1880, which guaranteed fair treatment. Arthur vetoed the first bill, but accepted a second, less stringent in its terms. After this victory, the labor forces turned upon immigration in general.

No idea had been fixed more firmly in the American mind than that the oppressed of Europe were here to find opportunity. Immigrants had always been welcomed and assimilated, while Congress had, in 1864, organized a bureau to encourage and safeguard immigration. The influx always increased in prosperous, and declined in adverse, years. After 1878 the annual number broke all records. Western railway corporations were inviting immigrants to use their lands, manufacturers called them to the mills, and the total rose from 177,000 in 1879 to 788,000 in 1882. This latter year was the greatest of the century, its newcomers attracting the attention of the press, of the city charities who felt their growing responsibilities, and of the unions who felt their competition. Nearly all the immigrants were producers, a high percentage being able-bodied young men and women. The greatest number came from Great Britain, among whom the Irish settled in the Eastern cities. Next were the Germans, who moved toward Chicago or St. Louis, while the Scandinavians filled up the wheat-lands of the Northwest.

Under the demand of the labor vote, Congress provided, in 1882, for the inspection of immigrants and the deportation of undesirable aliens, and in 1885 it forbade the importation of skilled laborers under contract. As yet the labor movement was largely aristocratic, safeguarding the skilled workmen, but disregarding the common laborers.

The labor and immigration movement in its new aspect widened the field for economic legislation, for few States had factory laws, employers' liability laws, or laws protecting the weak, — the women and the children. It also complicated the situation in politics.

rative of the eighties is covered by E. E. Sparks, *National Development*, and D. R. Dewey, *National Problems* (in *The American Nation*, vols. 23 and 24, 1907), and E. B. Andrews, *The United States in Our Own Time*. A thoughtful economic analysis of the period is D. A. Wells, *Recent Economic Changes* (1890). The Report of the Tariff Commission of 1882 is valuable for the study of tariff revision, as are also the standard tariff histories by E. Stanwood, I. M. Tarbell, and F. W. Taussig. The Annual Reports of the Commissioner of Labor (1884–   ) are fundamental for the labor problem. Useful monographs are C. D. Wright, *An Historical Sketch of the Knights of Labor* (in *Quarterly Journal of Economics*, vol. I), T. V. Powderly, *Thirty Years of Labor* (1889), G. E. McNeill, *The Labor Movement* (1887), and M. A. Aldrich, *The American Federation of Labor* (in American Economic Association, Economic Studies, vol. III).

CHAPTER VIII

GROVER CLEVELAND

THE Administration of Chester A. Arthur proved that the President had never been so discreditable a spoilsman as the reformers had believed, or else that he had changed his spots. The term ended in dignity and Arthur hoped to secure a personal vindication through renomination by his party. His struggle precipitated a contest of leaders, and until the nominations were made, none could say where either party stood.

The independents, chiefly of Republican antecedents, hoped to retain what had been gained in the last Administration. They hoped to extend the reform in the civil service and to focus attention upon the tariff. The failure of downward revision in 1883 had strengthened their hands and increased their hopes. They had dallied with bolting movements and threats so long that party regularity meant little to them. Either party could obtain their support by nominating men who could be trusted to stick to their platform. Arthur was not acceptable to them, and Blaine was anathema.

The candidacy of Arthur was doomed to failure. He had alienated the Stalwarts by his independence, while he had failed to win the reformers because he had not invariably refrained from playing the poli-

tician. In the fall of 1882 he had interfered in the
campaign in New York, allowing his Secretary of
the Treasury, Charles J. Folger, while retaining that
office, to be the Republican candidate for governor.
This had led to the belief that the patronage was
being used for local purposes, and had stirred up an
opposition to Folger which defeated him. Arthur's
veto of the Chinese Exclusion Bill and the River and
Harbor Bill further increased his unpopularity in
various sections. He failed to win over the Blaine
faction, who regarded him as an intrusive accident
and waited impatiently for the next national convention.

Blaine was the leader of the Republican party in
1884, so far as it had a leader, and he possessed all
the weaknesses of such a leader as well as personal
weaknesses of his own. Rarely has it been possible
to nominate or to elect one who has gained a dominant place through party struggles. Such men, Clay,
Webster, Calhoun, and their kind, have commonly
created enough enemies, as they have risen, to make
them unavailable as leaders of a national ticket.
Blaine was handicapped like these. His prolonged
fight against Conkling and the Stalwarts created a
breach too deep to fill, while the old questions respecting his honor would not down.

Early in 1884 Blaine was the leading candidate
for the nomination in spite of all opposition. The
Republican National Committee was in charge of
men who sympathized with him. Dorsey had resigned as its secretary after the star-route exposure,
though his associate in land speculations, Stephen

B. Elkins, remained as one of the managers. The control was in the hands of men who had close affiliation with the old organization, and of the manufacturers who had blocked tariff revision in 1883. It was improbable, in the opinion of many independents, that a tariff reduction could be got from an Administration headed by Blaine; they questioned his sincerity upon civil service reform; and they thought it not right that any man, concerning whose character there was a doubt, should be President. They put forward, within the party, Senator George F. Edmunds, whom they had desired in 1880, and who had since become President of the Senate. Other candidates with local followings were General John A. Logan, of Illinois, John Sherman, and the President himself.

The Chicago Convention of the Republican party, meeting early in June, was the scene of a battle between the two elements in the party. At the outset, the old independents, headed by Curtis, and reinforced by younger men like Henry Cabot Lodge, of Massachusetts, and Theodore Roosevelt, of New York, broke the slate of the National Committee and seated a chairman of their own choice. But the regulars rallied, controlled the platform, and made the nomination. Blaine and John A. Logan were selected, the former accepting the honor with secret misgivings, for he had a clear understanding of the intensity of the opposition within the party. The reformers went home discouraged, many of them determined not to let party regularity hold them to Blaine.

Out of the nomination of Blaine grew the " Mugwump " movement, whose influence was greater than that of the last bolt. The origin of the name " Mugwump " is not entirely clear, but it was well known as an opprobrious epithet, and was applied now by party regulars to the " holier-than-thou " reformers. One of the regulars later quoted Revelation at them : " Thou art neither hot nor cold . . . so, then, I will spew thee out of my mouth." They were more offensive to Republicans than were the Democrats, while the latter were bewildered but cynical. " I know that to-day we are living in a very highly scented atmosphere of political reform," said one of the Democratic Senators a little later, " I know that under the saintly leadership of the Eatonian school of political philosophers we are all ceasing to be partisans, that we no longer recognize party obligations, party duty, party discipline, and party devoirs ; that we are all to become reconciled to a life of political monasticism ; but I will continue to have one failing, and that is in my humble way to be as watchful and as vigilant of the purposes, designs, and craft of the Republican leaders as I have endeavored to be in the past."

The Mugwumps left Chicago and at once opened negotiations with the Democratic leaders. The *Nation* and the *Evening Post* were already with them. *Harper's Weekly*, which had been a Union journal in the war, and Republican ever since, abandoned the party ticket. George William Curtis, its editor, led in the revolt, and the Mugwumps met at the house of one of the Harpers for organization, on

June 17, 1884. Their problem was whether to nominate an independent ticket and be defeated, or to support and help elect a Democratic President, in case the Democrats should be willing to coöperate with them.

Not all the reformers turned from Blaine. Whitelaw Reid, the successor of Horace Greeley on the New York *Tribune*, remained regular. Lodge went back to Massachusetts and persuaded himself to take part in the canvass. Roosevelt, discouraged by the nomination of Blaine, remained regular, but stepped out of the campaign and began his ranch life in the Far West. With him, as with many others, it was a matter of conviction that reform, to be effective, must be urged within the party. But enough of the reformers went with the Mugwumps to lessen Blaine's chances of election.

When the Mugwumps made overtures for fusion to the Democratic leaders, they had in mind as a candidate a young Democratic lawyer who had appeared as Mayor of Buffalo in 1881 and had been elected as reform Governor of New York in 1882. He had secured the aid of independent reformers in that campaign, — men who resented the candidacy of Folger and the intrusion of the National Administration in local politics. As governor he had speedily established his reputation for stubborn honesty and independent judgment. Grover Cleveland had become, like Tilden, the most promising candidate in a party that had no admitted leader.

The opposition from two elements in his party, at the Democratic Convention in Chicago, strengthened

Cleveland as the candidate of reform. Ben Butler, who had himself been nominated for the Presidency by an Anti-Monopoly Convention, denounced him as a foe of labor; and such was Butler's reputation that his enmity was one of Cleveland's assets. John Kelly, the chief of Tammany Hall, opposed him, too, having learned to know him as Governor of New York. Well might Cleveland's friends say, " We love him for the enemies he has made." They nominated him on the second ballot, selecting Thomas A. Hendricks, of Indiana, to run with him. Their platform was full of reform, even of the tariff, but on the latter subject it was less specific than the tariff reformers had hoped.

As the parties stood in 1884, personal character meant more than platform or party name. Cleveland possessed qualities that made his appeal to independents quite as strong as it was to Democrats. With older brothers in the army he had supported his mother during the war, and had kept clear of copperheadism. He stood for sound money; he believed in a tariff for revenue; he had proved his devotion to civil service reform; he lacked the factional enemies who weakened the candidacy of a prominent leader like Blaine; and his peculiar appeal to Republican dissenters led the canvass away from issues into the field of personalities.

The charge of the independents upon Blaine's personal honor caused the Republican schism and drove the party regulars into a retort in kind. The private life of the candidates was uncovered to the annoyance of both and to the greater embarrassment of Cleveland. Nothing discreditable to his honesty could be found, but an apparent lapse in his private conduct gave the pretext for wild and dishonest attacks upon his character. A few years later the novelist, Paul Leicester Ford, in a keen study of New York politics entitled *The Honorable Peter Stirling*, portrayed a situation somewhat resembling that of Cleveland, though disclaiming Cleveland as his model. The Boston *Journal* led in the exploitation of the charges, and partisans forgot decency on both sides. Nast, having formerly cartooned Blaine in the " Bloody Shirt," now turned to " A Roaring Farce — The Plumed Knight in a Clean Shirt," while others pointed out the fact that the admirer who coined the "plumed knight" epithet had been counsel for the fraudulent star-route contractors.

Attempts were made to appeal to class hatred on both sides. Butler had hesitated for several weeks in his acceptance of the nomination by the Anti-Monopoly Convention. Greenbackers and a few labor leaders made up his following, and it was supposed that they would draw votes from the Democrats. After conference with Republican leaders, Butler agreed to run, and it was freely charged that these leaders financed his campaign to injure Cleveland. Republicans appealed to the Irish vote by recalling Blaine's vigorous diplomacy against Great Britain; their opponents caricatured Blaine by representing him as consorting with Irish thugs and dynamiters. At the very end of the canvass a chance remark may have decided the result.

So much had been said of character in the campaign that both candidates brought out the clergy to give them certificates of excellence. In October a meeting of clergymen of all denominations was held at the Fifth Avenue Hotel to greet Blaine. The oldest minister, Burchard by name, was asked to deliver the address, and while he spoke Blaine thought of other matters. He thus missed a phrase which other hearers caught and which the Democrats immediately advertised. It denounced the Democrats as adherents of "rum, Romanism, and rebellion," and was reported as conveying a gratuitous insult to the Irish vote. How many Irish turned from Blaine to Cleveland in the last week of the campaign cannot be said, but the election was so close that a few votes, swung either way, could have determined it. Cleveland carried New York and won a majority of the electoral college, but his popular plurality over Blaine was only 23,000, while he had some 300,000 fewer than his combined rivals. Butler drew 175,000 votes without defeating Cleveland. Purists, disgusted with the personalities of the campaign, swelled the Prohibition vote to 150,000.

On March 4, 1885, Grover Cleveland was inaugurated as the first Democrat elected President since James Buchanan. His Cabinet was necessarily filled with men inexperienced in national administration, for the party had been proscribed for six terms. The greatest attention was attracted by the two former Confederates, Garland and Lamar, whose career did much to disprove the "gloomy and baseless superstition" of twenty years, "that one half of the nation had become the irreconcilable enemies

of the national unity and the national will." It was
an American Administration, and of its chief, James
Russell Lowell, who had known men in many lands,
wrote, " He is a truly American type of the best
kind — a type very dear to me, I confess."

The State Department was entrusted to Thomas
F. Bayard, who had been a competitor for the nomination in 1884, and who sustained the tradition that
only first-rate men shall fill this office. Bayard proceeded at once to undo the work of the last five
years and to reverse a policy of Blaine. A treaty
with Nicaragua, negotiated by Frelinghuysen in December, 1884, ran counter to the English treaty of
1850. After a vain attempt to persuade Great Britain
to abandon the Clayton-Bulwer Treaty respecting
an isthmian canal, Frelinghuysen had disregarded it
and acquired a complete right-of-way from Nicaragua.
This was pending in the Senate when Cleveland was
inaugurated, and was withdrawn at once. The United
States reverted to the old Whig policy of a neutralized canal.

In all departments the new Administration was
forced to test the strength of its convictions upon
civil service reform. During its long years of opposition the party had often voiced a demand for reform, but now in office its workers demanded the
usual rewards of success. Cleveland had fought the
spoils politicians in New York, and had taken counsel
of Carl Schurz after his election as President. In the
next four years he nearly doubled the number in
the classified service in the face of opposition from
his most intimate associates.

The problems of prosperity and national growth, developing in the eighties and culminating between 1885 and 1889, involved administrative efficiency rather than party policy. On every side the Government was forced to expand its activities, and Cleveland was occupied in getting new machinery into operation and meeting conditions for which no precedents existed.

Organized labor had gained concessions from Congress in a Bureau of Labor, in 1884, and an Anti-Contract Labor Law in 1885. These called for sympathetic administration and encouraged labor to hope for more. During 1886 and 1887 the views of labor leaders attracted much attention because of a series of strikes and riots. In the greatest of these the local chapters of the Knights of Labor fought against the Gould railways of the Southwest — the Missouri Pacific and the Texas Pacific. The strike originated in March, 1886, in sympathy with labor organizers who had been discharged by the railroad. Under the leadership of Martin Irons it spread over the Southwest, causing distress in those regions which were dependent upon the railroad for fuel and food and causing disorder in the towns where the idle workmen congregated. Powderly and the other chief officials of the Knights tried to stop the strike, but were ineffective, while the railroad managers shaped events so as to divert the sympathies of the Western people against the strikers. The Knights never recovered from the blow which the loss of the strike inflicted upon them.

In May, 1886, a general demonstration in favor

of the eight-hour day was planned and carried out. In Milwaukee riots ensued, the militia was called out by Governor Rusk, and a volley was fired into the mob. In Chicago the union movement was combined with anarchy and socialism, and opponents of all did not discriminate among them. A meeting of the anarchists was broken up by the police, several of whom were killed by the explosion of a bomb thrown in the tumult. In 1887 a group of the anarchist leaders were hanged, having been convicted of what may be called constructive conspiracy. The unrest revealed by the strikes and riots showed that the old period of uniform well-being and satisfaction was over.

The demands made upon politics by organized labor were exceeded by the demands of organized patriotism. The veterans of the Civil War, who were in early manhood in 1865, were now in middle life, were possessed of political influence, and turned to the National Government for personal advantage. Advocates of protection acted upon the theory that for national purposes special advantages ought to be given to manufacturers. The same idea of government readily bestowed these advantages in return for a past service.

The machinery of the veterans was the Grand Army of the Republic, which, from being an unimportant, reminiscent league, had grown to be an instrument for the procuring of pensions. The surplus tempted citizens to make demands upon it; the number of soldier votes encouraged politicians to comply with the demands. In 1879 the movement began with an Arrears of Pensions Act, by which pensioners were entitled to back pay from their mustering-out dates, regardless of the period at which their incapacity set in. The next step involved the issuing of pensions for incapacity and dependence, regardless of their cause, and opened the way for pensions for service only. In 1887 Cleveland vetoed a pension bill of this character, and prevented its passage until the term of his successor, in 1890. He had already offended many of his supporters by guarding the offices; his pension veto offended more by checking the attack of the old soldiers on the Treasury. No one opposed the granting of pensions to soldiers who had been injured in the Civil War, but the demands of the leaders of the Grand Army, supported by the interests of hundreds of attorneys who lived on pension claims, now assumed the appearance of an organized raid on the Treasury. The general laws were supplemented by special private pension laws, of which 1871 were sent to Cleveland in four years. He vetoed 228 of these, often to his political injury. In many cases these made allowances to persons whose claims had been rejected by the Pension Bureau as inadequate or fraudulent. In the course of time Cleveland became "thoroughly tired of disapproving gifts of public money to individuals who in my view have no right or claim to the same." The pension fund, he maintained, was "the soldiers' fund," and should be distributed so as to "exclude perversion as well as to insure a liberal and generous application of grateful and benevolent designs." In the ten years ending in 1889, Congress spent

$644,000,000 on pensions; in the next ten it spent
$1,350,000,000.

The surplus incited extravagance, and its reduction had been demanded on this ground, the tariff
appearing to afford the best method of reduction.
When the Democratic party gained control of the
House, in 1883, it proceeded at once to discuss revision, and promptly uncovered a difference of opinion among its members. The last Democratic Speaker
of the House had been Samuel J. Randall, of Pennsylvania, a Democrat who had been trained in the
philosophy of Henry Clay and in the interests of a
great manufacturing State. He was by conviction
and association a protectionist, and was a candidate
for his party's nomination as Speaker in the Forty-
eighth Congress, which met in December, 1883.
From this date he ceased to lead his party in the
House and became the leader of an internal faction.
John G. Carlisle, of Kentucky, supplanted him, was
elected Speaker, and organized the House in the interest of a tariff for revenue only. For the next six
years the Democratic organization of the House was
pledged to revision, but operated in the face of a
growing Republican opposition, and with Randall
and the protectionist Democrats attacking from the
rear.

The election of Cleveland gave the Democrats
control of two branches of the Government, but left
the Senate in the hands of the Republicans. It was
vain to talk of serious revision or any other party
measure in a divided administration, yet the President chafed under his inability to fulfill party pledges.

The surplus continued to accumulate, to permit extravagance in Congress, and to arouse the cupidity of citizens. In his message to his second Congress, in 1887, Cleveland startled the country by devoting his undivided attention to this single topic. He set his party a text which could not be evaded, although there was even yet no reason to believe that a tariff bill could pass both houses. He had taken Carlisle into his confidence before sending the message; the latter entrusted the leadership in revision to Roger Q. Mills, of Texas, a free-trader, whom he appointed as chairman of the Committee on Ways and Means.

With the opening of the debate on the Mills Bill, in April, 1888, there began "the first serious attempt since the war to reduce toward a peace basis the customs duties imposed during that conflict almost solely for purposes of revenue." Mills and William L. Wilson, who had been a college president in West Virginia, bore the burden of advocacy of a reduction of the revenue to the extent of $50,000,000. They were opposed by a united Republican party, both frightened and gratified because the issue had been made so clear. It was charged that the Committee on Ways and Means had drawn up the bill in secrecy, and that a majority of its Democratic members were Southerners who knew nothing of the needs of manufactures. The danger to American labor from the competition of the pauper labor of Europe was urged against it. It was asserted to be a pro-British measure, and stories were circulated of British gold, coming from the Cobden Club, a free-trade organization, to subvert American institutions.

The Democratic organization drove the bill through the House of Representatives in spite of all resistance. In the Senate, with the Republicans in control, the bill never came to a vote, and was used to manufacture campaign materials for the campaign then pending. Many of the advisers of Cleveland had urged him to withhold the tariff message, lest he arouse the enemy and defeat himself, but he had risked personal and party defeat in order to get an issue definitively accepted — the first issue so accepted in politics since 1864.

The Mills Bill fiasco was the most important party measure of Cleveland's Administration, yet it served only to accentuate the difficulties in tariff legislation which had been experienced in 1883, and to provide an issue for the campaign of 1888. The laws that were passed between 1885 and 1889 were generally non-partisan in their character and were of most influence when they helped to readjust federal law to national economic problems. The Federal Government was unfolding and testing powers that had existed since the adoption of the Constitution, but had not been needed hitherto in an agricultural republic. The change that forced the resort to these powers came largely from the completion of a national system of communication.

BIBLIOGRAPHICAL NOTE

For the election of 1884, consult, in addition to Stanwood, J. F. Rhodes, " The National Republican Conventions of 1880 and 1884 " (*Scribner's Magazine*, September, 1911), and " Cleveland's Administrations " (*Scribner's Magazine*, October, 1911).

There is an annotated reprint of the "Mulligan Letters" in *Harper's Weekly* (1884, pp. 643–46). The biographies of Blaine by Hamilton and Stanwood should be examined, as well as the sketches of Cleveland (who left few literary remains), by J. L. Williams, G. F. Parker, and R. W. Gilder. Among partisan party histories, the best are F. Curtis, *The Republican Party*, (2 vols., 1904), and W. L. Wilson, *The National Democratic Party* (1888). J. H. Harper recounts details of the Mugwump split in his history of *The House of Harper* (1912). The standard compilation on the pension system, which has not yet received adequate treatment, is W. H. Glasson, *Military Pension Legislation in the United States* (in Columbia University Studies, vol. XII). C. F. Adams and W. B. Hale published useful essays on the pension system in *World's Work, 1911.* H. T. Peck begins his popular *Twenty Years of the Republic* (1907) with the inauguration of Cleveland in 1885. Consult also Sparks, Dewey, Andrews, and the *Annual Cyclopædia*.

CHAPTER IX

THE LAST OF THE FRONTIER

FIVE statutes that received the signature of Grover Cleveland are documentary proof of the new problems and the changing attitude of the National Administration during the eighties. They indicate that the chief function of the National Government had ceased to be, to moderate among a group of self-sufficient States and had come to be the direction of such interests as were national in importance or extent. On February 4, 1887, the Interstate Commerce Law was passed in recognition of a transportation system that had become national; and four days later the Dawes Bill, providing that lands should be issued to Indians in severalty, marked the disappearance of the wild Indian from the border. In 1889 a Department of Agriculture, with a seat in the Cabinet, and a law for the survey of irrigation sites in the Far West, mark the interest of a nation in the prosperity of its whole area and population; while laws of 1889 and 1890 admitting six new States extended the chain of commonwealths for the first time from ocean to ocean. A process that had been under way since Jamestown and Plymouth Rock had culminated in the occupation of the whole breadth of the continent.

The first continental railroad, the Union Pacific,

chartered in 1862 and finished in 1869, was admittedly a national project. Its purpose was to bind the Pacific Slope to the East in a period when sectionalism was a menace to national unity. Its opening was the first step in the completion of an intricate system of lines extending to the Pacific. Direct federal aid was given to the road in the form of land grants, right of way, and a loan of bonds.

Other continental railroads were authorized in the later sixties. In 1864 a Northern Pacific, to connect Lake Superior and Puget Sound, made its appearance. In 1866 the Atlantic & Pacific was given the right to run from a southwestern terminal at Springfield, Missouri, to southern California. In 1871 the Texas Pacific was designed to connect the head of navigation on the Red River, near Shreveport and Texarkana, with Fort Yuma and San Diego. Additional lines with continental possibilities received charters from the Western States, — the Denver & Rio Grande, the Chicago, Burlington & Quincy, and the Atchison, Topeka & Santa Fé, — and received indirectly a share of the public domain as an inducement to build. Congress stopped making land grants for this purpose in 1871, but not until more lines than could be used for twenty years had been allowed.

All the continental railways were begun before 1873, were checked by the five years of depression, and were revived about 1878. When they began again to build there was associated with them a new project for an old continental route.

The interoceanic canal had been foreseen ever

since the first white man stood on the Isthmus and
gazed at the Pacific. Its construction had been
stimulated by the gold discoveries and the California
emigration of 1848–49, and had been arranged for
in a treaty signed with Great Britain in 1850. No
means to build the canal were found, however, and
the project drifted along until De Lesseps finished
his canal at Suez, and the new interest in continental
communication in America resuscitated the canal at
Panama. In 1878 a French company, with De Lesseps at its head, obtained a concession from Colombia. It began work in 1880, at once arousing the
jealousy of the United States which was shown in
the efforts of Hayes, Garfield, and Arthur to abro-
gate the Clayton-Bulwer Treaty and procure for
the United States a free hand at the Isthmus. Cleveland reverted to the policy of a neutralized canal in
1885, but interest on either side was premature,
since no canal was built for thirty years.

The continental railways aroused keen interest in
problems of transportation by their completion between 1881 and 1885. The Northern Pacific was
finished under the direction of Henry Villard, a German journalist who had been a correspondent in the
Civil War and had managed the interests of foreign
investors after 1873. He gained control of the partly
finished Northern Pacific and the local lines of Oregon through a holding company known as the Oregon
& Transcontinental. In September, 1883, he took a
special train, full of distinguished visitors, over his
lines to witness the driving of the last spike near
Helena, Montana. On the way out, they stopped at

Bismarck to help lay the corner-stone for an ambitious new capitol of the Territory of Dakota. From Duluth to Tacoma the new line brought in immigrants whose freight made its chief business.

South of the Northern Pacific, the original main line of the Union Pacific ran from Omaha up the Platte Trail through Cheyenne to Ogden, with a branch from Kansas City to Denver and Cheyenne. Between the main line and the branch the Chicago, Burlington & Quincy constructed a road that reached Denver in May, 1882. Here it met, in 1883, the Denver & Rio Grande, a narrow-gauge road that penetrated the divide by way of the cañon of the Arkansas River, and extended to the Great Salt Lake. The two roads together offered a competition to the Union Pacific for its whole length from the Missouri River to Ogden, and drove that road to extend feeder branches south to the Gulf and north into Oregon.

Farther south the Atchison, Topeka & Santa Fé stretched the whole length of Kansas and followed the old trail to Santa Fé and the Rio Grande, and thence to Old Mexico. Its owners coöperated with the owners of the Atlantic & Pacific franchise, and the Southern Pacific of California, to build a connecting link between the Atchison, Topeka & Santa Fé at Albuquerque and the Colorado River at the Needles. From this point the Southern Pacific traversed the valleys of California. In October, 1883, trains were running from San Francisco to St. Louis over this road.

The Southern Pacific of California met the other

By 1870 the railway net had covered the eastern half of the United States and had just begun its Pacific extension. There were 52,914 miles of railroad.

THE WESTERN RAILROADS AND THE

(Based upon the maps showing density of population in the Eleventh
Rand-McNally Official Rail-

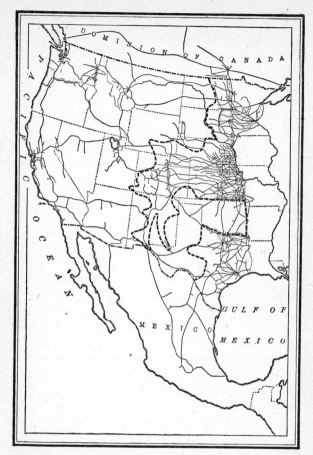

By 1890 the railway mileage of the United States had increased to
163,597, extending the railway net over the whole trans-Missouri region,
and reinforced by lines in Canada and Mexico.

CONTINENTAL FRONTIER, 1870-1890

Census, and upon Appleton's Railway Guide, November, 1871, and the
way Guide, August, 1891.)

continental lines at the Fort Yuma crossing of the Colorado River. The Texas Pacific had got only to Fort Worth before the panic of 1873. It now built across Texas toward El Paso. Subsidiary corporations owned by the Southern Pacific men built the line between El Paso and Fort Yuma, and enabled a through service to start to St. Louis in January, and to New Orleans in October, 1882. Yet another Southern Pacific line was opened through San Antonio and Houston, tapping the commerce of the Gulf shore, and running trains to New Orleans in February, 1883.

The opening of great lines in the United States in the early eighties was part of a similar movement throughout the world. In Canada, Sir Donald Smith, later raised to the peerage as Lord Strathcona, was beginning the Canadian Pacific from Port Arthur to Vancouver, while on the Continent of Europe the first train of the " Orient Express " left Paris for Constantinople in June, 1883. In November, 1883, the American railroads, realizing that they were a national system, agreed upon a scheme of standard time by which to run their trains. Heretofore every road had followed what local time it chose, to the confusion of the traveling public.

Most of the continental railways had extensive land grants, of from twenty to forty sections per mile of track, but whether they had lands to sell or not they were vitally interested in the settlement of the regions through which they ran. Each encouraged immigration and colonization. Their literature, scattered over Europe, was one factor in the heavy drift of population that started after 1878. Six new Western States were created in the ten years after their completion.

The youngest American Territory in the eighties was Wyoming, created in 1868, and the youngest State was Colorado, admitted in 1876. After Colorado, the political division of the West embraced eight organized Territories: Dakota, Montana, Idaho, and Washington along the Canadian line, Wyoming and Utah in the middle, Arizona and New Mexico on the Mexican border. Besides these Territories there was the unorganized remnant of the Indian country known as Indian Territory, and attracting the covetous glances of frontiersmen in all the near-by Western States.

Agriculture was the main reliance of the wave of pioneers that poured over the plains along the lines of the railroads. In the valley of the Red River of the North, wheat-farming was their staple industry. As the Old South had devoted itself to the staple crop of cotton, so this new region took up the single crop of wheat, bringing to its cultivation great machines, white labor, and a modified factory system. South of the wheat country, corn dominated in Kansas, Iowa, and Nebraska, and went to market either as grain or in the converted form of hogs or stock. In Texas the cotton-fields pushed into new areas. The farm lands completely surrounded the Indian Territory, in which a diversified agriculture was known to be both possible and profitable.

Across the United States, from Canada to Mexico, the advance line of farms pushed from the well-

watered bottoms of the Mississippi Valley into the
plains that rise toward the Rocky Mountains. Near
the ninety-seventh meridian the rainfall of this region becomes insufficient for general farming in
ordinary years. But the solicitations of land-sellers
brought settlers into the subhumid region, while for
a few years in the eighties the rainfall was greater
than the average. Permanent climatic changes were
imagined by the hopeful. A Governor of Kansas
stated, in 1886, "with absolute certainty, that great
areas in the Western third of Kansas are becoming
more fertile," while an Eastern Senator, who was
generally well informed, believed in 1888 that "the
whole Territory of Dakota is as capable of sustaining
population as Iowa."

Between the farming frontier and the mountains
the cattlemen expanded the grazing industry, with
profits that were enlarged because of the markets
that the railroads brought them. The "long drive"
from Texas to Montana became a familiar idea on
the border, while the cowboys in their lonely watches
developed a folk-song literature that is typically
American. Between the cattlemen and the sheep-
men there was permanent war, for the sheep injured
the grass they grazed over. Although both industries
were trespassers on the public lands the herders resented the appearance of the flocks as an intrusion
upon their domain.

Kansas City rose suddenly to prominence as the
meeting-place of the railways of the West and Southwest with those of the East. Near to the line that
divided steady agriculture from the nomadic life of

the plains it became a convenient market for both. Here the packers developed the traffic in fresh beef that the new railways with their refrigerator cars made possible. The cities of the East, in need of more fresh meat than the local farmers could provide, found their supply on the plains of the Far West.

Beyond the plains, the mountain regions changed less from the advent of the railways than any other section of the remote West. They had attracted population to their camps during the Civil War, and now they grew in size and permanence. But only such regions reached permanent importance as had valleys to be irrigated and fields to be cultivated. Without agriculture no important region has flourished in the West.

Toward the end of the eighties the pressure of the population for more homestead lands brought about the opening of Oklahoma. Here, for over half a century, the Indian tribes had lived in full possession. After the Civil War the plains tribes had been colonized here too. Now, as the lands were awarded to the Indians in severalty under the Dawes Act, the old tribal holdings were surrendered and large areas were offered to white settlement. After ten years of ejectment and restraint the Oklahoma boomers were let into the country in 1889. Guthrie and Oklahoma City were created overnight, and in 1890 the Territory of Oklahoma received permanent organization.

Before the last continental railway was finished, the Territories were asking for statehood and were showing advance in population to justify it. When

Villard aided in the corner-stone laying at Bismarck in 1883 there were already three clearly defined groups of population in Dakota and an ultimate division had been determined upon by the settlers. Repeatedly, in the decade, the Dakota colonists framed constitutions and signed petitions, and the Republicans in Congress sought to give them statehood. The Democratic House, which prevailed from 1883 to 1889, saw no reason for creating more Republican States, as these would likely be, and found pretexts for holding up the bills. Montana, less advanced than Dakota, and Idaho and Wyoming which were yet more primitive, joined the forces of the statehood advocates. Arizona and New Mexico did the same, and Utah had been a suitor since 1850. Washington, with a growing population on Puget Sound and in the Spokane country, was obviously not long to be denied.

For party purposes, the Democrats resisted the demands for statehood until the election of 1888 insured Republican control through every branch of the United States Government. Thereafter there was no point to resistance, and Cleveland, in 1889, signed an " omnibus " bill under which North Dakota, South Dakota, Montana, and Washington were admitted. Idaho and Wyoming, defeated at this time, were let in by the Republicans in 1890. The unorganized frontier was now all but gone, and the pioneers of these new States used Pullman cars and read the monthly magazines like any other citizens.

Arizona and New Mexico were excluded from the new States of 1889 and 1890 because a Republican

THE DISTRIBUTION OF THE PUBLIC DOMAIN, 1789-1904

The large rectangle represents the total land area of the United States, excluding Alaska and the Islands 1,902,000,000 Acres

Public lands remaining in the possession of the United States in 1904 about 700,000,000 Acres			Land area of the thirteen original states and Maine, Vermont, West Virginia, Kentucky, Tennessee, and Texas, in none of which has the public domain ever existed 460,000,000 Acres
Area given to individuals in the form of homesteads or allotments 122,000,000 Acres	Land grants for internal improvements and railroads 137,000,000 Acres	Donations to the states for education and other local purposes 164,000,000 Acres	Sales to companies or individuals under preëmption and general laws, and private land claims allowed 319,000,000 Acres

(Diagram based upon the Report of the Public Lands Commission and the Report of the Commissioner of the General Land Office, 1905)

Land area of the twenty-nine states constituting the public domain, 1,442,000,000 Acres

Congress expected them to be Democratic, and both
remained Territories for more than twenty succeeding years. Utah, with ample population, was kept
where the Federal Government could control it because of the practices taught by its Church. The
Mormons had made a prosperous Territory in Utah
by 1850. They had flourished ever since, but their
institution of polygamy frightened the United States
and created permanent hostility to their admission.
In 1882 the Territory was placed under a commission, and thereafter polygamous citizens were brought
to punishment. In 1890 the Church gave up the
fight and formally abandoned the obnoxious doctrine,
but the surrender came too late to accomplish admission at this time.

By 1890 the good agricultural lands of the United
States were nearly all in private hands. Their occupation had been hastened in the last five years by
facility of access and the efforts of the railways.
With the disappearance of free lands a new period
in America began, as was recognized at the time,
and has become clearer ever since.

Out of forty-eight States comprising the United
States in 1912, and including about 1,902,000,000
acres, twenty-nine with 1,442,000,000 acres had been
erected in the public domain to which Congress had
once owned title. By cession, purchase, or conquest
this domain had been acquired between 1781 and
1853; it had been treated as a national asset and
governed with what efficiency Congress possessed.
By 1903 the United States had transferred to individuals about half its public land and nearly all

its farm land. It retained many millions of acres, but these were mountain or desert, and were not usable by the individual farmer who had been the typical unit in the occupation of the West.

Already, by 1880, the statisticians had recognized that the period of free land was at an end, and had turned their attention to the abuses which had arisen in the administration of the estate. From the beginning, it had been difficult to compel the West to respect national land laws. The squatter who occupied lands without title had always been an obstacle to uniform administration. Evasion of the law had rarely been frowned upon by Western opinion, which had hoped to get the public lands into private hands by the quickest route. In the region where the laws had to be enforced, opinion prevented it, while the National Administration, before the adoption of civil service reform, was incapable of directing with accuracy and uniform policy any administrative scheme which must be so highly technical as a land office. The Preëmption, Homestead, and Timber Culture Laws were all framed in the interest of the small holder, but were all perverted by fraud and collusion. The United States invited much of the fraud by making no provision by which those industries which had a valid need for a large acreage could get it legally.

Among the special abuses that were observed now that it was too late to remedy them were the violations of the law and the lawless seizures of the public lands. The cattle companies took and fenced what they needed and drove out "trespassers" by force.

Mail contractors complained of illegal inclosures which they dare not cross, but which diverted the United States mail from its lawful course. Yet such was the general land law that against all but the United States Government the possessors could maintain their possession. If the Government could not or would not interfere, there was no redress.

These abuses had been noticed for many years, and were specially advertised in the early eighties by the enormous holdings of a few British noblemen. The problem of absentee landlordism was exciting Ireland in these years. When Cleveland became President his Commissioner of the General Land Office, Sparks, turned cheerfully and vigorously to reform, and denounced the discreditable condition the more readily because it had appeared under Republican administration. He held up the granting of homestead and preëmption titles for the purpose of examination and inspection, and demanded the repeal of the Preëmption Law. He was successful in recovering some of the lands that had been offered to the railways to aid in their construction.

The railway land grants were notorious because the railways had rarely been done on contract time, and had in theory forfeited their grants. The estimated area offered them was about 214,000,000 acres, and the question arose as to the extent to which forfeiture should be imposed upon them. The spectacular completion of their lines and their efforts to bring a population into the West, and the vast size of the corporations that owned them, had aroused a hostile opinion that supported the Democratic

Administration in its efforts to save what lands it could. Some fifty million acres were restored to the domain by this fight, but the restoration only emphasized the fact that most of the good lands were gone.

Out of the demand for the reform of the public lands grew a new interest in the condition of the lands that were left. The Department of Agriculture was created at the end of Cleveland's term, and Governor Jeremiah Rusk was appointed as its first Secretary by Harrison. Rusk accepted cheerfully his place as "the tail of the Cabinet," asserting that as such he was expected "to keep the flies off," and set about rearranging or organizing a group of scientific bureaus. Since most of the remaining lands could not be used without irrigation, the surveys undertaken by Congress started a new phase of public science, and led ultimately to the rise of a positive theory of conservation.

The problems of national communication, Western settlement, and public lands resulted from the completion of the continental railways, while the railways themselves gave a new significance to transportation in America. During the years of the Granger movement the doctrine had been established that railroads are quasi-public and are subject to regulation by public authority. In the Granger Cases in 1877 the Supreme Court recognized the right of the States to establish rates by law, even when these rates, by becoming part of a through rate, had an incidental effect upon interstate commerce. The problem had been viewed as local or regional during the seventies. Most of the States had passed railway laws and had proceeded to accumulate a volume of statistical information upon the railway business, that was increased by such public investigations as the Windom and Hepburn Reports and by lawsuits that revealed the nature of special favors and rebates.

Before the States had gone far in the direction of railway regulation it was discovered that no State could regulate an interstate railway with precision and justice. The great systems built up by Villard and Gould and Vanderbilt and Huntington dominated whole regions and precipitated the question of the effectiveness of state action. The continental lines, necessarily long and traversing several States, emphasized the inequality between the powers of a State and the problem to be met. Their national character pointed to national control.

In Congress there were repeated attempts after 1873 to secure the passage of an Interstate Commerce Act. In continuation of this campaign a committee headed by Senator Shelby M. Cullom, of Illinois, made a new investigation in 1885, and reported early in 1886 that supervision and publicity were required, and that these could best be obtained through a federal commission with large powers of taking testimony and examining books. The committee was convinced, as the public was already convinced, that the problem had become national.

The Supreme Court reached the same opinion in 1886 when it handed down a new decision in the case of the Wabash Railway Company *vs.* Illinois. Here it reversed or modified its own decision in the Granger Cases. In 1877 it had ruled that railways are subject to regulation and that the States under their police powers may regulate. It now adhered to its major premise, but declared that such regulation as affected an interstate rate is exclusively a federal function. In effect it determined that if there was to be regulation of the great systems it could only be at the hands of Congress.

The regulation of interstate commerce was not a party measure. It had its advocates in both parties, and found its opponents in the railroad lobby that resented any public interference with the business of the roads. The railway owners and directors were slower than the public in accepting the doctrine of the quasi-public nature of their business. It was a powerful argument against them that their size and influence were such that they could and did ruin or enrich individual customers, and that they could make or destroy whole regions of the West. Enough positive proof of favoritism existed to give point to the demand that the business must cease to discriminate.

The Interstate Commerce Act became a law February 4, 1887. It created a commission of five, with a six-year term and the proviso that not more than three of the commissioners should belong to one party. It forbade a group of practices which had resulted in unfair discrimination and gave to the commission considerable powers in investigation and interference. The later interpretation of the law deprived the commission of some of the powers that, it was thought, had been given to it, but during the next nineteen years the Interstate Commerce Commission was a central figure in the solution of the railroad problem. The work of this commission, like the work of irrigation and agriculture, was technical, calling for expert service, and aiding in the process that was changing the character of the National Administration as one function after another was called into service for the first time.

BIBLIOGRAPHICAL NOTE

In 1893 F. J. Turner called attention to the *Significance of the Frontier in American History* (in American Historical Association, Annual Report, 1893). His theory has been elaborated by F. L. Paxson, *The Last American Frontier* (1910), and K. Coman, *Economic Beginnings of the Far West* (1912). There is no good account of the public lands. T. Donaldson, *The Public Domain* (1881), is inaccurate, antiquated, and clumsy, but has not been supplanted. Many useful tables are in the report of the Public Lands Commission created by President Roosevelt (in 58th Congress, 3d session, Senate Document, No. 189, Serial No. 4766). The general spirit of the frontier in the eighties has been appreciated by Owen Wister, in *The Virginian* (1902), and *Members of the Family* (1911), and by E. Talbot, in *My People of the Plains* (1906). J. A. Lomax has preserved some of its folklore in *Cowboy Songs and Other Frontier Ballads* (1910). The best narratives on the continental railways are J. P. Davis, *Union Pacific Railway* (1894), and E. V. Smalley, *The Northern Pacific Railroad* (1883). Many contributory details are in H. Villard, *Memoirs* (2 vols., 1904), E. P. Oberholtzer, *Jay Cooke* (2 vols., 1907), and in the appropriate volumes of H. H. Bancroft, *Works*. L. H. Haney has compiled the formal documents in his *Congressional History of Railroads* (in Bulletins of the University of Wisconsin, Nos. 211 and 342). The debate over the Isthmian Canal may be read in J. D. Richardson, *Messages and*

Papers of the Presidents; the Foreign Relations Reports, 1879–83 ; L. M. Keasbey, *The Nicaragua Canal and the Monroe Doctrine* (1896) ; J. B. Henderson, *American Diplomatic Questions* (1901) ; and J. Latané, *Diplomatic Relations of the United States and Spanish America* (1900).

CHAPTER X

NATIONAL BUSINESS

TRANSPORTATION was a fundamental factor in the two greatest problems of the eighties. In the case of the disappearance of free land and the frontier, it produced phenomena that were most clearly visible in the West, although affecting the whole United States. In the case of concentration of capital and the growth of trusts, its phenomena were mostly in the East, where were to be found the accumulations of capital, the great markets, and the supply of labor.

Through the improvements in communication it became possible to conduct an efficient business in every State and direct it from a single head office. Not only railroad and telegraph helped in this, but telephone, typewriter, the improved processes in photography and printing, and the organization of express service were of importance and touched every aspect of life. Journalism both broadened and concentrated. The effective range of the weeklies and monthlies and even of the city dailies was widened, while the resulting competition tended to weed out the weaker and more local. Illustrations improved and changed the physical appearance of periodical literature.

Social organizations of national scope or ambition took advantage of the new communication. Trade

unions, benevolent associations, and professional societies multiplied their annual congresses and conventions, and increased the proportion of the population that knew something of the whole Union. A
few periodicals and pattern-makers began to circulate styles, which clothing manufacturers imitated
and local shopkeepers sold at retail. Mail-order
business was aided by the same conditions. A new
uniformity in appearance began to enter American
life, weakening the old localisms in dress, speech,
and conduct. Until within a few years it had been
possible here and there to sit down to dinner " with
a gentleman in the dress of the early century —
ruffles, even *bag-wig* complete "; but the new standards were the standards of the mass, and it became
increasingly more difficult to keep up an aristocratic
seclusion or a style of life much different from that
of the community.

With the growth of national uniformity went also
the concentration of control. As the field of competition widened, the number of possible winners declined.
Men measured strength, not only in their town or
State, but across the continent, and the handful of
leaders used the facilities of communication as the
basis for the further expansion of their industries.
Business was extended because it was possible and
because it was thought to pay.

Many of the economies of consolidation were so
obvious as to need no argument. If a single firm
could do the business of five, — or fifty — it increased
its profit through larger and better plants, greater
division of labor, and a more careful use of its by-

products. It could cut down expenses by reducing the army of competing salesmen and by lessening the duplication of administrative offices. The same economics in management which had driven the Old South to the large plantation as a type drove American industrial society toward economic consolidation and the trusts.

The technical form of organization of the trust was unimportant. Strictly speaking, it was a combination of competing concerns, in which the control of all was vested in a group of trustees for the purpose of uniformity. The name was thus derived, but it spread in popular usage until it was regarded as generally descriptive of any business so large that it affected the course of the whole trade of which it was a part. The logical outcome of the trust was monopoly, and trusts appeared first in those industries in which there existed a predisposition to monopoly, an excessive loss through competition, or a controlling patent or trade secret.

The first trust to arouse public notice was concerned in the transportation and manufacture of petroleum and its products. Commercial processes for refining petroleum became available in the sixties, enabling improvements in domestic illumination that insured an increasing market for the product. The industry was speculative by nature because of the low cost of crude petroleum at the well and the high cost of delivering it to the consumer. Slight rises in price caused the market to be swamped by overproduction, and threw the control of the industry into the hands of those who controlled its transportation.

Once above ground, the cheap and bulky oil had to be hauled first to the refiner and then to the consumer. The receptacles were expensive, and the methods of transportation that were cheapest in operation had the greatest initial cost. Barrels were relatively cheap to buy, but were costly to handle. Tank-cars were more expensive, but repaid those who could afford them. Pipe-lines were beyond the means of the individual, but brought in greater returns to the corporations that owned them.

It was inevitable that some of the dealers who competed in the oil-fields of Ohio, Pennsylvania, and West Virginia in the sixties should realize the strategic value of the control of transportation and profit by it. John D. Rockefeller happened to be more successful than others in manipulating transportation. His refineries grew in size, as they bought out or crushed their rivals, until by 1882 most of the traffic in petroleum was under his control. Economy and sagacity had much to do with the success, but were less significant than transportation. Railway rates were yet unfixed by law and every road sold transportation as best it could. Rockefeller learned to bargain in freight rates, and through a system of special rates and rebates gained advantages over every competitor. His lobby made it difficult to weaken him through legislative measures, while his attorneys were generally more skillful than his prosecutors before the courts. The recognition of the existence of rebates did much to hasten the passage of the Interstate Commerce Law. The group of corporations that flourished because of them became the greatest of the trusts. By 1882 the affiliated Rockefeller companies were so numerous and complicated that they were given into the hands of a group of trustees to be managed as a single business.

The Whiskey and Sugar Trusts, formed in 1887, had to do with commodities in which transportation was not the controlling element. These industries suffered from overproduction and ruinous competition, to eliminate which the distilleries and sugar refineries entered into trust agreements like that of the Standard Oil companies. Other lines of manufacture followed as best they could. Before Cleveland was inaugurated the trend was noticed and attacked.

Most of the agitation against the trusts came from individuals whose lives were touched by them. Competition was ruthless and often unscrupulous. Every man who was crushed by it hated his destroyer. There was much changing of occupations as firms merged and reorganized and as plants grew in size and ingenuity. Perhaps more workers changed the character of their occupation in the eighties than in any other decade. As each individual readjusted himself to his new environment, he added to the mass of public opinion that believed the trusts to be a menace to society.

As early as 1881 there was a market for anti-trust literature, for in March of that year the *Atlantic Monthly* printed the " Story of a Great Monopoly," by Henry Demarest Lloyd, who became one of the leaders in the attack. It had been fashionable to regard success as a vindication of Yankee cleverness and worthy of emulation, without much examination of the methods by which it was attained. The Standard Oil Company, attracting attention to itself, raised the question of the effect of industry upon society.

The evils ascribed to the trusts were social or political. In a social way they were believed to check individualism and to create too large a proportion of subordinates to independent producers. As monopolies, they were believed to threaten extortion through high price. It was strongly suspected of the largest trusts that having destroyed all competition they could fix prices at pleasure. Economists pointed out that such price could hardly be high and yet remunerative to the trusts, because the latter did not dare to check consumption. But fear of oppression could not be dispelled by any economic law.

The trust was believed to have an evil influence in politics, and to obtain special favors through bribery or pressure. The United States was used to the influence of money in politics, and distrusted public officials. The state constitutions framed in this period were being expanded into codes of specific law in the hope of safeguarding public interests. There was little belief that corrupt overtures, if made by the trusts, would be resisted.

Lloyd, and men of his type, believed in regulation and control. Some of them became socialists. Others hoped to restore a competitive basis by law. The greatest impression on the public was made by one of their literary allies, Edward Bellamy.

Early in 1888 Edward Bellamy published a ro-

mance entitled *Looking Backward*, in which his
hero, Mr. Julian West, went to sleep in 1887, with
labor controversy and trust denunciation sounding
in his ears, to awake in the year 2000 A.D. The so-
cialized state into which the hero was reborn was a
picture of an end to which industry was perhaps
drifting. It caught public attention. Clubs of enthusiasts tried to hasten the day of nationalization
by forming Bellamistic societies. Those who were
repelled by a future in which the trusts and the
State were merged became more active in their demand for regulation.

The legislative side of trust regulation, like that
of railway regulation, was made more difficult because
of the division of powers between Congress and the
States. It was an interesting question whether one
State could control a monopoly as large as the nation. But the States passed anti-trust laws by the
score, as they had passed the railway laws. As in
the earlier case they found their model in the common law, which had long prohibited conspiracies in
restraint of trade. One of the States, Ohio, with
only the common law to go upon, brought suit
against the Standard Oil Trust and secured a prohibition against it in 1892. It was relatively easy to
attack the formal organization of the trust, but in
spite of such attacks concentration continued to produce ever greater combinations, as though it were
fulfilling some fundamental economic law.

Those of the anti-monopolists who were also tariff
reformers had a weapon to urge besides that of regulation. They maintained that part of the power of

the corporations was due to the needless favors of
protection, which deprived the United States of the
aid that competition from European manufacturers
might have given. They insisted that a revision of
the tariff would do much to remove the burden of
the trusts. The House ordered an investigation of the
trusts while it was engaged on the futile Mills Bill
in 1888, but it was the latter that furnished the text
for the ensuing presidential campaign.

So far as the parties were concerned the Republicans took the aggressive in 1888. Cleveland's emphasis upon tariff reduction was personal and never
had the cheerful support of the whole party. The
manufacturers, however, were thoroughly scared by
the continued threats of revision. As they had come,
by supporting the party in power, to support the
Republicans, so they now organized within that party
to save themselves. Their leaders sang a new note
in 1888, no longer apologizing for the tariff or urging reduction, but defending it on principle, — on
Clay's old principle of an American system, — and
asking that it be made more comprehensive. From
Florence, and then from Paris, Blaine replied to
Cleveland's Message of 1887, and his friends continued to urge his nomination for the Presidency.
Only after his positive refusal to be a candidate did
the Republican Convention at Chicago make its
choice from a list of candidates including Sherman,
Gresham, Depew, Alger, Harrison, and Allison.
The ticket finally nominated consisted of Benjamin
Harrison, a Senator from Indiana, and Levi P. Mor-
ton, a New York banker. The platform was "un-

compromisingly in favor of the American system of protection." It denounced Cleveland and the revisionists as serving "the interests of Europe," and condemned "the Mills Bill as destructive to the general business, the labor, and the farming interests of the country."

The Democrats, as is usual for the party in power, had already held their convention before the Republicans met. They had renominated Grover Cleveland by acclamation, and Allen G. Thurman, of Ohio, as Vice-President, and had indorsed, not the Mills Bill by name, but the views of Cleveland and the efforts of the President and Representatives in Congress to secure a reduction. For many of the Democrats the need to defend tariff reform was so distasteful that they left the party, blaming Cleveland as the cause of their defection.

The canvass of 1888 was not marred by the personalities of 1884. The issue of protection was discussed earnestly by both parties, Blaine, who returned from Europe, leading the Republican attack. The only exciting incidents of the campaign had to do with the "Murchison Letter" and the campaign fund.

Matthew S. Quay, whose career as Treasurer of Pennsylvania had not been above reproach, was chairman of the Republican campaign committee. During the contest it was asserted that he was assessing the protected manufacturers and guaranteeing them immunity in case of a Republican victory. He was at least able to play upon their fears and bring a vigorous support to the protective promises of his party. His committee circulated stories of the un-Americanism of Cleveland, charging that free-trade was pro-British, and making capital out of the pension vetoes. Toward the end of the canvass Sir Lionel Sackville-West, the British Minister, fell into a Republican trap and wrote to a pretended naturalized Englishman, who called himself Murchison, that a vote for Cleveland would best serve Great Britain. His tactless blunder caused his summary dismissal from Washington and aided the Republican cause much as the Burchard affair had injured it four years before.

Harrison was elected in November as a minority President, Cleveland actually receiving more popular though fewer electoral votes. He came into office with a Republican Senate and a Republican House, able to carry out party intentions for the first time since 1883.

Benjamin Harrison was never a leader of his party. He had a good war record and had been Senator for a single term. His nomination was not due to his strength, but to his availability. Coming from the doubtful State of Indiana, he was likely to carry it, particularly since the Republican candidate for governor was a leader of the Grand Army of the Republic. Harrison's personal character and piety were valuable assets in a time when party leaders were under fire. Once in office he had a cold abruptness that made it easy to lose the support of associates who felt that their own importance was greater than his.

Blaine, the greatest of these associates, became

Secretary of State, and soon had the satisfaction of meeting the Pan-American Congress that he had called eight years before. In his interest in larger American affairs he lost some of his keenness as a protectionist and acquired a zeal for foreign trade. With England he had another unsuccessful tilt, this time over the seals of Bering Sea.

In some of the appointments Harrison paid the party debts. Windom came back to the Treasury, although ex-Senator Platt, of New York, claimed that he had been promised it. John Wanamaker, who had raised large sums in Philadelphia to aid Quay in the campaign, became Postmaster-General. The Pension Bureau, important through the alliance with the soldiers, went to a leader of the Grand Army of the Republic, one "Corporal" Tanner, whose most famous utterance related to his intentions: "God save the surplus!"

The Fifty-first Congress, convening in December, 1889, took up with enthusiasm the mandate of the election, as the Republicans saw it, to revise the tariff in the interest of protection. It chose as Speaker Thomas B. Reed, of Maine, and revised its rules so as to expedite legislation. William McKinley prepared a revision of the tariff in the House, while another Ohioan, John Sherman, took up the matter of the trusts in the Senate.

The Sherman Anti-Trust Law was enacted in July, 1890, after nearly ten years of general discussion. Although formulated by Republicans — Sherman, Edmunds, and Hoar — it was not more distinctly a party measure than the Interstate Commerce

Act had been. It relied upon the interstate commerce clause of the Constitution as its authority to declare illegal " every contract, combination in the form of trust or otherwise, or conspiracy, in restraint of commerce among the several States, or with foreign nations," and it provided suitable penalties for violation. The most significant debate in connection with it occurred upon an amendment offered by Representative Richard P. Bland, of Missouri, who desired to extend the scope of the prohibition, specifically, to railroads. The Senate excluded the amendment on the ground that the law was general, covering the railroads without special enumeration. The full meaning of the law remained in doubt for nearly fifteen years, for few private suitors invoked it and the Attorneys-General were not hostile to the ordinary practices of business. A great financial depression which appeared in 1893 acted well as a temporary deterrent of trusts. There was a suspicion that the law had been intended not to be enforced, but to act as a popular antidote to the McKinley Tariff Bill which was pending while it passed.

There were two reasons for a revision of the tariff in 1890. The surplus, still a reason, added $105,000,000 in 1889, and continued to embarrass the Treasury with a wealth of riches. Secondly, the election of 1888 had gone Republican, and party leaders chose to regard this as a popular condemnation of Cleveland and tariff reform, and a popular mandate for higher protection, in spite of the fact that more Americans voted for Cleveland than for Harrison. A third reason, alleged by the opposition, was the

which further relieved the surplus. The sugar clause was one of the notable features of the McKinley Bill, and was closely related to a group of duties upon agricultural imports. There had been complaint among the farmers that protection did nothing for them. The agricultural schedule was designed to silence this complaint.

Another novelty in the bill was the extension of protection to unborn industries. In the case of tin plate, the President was empowered to impose a duty whenever he should learn that American mills were ready to manufacture it. This was an application of the principle that went beyond the demands of most advocates of protection.

A final novelty, reciprocity, was the favorite scheme of the Secretary of State. Blaine, in his foreign policy, saw in the tariff wall an obstacle to friendly trade relations, and induced Congress to permit the duties on the chief imports from South America to be admitted on a special basis in return for reciprocal favors. McKinley, as his experience widened, accepted this principle in full, and died with an expression of it upon his lips. But in 1890 most protectionists inclined toward absolute exclusion, regardless of foreign relations, and were ready to raise the rate whenever the imports were large.

In the passage of the McKinley Tariff Bill it was noticed that a third body was sharing largely in such legislation. After each house had passed the bill and disagreements on amendments had been reached, it was sent to a Joint Committee of Conference whose report was, by rule, unamendable. In the

Conference Committee the bill was finally shaped, and so shaped that the Republican majority was forced to accept it or none. The party leaders who sat on the Committee of Conference were a third house with almost despotic power, and were, as well, men whose association with manufacturing districts or protected interests raised a fair question as to the impartiality of their decisions. The Republican reply, in their hands, to the assertion that the tariff was the mother of trusts was to raise the tariff still higher and to forbid the trusts to engage in interstate commerce.

BIBLIOGRAPHICAL NOTE

The *Life of Henry Demarest Lloyd*, by C. Lloyd (2 vols., 1912) contains an admirable and sympathetic survey of the growth of anti-trust feeling, and should be supplemented by the writings of H. D. Lloyd, more particularly, " The Story of a Great Monopoly " (in *Atlantic Monthly*, March, 1881), and *Wealth against Commonwealth* (1894). The philosophy of Henry George is best stated in his *Progress and Poverty* (1879), and is presented biographically by H. George, Jr., in his *Life of Henry George* (1900). The most popular romance of the decade is based upon an economic hypothesis : E. Bellamy, *Looking Backward* (1887). J. W. Jenks, *The Trust Problem* (1900, etc.), has become a classic sketch of the economics of industrial concentration. The histories of the Standard Oil Company, by I. M. Tarbell (2 vols., 1904) and G. H. Montague (1903), are based largely upon judicial and congressional investigations. The Sherman Law is discussed in the writings and biographies of Sherman, Hoar, and Edmunds, and in A. H. Walker, *History of the Sherman Law* (1910). For the election of 1888, consult Stanwood, Andrews, Peck, the *Annual Cyclopædia*, the tariff histories, and D. R. Dewey, *National Problems, 1885–1897* (in *The American Nation*, vol. 24, 1907).

CHAPTER XI

THE FARMERS' CAUSE

THE Republican protective policy had its strongest supporters among the industrial communities of the East where the profits of manufacture were distributed. In the West, where the agricultural staples had produced a simplicity of interests somewhat resembling those of the Old South in its cotton crop, the advantage of protection was questioned even in Republican communities. The Granger States and the Prairie States were normally Republican, but they had experienced falling prices for their corn and wheat, as the South had for its cotton, in the eighties, and had listened encouragingly to the advocates of tariff reform. Cleveland's Message of 1887 had affected them strongly. Through 1888 and 1889 country papers shifted to the support of revision, while farmers' clubs and agricultural journals began to denounce protection. The Republican leaders felt the discontent, and brought forward the agricultural schedules of the McKinley Bill to appease it, but dissatisfaction increased in 1889 and 1890 through most of the farming sections.

The farmer in the South was directly affected by the falling price of cotton, and retained his hereditary aversion to the protective tariff. He could not believe that either party was working in his interests. The dominant issues of the eighties did not touch his problems. He was not interested in civil service reform, which was a product of a differentiated society, in which professional expertness was recognized and valued. He knew and cared little about administration, and being used to a multitude of different tasks himself saw no reason why the offices should not be passed around. In this view American farmers generally concurred.

The Southern farmer was without interest in the pension system and was prone to criticize it. The Fourteenth Amendment had forced the repudiation of the whole Confederate debt, leaving the Southern veterans compelled to pay taxes that were disbursed for the benefit of Union veterans and debarred from enjoying similar rewards. They could not turn Republican, yet in their own party they saw men who failed to represent them.

In the North agriculture was depressed and the farmers were discontented. In many regions the farms were worn out. Scientific farming was beginning to be talked about to some extent, but was little practiced. The improvements in transportation had brought the younger and more fertile lands of the West into competition with the East for the city markets. Cattle, raised on the plains and slaughtered at Kansas City or Chicago, were offered for sale in New York and Philadelphia. Western fruits of superior quality were competing with the common varieties of the Eastern orchards. Here, as in the South, the farmers saw the parties quarreling over issues that touched the manufacturing classes, but disregarding those of agriculture.

It was in the West, however, that agricultural discontent was keenest. In no other region were uniform conditions to be found over so large an area. The Granger States had shown how uniformity in discontent may bring forth political readjustments. The new region of the late eighties lay west of Missouri and Iowa, where the railroads had stimulated settlement along the farther edge of the arable prairies. Texas, Kansas, Colorado, and the Dakotas had passed into a boom period about 1885, and had pushed new farms into regions that could not in ordinary years produce a crop. Only blinded enthusiasts believed that the climate of the sub-humid plains was changing. In good years crops will grow as far west as the Rockies: in bad, they dry up in eastern Kansas.

It served the interest of the railroads to promote new settlements, and speculation got the better of prudence. The rainfall coöperated for a few years, enabling the newcomers to break the sod and set up their dwellings and barns. The quality of the settlers increased the dangers attendant upon the community.

Under earlier conditions in the westward migration each frontier had been settled, chiefly, by occupants of the preceding frontier, who knew the climate and understood the conditions of successful farming. The greater distances in the farther West, and the ease of access which the railroads gave, brought a less capable class of farmers into the plains settlements. Some were amateurs; others knew a different type of agriculture. The population which had to deal with this new region was less likely to succeed than that of any previous frontier.

The frontier of the eighties presented new obstacles in its doubtful rainfall and its experimental farmers. It contained as well the conditions that had always prevailed along the edge of settlement. Transportation was vital to its life, — as vital as it had been in the Granger States, — yet was nearly as unregulated. The Interstate Commerce Law of 1887 had little noticeable immediate effect. Discrimination, unreasonable rates, and overcapitalization were still grievances that affected the West. The new activity of organized labor, shown in the Western strikes of 1885 and 1886, added another obstacle to the easy prosperity of farmers who needed uninterrupted train service. The germs of an anti-railroad movement were well distributed.

An anti-corporation movement, too, might reasonably be expected in this new frontier. Producing only the raw products of agriculture, its inhabitants bought most of the commodities in use from distant sections. They were impressed with the cost of what they had to buy and the low price of what they sold. They were ready listeners to agitators against the trusts.

Like all frontiers, this one was financed on borrowed money. The pioneer was dependent on credit, was hopeful and speculative in his borrowings, built more towns and railroads than he needed, and loaded himself with a mountain of debt that could be met only after a long series of prosperous years.

By necessity he was readily converted by the arguments of inflation. Greenback inflation had run its course, and after the resumption of specie payments in 1879 had been only a political threat without foundation or many followers. A Greenback party, affiliating with labor and anti-monopoly interests, had nominated Weaver in 1880 and Butler in 1884, but even inflationists had not voted for the ticket in large number. A new phase of inflation had become more interesting than the greenbacks, and had led to the demand for the free coinage of silver.

Among the demands of the Western farmer, whose greatest problem was the payment of his debts, none was more often heard than that for more and cheaper money. The Eastern farmer, though less burdened with debt, knew that more money would make higher prices, and believed it would bring larger profits. The Southern farmer, heavily in debt, not so much for purposes of development and permanent improvements, as because he regularly mortgaged his crop in advance and allowed the rural storekeeper to finance him, was also interested in inflation as a common remedy. Together the farmers of all sections kept pressing on the parties for free silver after the passage of the Bland-Allison Bill in 1878. As the price of silver declined the gain which silver inflation would bring them increased, and they were joined by another class of producers whose profits came from mining the silver bullion.

The silver mines furnished important industries in Montana, Idaho, Colorado, Utah, Nevada, Arizona, and California, and were highly valued in most of the Western communities. As their output declined in value after 1873, their owners turned to the United States Government for aid and protection, not differing much from the manufacturers of the East in their hope for aid. The restoration of silver coinage was the method by which they desired their protection, and they asserted that Congress could coin all the silver and yet maintain it at a parity with gold. They were allies with the farmer inflationists so far as means of relief were concerned, and both failed to see how incompatible were their real aims. The miners wanted free silver in order to increase the price of silver and their profits; the farmers wanted it to increase the volume of money and reduce its value. If either was correct in his prophecy as to the result of free coinage, the other was doomed to disappointment. But the combined demand was reiterated through the eighties. While times were good it was not serious, but any shock to the prosperity or credit of the West was likely to stimulate the one movement in which all the discontented concurred.

The crisis which precipitated Western discontent into politics came in 1889 when rainfall declined and crops failed. In the Arkansas Valley, with an average fall of eighteen inches, the total for this year was only thirteen inches. General Miles, who had chased hostile Indians across the plains for more than twenty years, and who had seen the new villages push in, mile by mile, saw the terrible results of drought. First suffering, then mortgage, then foreclosure and eviction, he prophesied. "And should this impending evil continue for a series of years," he wrote, "no one can anticipate what may follow." The glowing promises of the early eighties were falsified, whole towns and counties were deserted, and the farmers turned to the Government for aid.

The Western upheaval followed a period in which both great parties had been attacked as misrepresentative. There was a widely spread belief that politicians were dishonest and that the Government was conducted for the favored classes. It was natural that the discontented should take up one of the agricultural organizations already existing, as the Grangers had done, and convert it to their political purpose.

Since the high day of the Granger movement there had always been associations among the farmers and organizations striving to get their votes. The Grange had itself continued as a social and economic bond after its attack upon the railroads. There had been a Farmers' Union and an Agricultural Wheel. The great success of the Knights of Labor and the American Federation of Labor had had imitators who were less successful because farming had been too profitable to give much room for organized discontent, while in times of prosperity the farmer was an individualist. A new activity among the farmers' papers was now an evidence of a growing desire to get the advantage of coöperation.

The greatest farmer organization of the eighties was the Farmers' Alliance, a loose federation of agricultural clubs that reflected local conditions, West and South. In the South, it was noted in 1888 as "growing rapidly," but "only incidentally of political importance." In Dakota, it had been active since 1885, conducting for its members fire and hail insurance, a purchasing department, and an elevator company. In Texas it was building cotton and woolen mills. The machinery of this organization was used by the farmers in stating their common cause, and as their aims broadened it merged, during 1890, into a People's Party. In Kansas, during the summer of this year, the movement broke over the lines of both old parties and had such success that its promoters thought a new political party had been born.

Agricultural discontent, growing with the hard times of 1889, had been noticed, but there had been no means of measuring it until Congress adjourned after the passage of the McKinley Bill and the members came home to conduct the congressional campaign of 1890. They found that the recent law had become the chief issue before them. The so-called popular demand for protection, revealed in the election of 1888, had after all been based upon a minority of the votes cast. The tariff and the way it had been passed were used against them by the Democrats and the Farmers' Alliance.

The act was passed so close to election day that its real influence could not then be seen and its opponents could not be confuted when they told of the evils it would do. Before the election of 1888, as again in 1892, Republican manufacturers frightened their workmen by threats of closing down if free-traders won. This time the tables were turned against them by the recital of prospective high prices.

Corrupt methods in framing the schedules furnished an influential argument throughout the West. Even in the East the tariff reformers asserted that undue favors had been done for greedy interests; that manufacturers who had bought immunity by their contributions to Quay's campaign fund had been rewarded with increased protection. The farmers believed these charges, plausible though unprovable, for they were disposed to believe that both the great parties were interested only in selfish exploitation of the Government to the advantage of politicians.

In every State Republican candidates had to meet this fire as well as the local issues. In Maine, Reed met it and was elected with enlarged majority from a community that wanted protection. In Ohio, McKinley lost his seat, partly from the revulsion of feeling, but more because the Democrats, who controlled the State Legislature, had gerrymandered his district against him. Cannon, of Illinois, who had already served nine terms and was to serve ten more, lost his seat, and LaFollette, of Wisconsin, whom the protectionists had made much of, was checked early in a promising career because of an educational issue in his State. Pennsylvania, protectionist at heart, elected the Democratic ex-governor Pattison again in one of its revulsions against the Quay machine.

The Democrats defeated the Republicans in the East while the Farmers' Alliance undermined them in the West. In Kansas and Nebraska the Alliance controlled the result, sent their own men to Washington, and secured the Kansas Legislature which returned the first Populist Senator. In several States fusion tickets were successful with Democratic and Alliance support. In the South, Democrats found it aided them in winning nomination — for the real

Southern election was within this party and not at the polls — to assert that they were and had been farmers.

When the votes were counted the extent of the reaction was realized. The last Congress had contained a safe majority of Republicans in each house. The new Congress, the Fifty-second, chosen in 1890, had lost the high-tariff majority in the lower body. Only 88 Republicans were elected, against 236 Democrats and 8 of the Alliance. The Republicans retained the Senate partly because of the "rotten borough" States, Idaho and Wyoming, which they had just admitted.

The greatest factor in the landslide was the tariff, but this was, largely, only the occasion for an outburst of discontent that had been piling up for a decade. The dominant party was punished because things went wrong, because the trusts throve and labor was uneasy, because prices declined, because there were scandals in the Public Lands and Pension Bureaus, and because the rainfall had diminished on the plains. The new House elected a Georgian, Crisp, as Speaker, and the second half of Harrison's term passed quietly. Among the people, however, there was much conjecture upon the future of the Farmers' Alliance. A convention at Cincinnati, six months after the election, tried to unite the new element and form a third party of importance.

Union between the Knights of Labor and the Farmers' Alliance for political purposes was the aim of the promoters of the People's Party, a party that was to right all the wrongs from which the plain

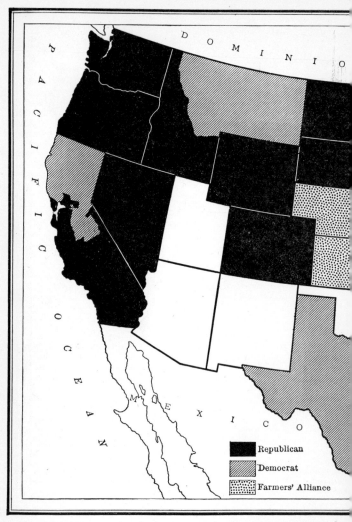

Republican

Democrat

Farmers' Alliance

THE CONGRESS

(Based upon a manuscript thesis by B. C

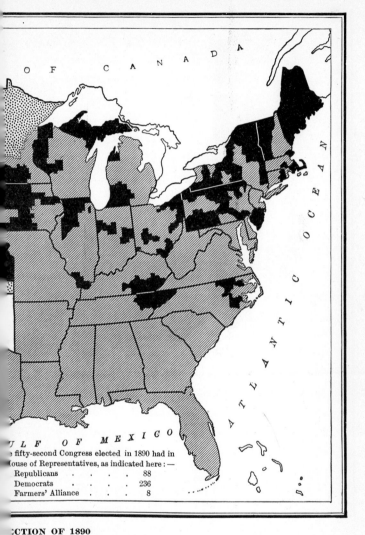

The fifty-second Congress elected in 1890 had in [its] House of Representatives, as indicated here : —

Republicans	.	.	.	88
Democrats	.	.	.	236
Farmers' Alliance	.	.	.	8

[ELE]CTION OF 1890

[From] the University of Wisconsin Library)

people suffered and restore the Government to their hands. Until the next presidential election they had time to organize for the crusade.

The United States, by 1890, had begun to feel the influence of the agencies of communication in breaking down sectionalism and letting in the light of comparative experience. Men who survived from the generation that flourished before the war found their cherished ideas undermined or shattered. In public life, administration, literature, and religion the old order was being swept away. The United States had become a nation because it could not avoid it. Even the Congregational churches, with whom parish autonomy was vital, had seen fit to erect a National Council. Every important activity of trade had become national, and the only agency that retained its old localism was the law, which must cope with the new order. In many ways the trust problem was the result of an inadequate legal system which left a wide " twilight zone " between the local capacity of the State and the activity of the Nation. Yet the Nation was unfolding and expanding its powers. Railroad control, immigration and labor control, agricultural experiment, irrigation, and reclamation were only samples of the new lines of activity that created new administrative machinery and advanced abreast of the new idea of appointment because of merit and tenure during good behavior. Men who continued to see the center of political gravity in the State Governments were behind the times.

An indigenous literature was rising in the United

States. Dickens had lived long enough to recognize
the spirit of a new school in *The Luck of Roaring
Camp*, and *The Outcasts of Poker Flat*, which appeared in 1868. Before 1890 the fame of their author,
Bret Harte, was secure. Samuel Langhorne Clemens
(Mark Twain), too, had seen the native field and had
exploited it. The New England school, Emerson and
Longfellow, Whittier, Holmes, and Lowell, lived into
or through the eighties, but were less robust in their
American flavor than their younger contemporaries
who picked subjects from the border. *Tom Sawyer*,
Huckleberry Finn, and the *Connecticut Yankee* were
life as well as art. Another writer of the generation,
William Dean Howells, gave *The Rise of Silas
Lapham* to the world in 1885, and revealed a different
stratum of the new society, while the vogue of *Little
Lord Fauntleroy* tells less of the life therein described than of the outlook of American readers.

Pure literature was in 1890 turning more and more
to American subjects; applied literature was searching
for causes and explanations. The writings of Henry
George, particularly his *Progress and Poverty*,
brought him from obscurity to prominence in six
years, and by 1885 had "formed a noteworthy epoch
in the history of economic thought." The success of
Bellamy's utopian romance proved the avidity of the
reading public. Parkman and Bancroft, of the older
generation, Henry Adams, McMaster, and Rhodes,
of the younger, led the way through history to an
understanding of American conditions. Economics,
sociology, and government were beginning to have a
literature of their own, the last receiving its strong-

est impulse from the thoughtful *American Common-wealth* of James Bryce.

In the field of periodical literature the rising American taste was supporting a wider range of magazines. The old and dignified *North American Review* was still an arena for political discussion. During 1890 it printed an important interchange of views between William E. Gladstone and James G. Blaine, on the merits of a protective tariff. *Harper's Monthly* and the *Atlantic* had given employment to the leading men of letters since before the Civil War. *Leslie's* and *Harper's Weeklies* had added illustration to news, making their place during the sixties, while the *Independent* held its own as the leading religious newspaper and the *Nation* appeared as a journal of criticism. *Scribner's* and the *Century* had been added more recently to the list of monthlies, the latter running its great series of reminiscences of the battles and leaders of the Civil War and its life of Lincoln by Nicolay and Hay. Improvements in typography and illustration, combined with greater ease in collecting the news and distributing the product, made all the periodicals more nearly national.

The periodicals, in a measure, took the place as national leaders that the newspapers had before. The newspaper as a personal expression was passing away, as the great editors of Horace Greeley's generation died. The younger editors were making investments rather than journalistic tools out of their papers. Trade and advertisement used this vehicle to approach their customers. News collecting became more prompt and adequate, but the opinion of the papers dwindled. They bought their news from syndicates or associations, as they bought paper or ink. The counting-house was coming to outrank the editorial room in their management.

Through the new literature the changing nature of American life was portrayed, and as the life reshaped itself under nationalizing influences theology lost much of its old narrowness. Among religious novels *Robert Elsmere* was perhaps most widely read. The struggle between orthodoxy and the new criticism had got out of the control of the professional theologians and had permeated the laity. A revised version of the Old and New Testaments gave new basis for textual discussion. The influence of the scientific generalizations of Darwin and his school had reached the Church and forced upon it a rephrasing of its views. It was becoming less dangerous for men to admit their belief in scientific process. The orthodox churches lost nothing in popularity as the struggle advanced, and outside them new teachers proclaimed new religions as they had ever done in America.

The greatest of the new religions was that of Mrs. Mary Baker Eddy, in whose teachings may be found a religious parallel to the political revolt of the People's Party. Christian Science was a reaction from the " vertebrate Jehovah " of the Puritans to a more comfortable and responsive Deity. It was the outgrowth of a well-fed and prosperous society, presenting itself to the ordinary mind as " primarily a religion of healing."

Intellectual, spiritual, economic, and political revolt were common in America in 1890, as they must have been after the industrial revolution of the last ten years. The whole nation was once more acting as a unit, for the South had outlived the worst results of war and reorganization and was again developing on independent lines. The immediate problem was the effect of the revolt upon political control.

BIBLIOGRAPHICAL NOTE

The materials upon the unrest of the later eighties are yet uncollected, and must be pursued through the files of the journals, many of which are named above in the text. The new scientific periodicals : *Quarterly Journal of Economics, Political Science Quarterly, Yale Review, Journal of Political Economy*, etc., devoted much space to current economic and social analysis. F. L. McVey, *The Populist Movement* (in American Economic Association, Economic Studies, vol. I), is useful but only fragmentary. The materials on free silver are mentioned in the note to chapter XIV, below. A. B. Paine, *Mark Twain*, gives many cross-references to the literary life of the decade. J. F. Jameson discusses the fertile field of American religious history in "The American Acta Sanctorum" (in the *American Historical Review*, 1908).

CHAPTER XII

THE NEW SOUTH

THE Old South, in which two parties had always struggled on fairly equal terms, was destroyed during the period of the Civil War, while reconstruction failed completely to revive it. The New South, in politics, had but one party of consequence. With few exceptions white men of respectability voted with the Democrats because of the influence of the race question which negro suffrage had raised. From the re-establishment of Southern home rule until the advent in politics of the Farmers' Alliance no issue appeared in the Southern States that even threatened to split the dominant vote. But under the economic pressure of the late eighties the old white leaders parted company and even contended with each other for the negro vote to aid their plans.

The political influence of the Alliance cannot be measured at the polls in the South as easily as in the West. In most States, in 1888 and 1890, Alliance tickets were promoted, often in fusion with the Republican party. The greater influence, how-ever, was within Democratic lines, at the primaries or conventions of that party. Here, among the candidates who presented themselves for nomination, the professional politician found himself an object of suspicion. The lawyer lost some of his political availability. Men who could claim to be close to the soil had an advantage.

The value placed upon the dissatisfied farmer vote is shown in the autobiographical sketches which Senators and Representatives wrote for the *Congressional Directory* of the Fifty-second Congress. Some who had never before held office stated the fact with apparent pride. One, who appeared from the Texas district which John H. Reagan had represented through eight Congresses, announced that he "became a member of the Order of Patrons of Husbandry, and took an active interest in advocating the cause of progress among his fellow laborers; is now Overseer of the Texas State Grange and President of the Texas Farmer Coöperative Publishing Association." From Georgia came several Representatives of this type. One "has devoted his time exclusively [since 1886] to agricultural interests, and is a member of the Farmers' Alliance." Another was elected "as an Alliance man and Democrat." A third "was Vice-President of the Georgia State Agricultural Society for eleven years, and President of the same for four years; he is now President of the Georgia State Alliance." A fourth, Thomas E. Watson, lawyer, editor, historian, and leader of the new movement, "has been, and still is, largely interested in farming." A South Carolina Representative covered himself with the generous assertion that he was "member of all the organizations in his State designed to benefit agriculture."

The agricultural bases of the Southern political disturbance lay in the changes in tenure and finance that had recently appeared. The South was not without a pioneer immigration resembling that of the West. Many of the carpet-baggers had undertaken to develop farms there. There was much opportunity for rural speculation that increased in attractiveness as the area of free Western lands diminished. So far as this went, it produced a debtor class and prepared the way for inflation.

But the development of new areas in the South was less significant than the method of its industry. The disintegration of plantations continued steadily through the seventies and eighties. The figures of the census, showing tenure for the first time in 1880, and color in 1890, exaggerated this, since many of the small holdings there enumerated were to all intents farmed by hired labor and were only matters of bookkeeping. Yet there was a marked diminution in the size of the estates. A class of negro owners was slowly developing to account for a part of the diminution. Frugality and industry appeared in enough of the freedmen to bring into negro ownership in 1900, within the slave area, 149,000 farms, averaging 55 acres. There were at this time 2,700,000 farms in the South, and 5,700,000 in the whole United States. Negro renters and negro croppers, many of whom labored under the direct supervision of the white landlords, increased the number of individual farmers, and like the rest lived upon the proceeds of the cotton crop that was not yet grown.

Much of the capital that was used in Southern agriculture came from the North through the manufacturers and wholesalers who supplied the retail merchants of the South. These merchants advanced credit to their customers, measuring it by the estimated value of the next crop. Once the bargain had been struck, the farmer bought all his supplies from his banker-merchant, paying such prices as the latter saw fit to charge. There could be little competition among merchants under this system, since the burden of his debt kept the planter from seeking the cheapest market. The double weight of extortionate prices and heavy interest impressed a large section of the South with the scarcity of cash and the evils of existing finance.

In agricultural method as well as in finance the South was oppressed by its system. The merchant wanted cotton, for cotton was marketable, and could not be consumed by a tricky debtor. Single cropping was thus unduly encouraged ; diversified agriculture and rotation of crops made little progress. The use of commercial fertilizers was greatly stimulated, but agriculture as a whole could not advance.

Tied fast to a system nearly as inflexible as that of the ante-bellum plantation, the South suffered disproportionately in years when cotton was low. Depression in the later eighties and the early nineties intensified the suffering of the debtor class and produced an inflation movement that allied the South and West in the demand for cheaper money and more of it. The Farmers' Alliance, with its demands for railroad control, trust regulation, banking reform, and free silver, was the logical vehicle for the expression of Southern discontent.

The white population of the South, undivided

since the Civil War, was confronted in 1890 by an issue that bore no relation to race and that divided society into debtor and creditor classes. For twenty years, by common agreement in which the North had tacitly concurred, the negro had been suppressed outside the law. Occasional negroes had got into office and even to Congress in reconstruction days. One, who described himself as "a bright mulatto," sat in the Fifty-first and Fifty-second Congresses, but in most regions of the South the negro had not been allowed to vote or had been "counted out" at the polls, while only in sporadic cases, mostly in the mountain sections, was the Republican party able to get enough votes to elect its candidates.

The Farmers' Alliance split the white vote and gave to the negro an unusual power. From being suppressed by all to being courted by many involved a change that raised his hopes only to destroy them. The South no sooner saw the possibility that the negro vote might hold a balance of power between two equal white factions than it took steps to remove itself from temptation and to disfranchise the undesired class.

The purpose of the Fourteenth and Fifteenth Amendments had been to raise the freedmen to civil equality and protect them there. Pursuant to the Fourteenth Amendment, Congress passed, in 1875, a Civil Rights Bill, which forbade discrimination against any citizen in "the full and equal enjoyment of the accommodations, advantages, facilities, and privileges of inns, public conveyances on land or water, theaters, and other places of public amusement." It was restrained from imposing coeducation of the races only by Northern philanthropists who were interested in Southern education. Its compulsion was disregarded at the South, where social equality between the races could not be attained. Innkeepers and railroads continued to separate their customers, and in time a few of them were haled into court to answer for violating the law. Their defense was that the Fourteenth Amendment forbade discrimination by the States, but did not touch the private act of any citizen ; that it protected the rights of citizens, but that these rights, complete before the law, did not extend to social relations, — that attendance at a theater is not a civil right at all, and may properly be regulated by the police power without conflict with the Constitution. In the Civil Rights Cases, decided in 1883, the Supreme Court released the defendants, ruling that the Fourteenth Amendment was too narrow in its intention to justify Congress in the passage of a code of social relations at the South. This part of reconstruction thus broke down, leaving the negro population at the discretion of its white neighbors.

The Fifteenth Amendment, too, had been limited in its protecting force before 1890. It forbade a denial of the right to vote by any State. The Supreme Court easily determined that no violation could occur when a hostile mob excluded negroes from the polls. It had been settled before 1890 that the negro was defenseless against personal discrimination. It remained to be seen whether he could be disfranchised by law and yet have no redress. Not till the South found some of its people appealing for the negro vote in the crisis of the Farmers' Alliance did it take the last steps in the undoing of reconstruction.

The Fifteenth Amendment was not explicit. Instead of asserting the right of the negro to vote, it said, by negation, that the right should not be denied on account of "race, color, or previous condition of servitude." The three qualities of race, color, and servitude separated the races, but the South learned that they were separated by other qualities that were not proscribed by the amendment as a basis for the franchise. The negro was generally poor, and any qualification based on property would exclude him. He was shiftless, and often vagrant, and hence could be touched by poll-tax and residence requirements. He was illiterate, and was unable to meet an educational test. Tired of using force or fraud, the South began in 1890 a system of legal evasion of the Fifteenth Amendment.

The State of Mississippi, in a new constitution framed in 1890, defined the franchise in terms that bore heavily upon the negro. In the debates of its convention members talked frankly and freely of their intention to disqualify the race; the clause bore no mention of discrimination. It permitted persons to vote who, being male citizens over twenty-one, and having reasonable residence qualifications, had paid a poll or other tax for two years preceding the election, and could read, or understand and interpret when read to them, any section of the constitution of the State. Under this clause, between

the cumulative tax and the large discretionary powers
vested in the officers of enrollment, the negro electorate was reduced until it was negligible in Mississippi ; and it was a subject of admiration for other
Southern States, which proceeded to imitate it.

All of the cotton States but Florida and Texas,
and most of the old slave States, revised their electoral clauses in the next twenty years. Arkansas, in
1893, based the franchise on a one-year poll-tax.
South Carolina, in 1895, used residence, enrollment,
and poll-tax, while the convention called to disfranchise the negro passed resolutions of sympathy for
Cuban independence. Delaware, in 1897, established
an educational test. Louisiana, in 1898, established
education and a poll-tax; North Carolina, in 1900,
did the same. Alabama, in 1901, made use of residence, registry, and poll-tax. Virginia based the suffrage on property, literacy, or poll-tax in 1902.
Georgia did the same in 1908, and the new State of
Oklahoma followed the Southern custom in 1910.

It was relatively easy to exclude most of the
negroes by means of qualifications such as these, but
every convention was embarrassed by the fact that
each qualification excluded, as well, some of the white
voters. In nearly every case revisions were accompanied by a determination to save the whites, and
for this purpose a temporary basis of enrollment
was created in addition to the permanent. Louisiana
devised the favorite method in 1898. Her constitution provided that, for a given period, persons who
could not qualify under the general clause might be
placed upon the roll of voters if they had voted in

the State before 1867 or were descended from such voters. The "grandfather clause," as this was immediately called, saved the poor whites, and was imitated by North Carolina, Alabama, Virginia, and Georgia. The governor of Louisiana, in 1898, sang the praises of the new invention: "The white supremacy for which we have so long struggled at the cost of so much precious blood and treasure is now crystallized into the constitution as a fundamental part and parcel of that organic instrument, and that, too, by no subterfuge or evasions. With this great principle thus firmly embedded in the constitution and honestly enforced, there need be no longer any fear as to the honesty and purity of our future elections." The Supreme Court declined to go behind the innocent phraseology of the clauses until 1915, and refused to overthrow them until most of them had become obsolete.

Before the courts had shown their unwillingness to interfere, Congress had done the same. Two methods of redress were discussed during the years of Republican ascendancy, 1889–91. One of these contemplated a reduction of the Southern representation in the House, under that part of the Fourteenth Amendment that requires such reduction in proportion to the number of citizens who are disfranchised. Although urged angrily more than once, this action was not taken, and would not have affected cases in which the denial was by force and not by law. To meet the former situation the Republican party pledged itself in 1888. A Force Bill, placing the control of Southern elections in federal hands was considered.

It received the enthusiastic support of Henry Cabot Lodge, and was the occasion for another waving of the "bloody shirt." It passed the House, with the aid of Speaker Reed, but in the Senate was abandoned by the caucus and allowed to die in 1891. The South was left alone with its negro problem. In the words of a Southern governor, "There are only two flags — the white and the black. Under which will you enlist?"

The New South removed the negro from politics, but he remained, in industry and society, a problem to whose solution an increasing attention was paid. At the time of emancipation he was almost universally illiterate and lived in a bankrupt community. Northern philanthropy saw an opportunity here. The teachers sent south by the Freedmen's Bureau stirred up interest by their letters home. In 1867 George Peabody, already noted for his benefactions in England and in Baltimore, created a large fund for the relief of illiteracy in the destitute region. His board of trustees became a clearing-house for educational efforts. Ex-President Hayes became, in 1882, the head of a similar fund created by John F. Slater, of Connecticut. Through the rest of the century these boards, in close coöperation, studied and relieved the educational necessities of the South. In 1901 the men who directed them organized a Southern Educational Board for the propagation of knowledge, while in 1903 Congress incorporated a General Education Board, to which John D. Rockefeller gave many millions for the subsidizing of educational attempts.

The negro advanced in literacy under the pressure of the new influences. In 1880 seventy per cent of the American negroes over ten years old were illiterate, but the proportion was reduced in the next ten years to fifty-seven per cent; to forty-five per cent by 1900; and to thirty per cent by 1910. As the negro advanced, his own leaders, as well as his white friends, differed in the status to which they would raise him and in the methods to be pursued. Some of his ablest representatives, W. E. B. DuBois among them, resented the discrimination and disfranchisement from which they suffered, and insisted upon equality as a preliminary. Others, like Booker T. Washington, who founded a notable trade school in Alabama in 1881, worried little over discrimination, and hoped to solve their problem through common and technical education which might lead the race to self-respect and independence.

Friction increased between the races at the South after emancipation. Freedom and political pressure demoralized many of the negroes, whose new feeling of independence exasperated many of the whites. Southern society still possessed many border traits. Men went armed and fought on slight provocation. The duel and the public assault aroused little serious criticism even in the eighties, and the freedmen lived in a society in which self-restraint had never been the dominant virtue. In Alabama, in 1880, the assessed value of guns, dirks, and pistols was nearly twice that of the libraries and five times that of the farm implements of the State. The distribution of the races varied exceedingly, from the Black Belt, where in the Yazoo bottom lands the negroes outnumbered the whites fifteen or more to one, to the uplands and mountains, where the proportions were reversed. But everywhere the less reputable of both races retarded society by their excesses.

In spite of its unsolvable race problem the South was reviving in the eighties and was changing under the influence of the industrial revolution. Northern capital was a mainstay of its agriculture. Transportation, manufacture, and city development found stimulation from the same source. In 1884 the National Planters' Association promoted a celebration of the hundredth anniversary of the export of the first American cotton. In a great exposition at New Orleans they showed how far the New South had gone in its development.

In the twenty years after 1880 the South became a modern industrial community. Its coal mines increased their annual output from 6,000,000 tons to 50,000,000; its output of pig iron grew from 397,000 tons to 2,500,000; its manufactures rose in annual value from $338,000,000 to $1,173,000,000, with a pay roll swelling from $76,000,000 to $350,000,000. The spindles in its cotton mills were increased from 610,000 to 4,298,000. With the industrial changes there came a shifting of Southern population. The census maps show a tendency in the black population to concentrate in the Black Belt, and in the white population to increase near the deposits of coal and iron. Factory towns appeared in the Piedmont, where cheap power could be obtained, and drew their operatives from the rural population of the neighborhood. Unembarrassed by the child-labor and factory laws of the North, the new Southern mills exploited the women and children, and were consuming one seventh of the cotton crop by 1900. In Alabama, Birmingham became a second Pittsburg.

The Southern railway system was completely rebuilt after the Civil War. In 1860 it included about one third of the thirty thousand miles of track in the United States, but war and neglect reduced it to ruin. Partly under federal auspices it was restored in the later sixties. After 1878 it suddenly expanded as did all the American railway systems.

Texas experienced the most thorough change in the fifty years after the Civil War. From 307 miles her railways expanded to more than 14,000 miles. Only one of the Confederate States, Arkansas, had a slighter mileage in 1860, but in 1910 no one had half as much as Texas. The totals for the Confederate area rose from 11,000 miles in 1870 to 17,000 in 1880, to 36,000 in 1890, to 45,000 in 1900, and to 63,000 in 1910. After 1880 no Confederate State equaled Texas, whose vast area, suddenly brought within reach of railway service, poured forth cotton until by the end of the century she alone raised one fourth of the American crop. Through the expanding transportation system the area of profitable cotton culture rose more rapidly than the demand for cotton, and in overproduction may be found one of the reasons for the decline in cotton values in the early nineties. In the decline may be found an incentive toward diversified agriculture. When cotton went down, farmers tried other crops. The corn acreage in the ten cotton States passed the cotton acreage before 1899, and with the diversification came no decrease in the total cotton output, but an increase in general agricultural prosperity. In many regions fruit culture and truck-raising forced their way to the front among profitable types of agriculture.

In spite of the changes in industry and transportation the South remained in 1910 a rural community when compared with the rest of the United States. Out of 114 cities of 50,000 population in 1910, only 15 were in the Confederate area. But when compared with its own past the South was developing cities at a rapid rate. Only New Orleans and Richmond, in 1880, had 50,000 inhabitants. Atlanta, Charleston, Memphis, and Nashville were added to this class by 1890. Texas had no city of this size until 1900. But in 1910 she possessed four, Dallas, Forth Worth, Houston, and San Antonio. As the cities increased in number, bound together, and bound to the cities of the rest of the United States by the ties of trade and society, the localisms of the South diminished. The essential fear of negro control remained untouched, but in superficial ways the Southerner came to resemble his fellow citizen of whatever section.

The sectionalism which had made a political unit of the South before the war was weakened. In the tariff debates of 1883 and later a group of Southern protectionists made common cause with Northern Republicans. Sugar, iron, and cotton manufactures converted them from the old regional devotion to free trade. A fear of national power had kept the old South generally opposed to internal improvements at the public cost. The Pacific railroads had been postponed somewhat because of this. But this repugnance had died away, and in the Mississippi River the United States found a field for work that was welcomed in the South.

The Mississippi never fully recovered the dominance that it had possessed before the war, but it remained an important highway for the Western cotton States. The whimsical torrent, washing away its banks, cutting new channels at will, flooding millions of acres every spring, was too great to be controlled by States that had been impoverished by war and reconstruction. In 1879 Congress created a Mississippi River Commission. Unusual floods in 1882 attracted attention to the danger, and thereafter Congress found the money for a levee system that restrained the river between its banks from Cairo to the Gulf.

The mouth of the river, always choked by mud flats, was opened by the United States in 1879. A Western engineer, James B. Eads, devised a scheme by which the current scoured out its own channel and converted itself into an ocean-going highway. He had already proved his power over the Father of Waters by building the railroad bridge that was opened at St. Louis in 1874. In 1892 other engineers completed a bridge at Memphis.

The active development of the New South lessened the difference between it and the rest of the United States, and brought it within the general industrial revolution. By 1884 the trend was not noticeable. By 1890 the white population had divided over a political issue like the North and West. In the years immediately following 1890 Populism was as much a problem in the South as anywhere.

BIBLIOGRAPHICAL NOTE

Most of the books relating to the South are partisan. The most useful economic analyses are to be found in the writings of W. L. Fleming, U. B. Phillips, and A. H. Stone. Special points of view are presented in A. B. Hart, *The Southern South* (1911), E. G. Murphy, *Problems of the Present South* (1904), E. A. Alderman and A. C. Gordon, *Life of J. L. M. Curry* (1911), J. L. M. Curry, *A Brief Sketch of George Peabody* (1898), J. E. Cutler, *Lynch Law* (1905), B. T. Washington, *Up from Slavery* (1905), W. E. B. DuBois, *Souls of Black Folk* (1903), and J. L. Mathews, *Remaking the Mississippi* (1909). The *Annual Cyclopædia* is full of useful details. The Annual Reports of the Peabody Fund, the Slater Fund, and the United States Commissioner of Education contain statistics and discussions upon Southern society. The Civil Rights Cases (109 U.S. Reports) give the best treatment of the legal status of the negro, and are supplemented by J. C. Rose, "Negro Suffrage" (in *American Political Science Review*, vol. I, pp. 17–43, — a partial sketch only), and J. M. Mathews, *Legislative and Judicial History of the Fifteenth Amendment* (in Johns Hopkins University Studies, vol. XXVII). There were interesting articles on the New Orleans Exposition, by E. V. Smalley, in the *Century Magazine* for April and May, 1885.

CHAPTER XIII

POPULISM

THE election of 1890 stunned and bewildered both old parties. The Republicans lost their control of the Lower House, while the Democrats paid for their victory the price of a partial alliance with a new movement whose weight they could only estimate. Populism was engendered by local troubles in the West and South, but its name now acquired a national usage and its leaders were encouraged to attempt a national organization.

In a series of conventions, held between 1889 and 1892, the People's Party developed into a finished organization with state delegations and a national committee. At St. Louis, in December, 1889, the Farmers' Alliance held a national convention and considered the basis for wider growth. The outcome was an attempt to combine in one party organized labor, organized agriculture, and believers in the single tax. The leaders of the Knights of Labor and the American Federation of Labor were not averse to such common action, although the latter preferred their own Federation to any party. The dangers of political action, seen in the decline of the National Labor Union of 1866, did not check the desires of the Knights in 1889, although the leaders found it easier then, as later, to promise the

support of organized labor than to deliver it at
the polls. After the St. Louis Convention the name
Farmers' Alliance merged into the broader name of
the People's Party, though the attempt to win the
rank and file of the unions failed.

In December, 1890, the farmers met at Ocala,
Florida, to rejoice over the congressional victory and
to plan for 1892. Since each of the great parties was
believed to be indifferent to the people and corrupt,
a permanent third party was a matter of conviction,
and in May, 1891, this party was formally created
in a mass convention at Cincinnati. Miscellaneous
reforms were insisted upon here, but were overshadowed by the demands of the inflationists. James
B. Weaver, of Iowa, the old presidential candidate
of the Greenbackers, was a leading spirit at Cincinnati. His best-known aide was Ignatius Donnelly,
of Minnesota, a devotee of the Baconian theory and
of the "Lost Atlantis," who was now devoting his
active mind to the support of free silver. A national
committee was created after another meeting, at St.
Louis in February, 1892, and on July 2, 1892, the
party met in that city in its first national nominating convention.

The platform of the People's Party was based on
calamity. "We meet in the midst of a nation brought
to the verge of moral, political, and material ruin,"
it declared. "Corruption dominates the ballot-box,
the legislature, the Congress, and touches even the
ermine of the bench. The people are demoralized.
. . . The newspapers are largely subsidized or muz-
zled; public opinion silenced; business prostrated;

our homes covered with mortgages; labor impoverished; and the land concentrating in the hands of the capitalists."

The greatest of the evils in sight was "the vast conspiracy against mankind," which had demonetized silver, added to the purchasing power of gold, and abridged the supply of money "to fatten usurers." To correct the financial evils the platform demanded "the free and unlimited coinage of silver at the present legal ratio of sixteen to one," and an issue of legal-tender currency until the circulation should reach an average of fifty dollars per capita. Postal savings banks, a graduated income tax, and economy in government were the subsidiary demands.

No demand of the Populists attracted so much attention as this for free silver, but its platform touched reform at every angle. In the field of transportation it asked for government ownership of railroads, telegraphs, and telephones. It asked that land monopolies be prevented, that the public lands be in part regained, and that alien ownership be forbidden. It wanted the Australian ballot, liberal pensions, restriction of immigration, an eight-hour day, a single term for President and Vice-President, direct election of United States Senators, abolition of the Pinkerton detectives, and was curious about the initiative and referendum. It was in many respects a prophecy as to the workings of reform for the next twenty years.

The People's Party entered the campaign of 1892 with this platform and with the support of advanced reformers, with a considerable following in the West and South, and with James B. Weaver and James G. Field as candidates. Few of the workers for its ticket were politicians of known standing, and its voters had a preponderance of youth. In several Western States the Democratic party supported it with fusion tickets. In the South it often coöperated with the Republicans. From the first the third party found it harder to stand alone than to unite with the weaker local party.

The disrupting force of hard times was increased by the acts of the Republican party. Harrison's first Congress had passed a series of laws that provoked opposition and criticism. The Interstate Commerce Law was still new when he took office. In quick succession in 1890 came the new States, and Oklahoma Territory, the Dependent Pensions Bill, the Sherman Anti-Trust Bill, the Silver Purchase Bill, and the McKinley Tariff. The dominant majority had used arbitrary methods to enforce its will and had given to its enemies more than one text. After 1891 the Democratic majority in the House reduced the Administration to the political incompetence that had prevailed from 1883 to 1889.

Benjamin Harrison gained little prestige as the result of the Administration. He had been nominated for his availability, and the campaign songs had said as much of his illustrious grandfather, the hero of Tippecanoe, as of himself. His appointments had pleased neither the politicians nor the reformers, while there was much laughter at the presence in the offices of numerous personal friends and relatives.

The most notable of his appointments was the most embarrassing.

James G. Blaine, as Secretary of State, found no topic in foreign relations as interesting as the canal had been in his earlier term. The wranglings with Great Britain and Germany over their treatment of naturalized Americans had subsided. The fisheries of the North Atlantic had been temporarily settled by President Cleveland. The regulation of the seal fisheries of Bering Sea brought no new glory to Blaine.

There was no doubt that the seal herd of the Pacific was being rapidly destroyed by careless and wasteful hunters from most of the countries bordering on that ocean. On the American islands the herds could be protected, and here they gathered every summer to mate and breed. But the men who hunted with guns at sea, instead of with clubs on land, could not be controlled unless the world would consent to an American police beyond the three-mile limit. In an arbitration with Great Britain, at Paris, Blaine tried to prove that the seals were American, and entitled to protection on the high seas, and that the waters of the northern Pacific were *mare clausum*. The arbitration went against him on every material point.

The only episode that threatened war occurred in Chile. Here Harrison had sent as Minister Patrick Egan, a newly naturalized Irishman and follower of Blaine. In a revolution of 1891 Egan sided with the conservative party that lost. His enemies charged him with improper interest in contracts and with instinctive antagonism to British interests in Chile.

After the revolution a mob in Valparaiso showed its dislike for Americans by attacking sailors on shore leave. Egan's extreme demands for summary punishment of the rioters were upheld by Harrison, who prepared the navy for war. Finally the Chilean Government was forced to make complete apologies.

In the same year an American mob in New Orleans lynched several Italians, and Blaine repelled with indignation the demand that indemnity be accorded before trial and conviction. He could not even promise trial because of the helplessness of the United States in local criminal proceedings. The Italian Minister, Baron Fava, was withdrawn from Washington on this account, and returned only when Congress had healed the breach by making provision for the families of the sufferers.

The internal relations of the Administration were not happier than the external. Harrison chafed under the influence of Blaine, and alienated so many of the regular Republican leaders that it became doubtful whether he could secure his own renomination. Both Quay and Platt had been offended, and the former had resigned his chairmanship of the National Committee after the failure of a political bank in Philadelphia. No one was anxious to manage the President's campaign, and he showed little skill in managing it himself. The future was still in doubt when, on June 4, 1892, three days before the meeting of the convention at Minneapolis, Blaine resigned his position without a word of explanation. Whether he was only sick and unhappy, or whether he desired the nomination, was uncertain.

The strength of Blaine and the rising influence of William McKinley were apparent in the Republican Convention. Harrison was renominated on the first ballot, but Blaine and McKinley received more than one hundred and eighty votes apiece. The former had reached the end of his career, and died the next winter. The latter was now Governor of Ohio. McKinley had lost his seat in the election of 1890, but had been raised to the governorship in the next year. He was chairman of the convention that renominated Harrison, reaffirmed the " American doctrine of protection," and evaded the issue of free silver.

The Democratic party had bred no national leader but Grover Cleveland since the Civil War, and he had earned the dislike of the organization before his defeat in 1888. His insistence upon the tariff offended the protectionist wing of his party, and he left office unpopular and lonely. He retired to New York City, where he took up the practice of law and regained the confidence of the people. Demands upon him for public speeches in 1891 revealed the recovery of his popularity. His friends began to organize in his behalf during 1892, and David B. Hill aided by his opposition.

The strength of Hill, who had been elected Governor of New York, and who was now Senator, was based upon Tammany Hall and those elements in the New York Democracy that reformers were constantly attacking. He was believed to have defeated Cleveland in 1888 by entering into a deal with the Republican machine by which Harrison received the electoral and he the gubernatorial vote of New York. Early in 1892, as interest in Cleveland revived, Hill called a " snap " convention and secured the indorsement of New York for his own candidacy. The solid New York delegation shouting for Hill was an item in Cleveland's favor at the Democratic Convention in Chicago. With tariff reformers in control, denouncing " Republican protection as a fraud, a robbery of the great majority of the American people for the benefit of a few," and reasserting Cleveland's phrase that " public office is a public trust," the convention selected Cleveland and Adlai E. Stevenson, of Illinois, as the party candidates. Its coinage plank, like that of the Republicans, meant what the voter chose to read into it.

There were two debates in the campaign of 1892. On the surface was the renewed discussion of the tariff, with the Republicans fighting for the McKinley Bill all the more earnestly because there was danger of its repeal, and the Democrats officially demanding reduction. " I would rather have seen Cleveland defeated than to have had that fool free-trade plank adopted," said one of the Eastern Democrats to " Tom " Johnson after the convention. But the Democratic protectionists were forced into surly acquiescence so long as Cleveland was the candidate and William L. Wilson the chairman of the convention. The partial insincerity of the tariff debate aided the Populists, who were directing a discussion upon the general basis of reform.

Cleveland was elected with a majority of electoral votes and a plurality of popular votes, but the vote for Weaver and Field measured the extent of the revolt against both parties. The Populists carried Colorado, Idaho, Nevada, and Kansas, gained twenty-two electoral votes, and polled over a million popular votes. Their protest, based on local hard times and discontent, probably defeated Harrison, while their organization was ready to receive a large following should the hard times spread.

Harrison was not unwilling to surrender the Government to Cleveland in March, 1893, for he had been struggling for weeks to conceal the financial weakness of the United States and to avoid a panic. The great surplus that had been a motive for legislation for more than ten years had nearly become a deficit. Continuous prosperity had tempted Congress to make lavish appropriations. The McKinley Bill had reduced the revenue through changes in the sugar schedule. The Pension Bill had used other millions. Internal improvements had been distributed to every section. The surplus, which had been at $105,000,000 for 1890, fell to $37,000,000 in 1891, and in the next two years to $9,900,000 and to $2,300,000. In the spring of 1893 the Treasury was so reduced that any unexpected shock might cause a suspension. Cleveland's first duty was with causes and cures.

The surplus had been affected both by increase in expenditures and by decrease in revenues. The latter had been due in part to the hard times, which had forced a curtailment of imports, with a resulting shrinkage in tariff receipts. At the same time an increasing nervousness, based upon the deterioration in quality of the assets of the United States, showed itself. The fear of free silver was hastening the day of panic.

Silver and gold had always been traditional American coins, but since 1834 little of the former had been coined or circulated, while between 1862 and 1879 neither variety of specie was ordinarily used as money. In 1873 a codification of coinage laws had omitted from the standard list the silver dollar, which had been unimportant for nearly forty years; and when, shortly thereafter, the decline in the price of silver made its coinage at the ratio of sixteen to one profitable, it was impossible. The demand for a restoration of silver coinage began with the silver miners who desired a stimulated market for their output. Some believed coinage would raise the price of bullion; others thought the Government would keep up the value of the silver coins, as it did the greenbacks, by redemption in gold. In 1878 a Free Coinage Act, pushed by R. P. Bland, was converted into the limited Bland-Allison Act. Under this the Treasury bought the minimum amount of silver bullion (two million dollars' worth) every month for twelve years, and protested continually that the silver coined from it was increasing the burden of redemption on the gold reserve. As the price of silver fell farther, the demand of the miners increased, and toward 1890 it was reinforced by the demands of inflationists who desired it for another reason.

In 1890 the free-silver movement was not political in the sense that parties had declared for or against it. In each great party it had supporters, and few politicians were actively opposing it. A movement in its favor, with the support of the Senate, was re-shaped under the influence of Sherman, and became a law in July, 1890. Under this the Treasury was forced to buy 4,500,000 ounces of silver each month, and to pay for it in a new issue of treasury notes. For the next three years the United States kept at par with gold the Civil War greenbacks, the Bland-Allison silver dollars, and the treasury notes of 1890. Only by its constant willingness to pay out any form of money at the option of the customer could it prevent the Gresham Law from operating and the currency from declining to the bullion value of silver.

Every creditor feared the establishment of the silver basis because of the loss which it would entail upon him. His dollars would shrink from their gold value to their silver value. A depreciated currency was bad enough when unavoidable, but the deliberate adoption of it would be frank repudiation. Continually, after 1890, popular apprehension of this grew more acute, discouraging the undertaking of new enterprises and leading to the insertion of " gold clauses " in contracts. Gold was hoarded whenever possible. The receipts at the New York Custom-House, which had been mostly gold before 1890, contained less than four per cent of gold in the winter of 1892–93. As the Treasury found its expenditures nearing its receipts, and the proportion of gold in its assets lessening, business men were badly worried over the future of the currency, and an actual limit of available capital appeared.

For fourteen years there had been prosperity in the United States. Financial and economic disturbances had been relatively slight, and every year had seen a greater business expansion than the last. Investment for permanent improvement had passed the amount of annual savings, and before 1893 the United States as a community had approached the point at which its economic surplus would be exhausted and an enforced liquidation would be due. As banks curtailed in 1893 to save themselves, stringency became general, and depression turned to panic. In April the gold reserve in the Treasury, on which the whole volume of silver and paper depended, passed below $100,000,000, which business had come to regard as the limit of safety. In the summer Great Britain closed her Indian mints to silver and that bullion dropped farther in value. Before July there was panic and failure everywhere in the United States.

Panic had been imminent before Harrison left office and remained for Cleveland to confront. Already Cleveland had taken a solid stand against free silver and the silver basis. He saw in the Sherman Silver Purchase Act the most striking cause of danger, and summoned Congress to meet in August, 1893, to repeal it, while he maintained the gold reserve for the next two years by borrowing on bonds. For the first time since the Civil War his party controlled every branch of the Government, yet it now met an issue on which it had not been elected and over which it broke to pieces.

An angry minority opposed the Message in which

Cleveland described the financial dangers and demanded the repeal of the Sherman Law. It was a sectional minority that included Western Representatives from both parties and many Democrats from the South. Men who had fought the Populists since 1890 now fraternized with them and raised their strength beyond their hopes. The President refused compromise, even to save his party from destruction, and found a majority for repeal among Easterners of both parties. The Sherman Law was repealed in November, and the liquidation following the crisis was effected during the next three years.

It was a bad beginning for tariff revision, to split the party at its first session and to drive into opposition those Democrats who were most genuinely interested in tariff reform. Cleveland had lost his influence with Western Democrats before the repeal of the McKinley Act was undertaken, and they, like the Populists, had decided that he was the tool of the corporations and the "gold-bugs" of the East. The anti-corporation feelings of the West were increased by the accident which threw the corporations and the farmers into different sides upon the silver question.

A tariff for revenue had been the winning issue in 1890 and 1892, and the Democratic organization was pledged to pass it. When Speaker Crisp made William L. Wilson chairman of the Committee on Ways and Means his act showed an intention to fulfill the pledge, for which purpose Wilson brought in his bill early in the regular session of 1893-94. Like previous bills, this tariff was passed in the House,

rewritten in the Senate, and again changed in conference committee. "The truth is," confessed Senator
Cullom long after, " we were all — Democrats as well
as Republicans — trying to get in amendments in
the interest of protecting the industries of our respective States." The surplus was no longer an argument in favor of reduction. The free-trade arguments
were flatly contradicted by a group of Democratic
Senators under whose leadership the bill lost most
of its reducing tendency. Out of doors the Republicans attacked the measure and noisily charged it
with having produced the panic of 1893. Fourteen
years later a Republican President still described it
as the measure " under the influence of which wheat
went down below fifty cents." When it finally came
to the President it was so little different from the
McKinley Bill that he denounced it violently. He
had tried in vain to hold his party to an honest revision, and now, in July, 1894, refused to sign the
bill. It became a law without his signature. It contained no novelty but an income tax, which was a
concession to the Populists and which the Supreme
Court soon declared to be unconstitutional.

In the fight over the Wilson Bill, Cleveland af-
fronted Eastern members of his party as he had the
Western members, in 1893, over the Sherman repeal. In the summer of 1894 he offended the whole
body of organized labor by intervening in a Western strike.

The panic of 1893 had unsettled labor and created a floating element among the unemployed.
These drifted toward Chicago, attracted by the Co-

lumbian Exposition held there during that summer,
and worried the police for many months. About
Easter, 1894, an "Army of the Unemployed"
marched on Washington under the command of
Jacob S. Coxey. A few weeks later a strike occurred
among the employees of the Pullman Palace Car
Company. The American Railroad Union, under the
leadership of Eugene V. Debs, established a sympathetic boycott against the Pullman cars. The
Knights of Labor indorsed the strike, and railway
travel was impeded over all the West. Around Chicago there was disorder and rioting which the Governor of Illinois, John P. Altgeld, did not suppress.
He held the militia in readiness, but had not intervened when Cleveland sent federal troops to Chicago
to remove obstructions to the carriage of the mails.

This federal intervention offended those who still
adhered to the doctrine of state rights, and angered
the strikers and organized labor as a whole. They
believed the President was a tool of the railroads,
and believed the same of the courts when a federal
judge issued an injunction to Debs forbidding him
to interfere in the strike. In the end the strikers
lost, leaving Cleveland's conduct in maintaining the
peace in sharp contrast with that of the Populist
Governor of Colorado, who intervened in a great
miners' strike at Cripple Creek to arrest, not the
strikers who had seized control of the mines, but the
sheriff and his posse who wished to dislodge them.
"It is better, infinitely better," Governor Waite had
declared, "that the blood should flow to the horses'
bridles than that our national liberties should be

destroyed." Congress made Labor Day a legal holiday in 1894, but failed to placate the unions.

By the summer of 1894 Cleveland's party was split beyond repair, and his friends were mostly among the Republicans. Consistent in his belief in sound money, tariff revision, and law and order, he had been forced by events to alienate the West, the East, and organized labor. His course had aided the Populist party by widening the belief that the Democrats had no interest in their welfare. The panic had aided it yet more, by multiplying the discontented who might be converted to the new faith. Every month the Populist party increased in strength, the East watching it with mingled fear and contempt and ignorance. The comic papers pictured as the typical Populist the raw-boned, booted, unkempt farmer, in shirt-sleeves and with flowing beard. It could not see the foundation of real reforms on which the movement stood. A satirist pictured the Populist as "The Kansas Bandit," declaiming

> "The People's Party, to
> Which me native instinct draws me because it
> Loves the rule of mediocrity, is now on top. I
> Love the rule of Ignorance."

BIBLIOGRAPHICAL NOTE

F. J. Turner discussed "The Problems of the West," in the *Atlantic Monthly* for September, 1896, and C. Becker has interpreted a similar point of view under the title "Kansas" in the *Turner Essays* (1910). Wildman and McVey are valuable guides. The external facts of the Populist movement are accessible in the *Annual Cyclopædia*; Stanwood, *History of the Presidency*; Annual Reports of the Secretary of the Treasury;

and Richardson, *Messages and Papers of the Presidents*. Standard writings on the silver problem are J. L. Laughlin, *History of Bimetallism in the United States* (1886, etc.), and F. W. Taussig, *Silver Situation in the United States* (1893). Useful details are added in the biographies of Blaine, Bland, Sherman, and Vance. W. E. Connelley, *Ingalls of Kansas* (1909), has included much material upon Populism, including E. Ware's satirical verses, *Alonzo, or the Kansas Bandit*. Light is thrown upon Governor J. P. Altgeld and his influence in the Democratic party by B. Whitlock, "Forty Years of It" (1914), and C. Lloyd, *Henry Demarest Lloyd*. The *Memoirs of a Varied Career*, William F. Draper (1908), gives a glimpse of the rigid protectionist attitude. A stimulating novel, based upon municipal politics in the nineties, is P. L. Ford's *The Honorable Peter Stirling* (1894).

discontent was serious, but had not come to be the primary interest of the West. Men were not yet willing to leave their parties for the sake of silver. The panic drove them to the final step.

Through the campaign of 1892 the major parties had dodged the issue of free silver by adopting evasive planks, while the general ignorance respecting the laws of money prevented the evasion from being seen. Until 1890 neither organization had been unfavorably disposed towards free silver and Congressmen catered to the movement when they dared. As its accomplishment became more probable, the selfish interests that would be adversely affected, and the economists who saw its theoretical danger, and the moralists who disliked repudiation, made common cause in a wide campaign of education.

With the exception of extreme inflationists, all had declared that they wanted " honest " or " sound " money, and both parties insisted, in 1892, that all dollars, of whatever sort, must remain equal in value and interchangeable. They insisted, too, that silver must be used as well as gold, and neither platform saw that the demands were either inconsistent or improbable of realization. The pledge of equality pleased the creditor East, while that of equal use of both metals satisfied the debtor West and South.

Bimetallism was a cry of many who disliked free silver, yet feared that a demand for the gold standard would wreck the party. As long as the traditional ratio of sixteen to one remained the commercial ratio, the free use of both metals was theoretically possible, but the experience of the United States showed that a slight variation in the commercial ratio inevitably drove the more valuable dollar into retirement and left the cheaper in use. The truth of Gresham's Law was believed by most economists, who doubted whether the commercial ratio was ever sufficiently permanent to make bimetallism possible. With the silver declining rapidly it was out of the question. If the silver in circulation ever got beyond the power of the government to control it through redemption in gold nothing could avoid the silver standard. No law of the United States could prevent it. There was only a bare possibility that an international agreement always to regard sixteen ounces of silver as worth one ounce of gold might establish the ratio, but to this straw the bimetallist turned, trying to ward off the demand for free silver with his plea for international bimetallism.

The panic of 1893, the decline of silver, and the repeal of the Sherman Law stimulated the activities of those who believed in free silver and produced formal steps to bring it into politics. A silver convention, held in Chicago in August, 1893, denounced the "Crime of 1873," and Governor Waite recommended to the Colorado Legislature that it open a mint of its own for the coinage of legal-tender silver dollars. At state conventions, in 1893 and 1894, both parties adopted silver planks. The Nebraska Democrats rejected such a plank in 1893, but in 1894, after a caucus of free-silver Democrats in Omaha, they adopted a demand for the immediate restoration of free-silver coinage "without waiting for the aid or consent of any nation on earth."

At the congressional election of 1894 the Republicans regained control of both Senate and House and many of the silver candidates were left at home. Some thirty, who had sat in the Fifty-third Congress, joined in March, 1895, in a call for the adoption of free silver as a party measure. To the iniquity alleged to exist in the gold standard was added the aggravating fact that its defenders had wealth and were often directors of corporations. The measure had become a class contest. Its textbook was found in *Coin's Financial School*, a little book with simple dialogue and graphic illustration, that popularized the Western view of free silver and reached hundreds of thousands with its apparent frankness. Free silver had by 1895 outgrown the Populists, and had overshadowed other measures of reform before either party had taken a frank attitude respecting it. " I have been more than usually despondent," wrote the originator of the Wilson Bill, who had lost his seat in 1894, " as I see how the folly of our Southern people, in taking up a false and destructive issue, and assaulting the very foundations of public and private credit, are throwing away the solid fruits of the great victory, solidifying the North as it never was solid in the burning days of reconstruction, and condemning the South to a position of inferiority and lessening influence in the Union she has never before reached."

When the Fifty-fourth Congress met in 1895, Reed was again enthroned as Speaker, but the spread of silver sentiment had undermined party loyalty. Cleveland's annual Message contained the usual range of items upon government and foreign relations, and devoted several pages to a résumé of the financial operations of the Treasury and the currency problem. It closed with an appeal to the enthusiastic multitude that approved free coinage to reëxamine their views " in the light of patriotic reason and familiar experience." It gave no hint that any other topic was likely to pass free silver in the public view. Fifteen days later, on December 17, 1895, the President sent a special Message to Congress, in reference to an old dispute between Great Britain and Venezuela, that startled the world, upset the stock markets, and brought to life once more the Monroe Doctrine.

For many years the unsettled boundary between Venezuela and British Guiana had been a source of irritation. The pretensions of both claimants were great and vague, while the continuous encroachment of British miners alarmed the weaker country. For nearly twenty years Venezuela had vainly appealed to the United States, asking that the dispute be arbitrated. The United States had taken a mild interest in the wrangle, but no one before Cleveland had felt vitally concerned. He undertook, in the summer of 1895, to persuade Great Britain to accept an arbitration, and pressed Lord Salisbury in a series of notes drafted by Richard Olney, Secretary of State.

The contention of Olney was that the dispute was suitable for arbitration because of the difference in physical strength between the two countries, and that the United States had an interest in an equitable territorial adjustment. He stated the doctrine that John Quincy Adams had advanced in the Administration of Monroe, that interference with the destiny of the South American Republics affects the United States, and asserted that this was now a part of the public law of the United States. He listed the precedents in which it had been advanced since 1823, finding none in which it had been flatly checked. His long arguments upon the interests and proper supremacy of the United States in all American questions failed to convince the British Foreign Office, which denied both Olney's correctness in applying the Monroe Doctrine and the binding force of the doctrine itself. Arbitration was declined, and Cleveland, in submitting the correspondence to Congress, urged that an American court be created to ascertain the true boundary and that the United States afterward maintain it. "In making these recommendations," he admitted, "I am fully alive to the responsibility incurred and keenly realize all the consequences that may follow."

The threat of war conveyed in the Message drove silver from the public mind. Business was aghast, and judicious publicists either questioned the value of the Monroe Doctrine or denied the propriety of its application. The general public supported the President without question, but many of his closest advisers turned against him. His political enemies charged him with raising a foreign issue to reunite his party, or with creating a scare to help his speculations in stocks. Great Britain blustered in her press, but opened her archives to the American Venezuelan

Commission. In 1897 she allowed an arbitration to take place, and the affair passed over.

Whatever Cleveland's motive in the Venezuela Message, it did not establish more than a transient calm in either party. His own was doubly split by silver and the tariff, while Republican plans for 1896 had become badly deranged. That party had organized to play upon protection, but found interest in its chosen subject silenced for the time.

In spite of its defeats in 1890 and 1892, the Republican organization had kept up its fight for protection. Quay had in 1888 completed the partnership between the manufacturers who had a cash interest in the tariff and the Republican voters. In manufacturing communities the doctrine had been accepted that prosperity and protection went together. Ruin was prophesied if the Democrats should win. The panic of 1893 seemed to prove this, and when the Democrats passed the Wilson Bill the Republicans asserted that the fear of this had caused the panic. In private, the leaders agreed with the president of the Home Market Club, who wrote in his memoirs, "The bill . . . was much less destructive than there was reason to fear." " Our business was not unprofitable during these lean years, but much less profitable than it had been and ought to have been." Prosperity was clearly lacking and to be desired, and among the candidates for the nomination in 1896 was the author of the McKinley Bill, in whom an Ohio cartoonist had discovered the " Advance Agent of Prosperity."

Associated with the name of William McKinley,

of Canton, Ohio, was that of Marcus Alonzo Hanna, a citizen of Cleveland who had acted on the borderland between business and politics since 1880. Hanna had been among the earliest to see the financial interest of the manufacturers in the tariff and to capitalize it for political purposes. For several years he had collected money in Ohio for campaign funds, assessing the manufacturers according to their interests and impressing upon them the duty of paying on demand. It had been a business transaction. Hanna had no extraordinary stake in the result, but combined a genuine interest in politics with business standards of the prevailing type. About 1890 he became a friend of the Ohio protectionist and worked steadily thereafter for his election to the Presidency.

McKinley was a tactful and successful Congressman. He believed in the tariff, spoke convincingly in its favor, had few enemies and many warm friends, and was widely advertised by the Tariff Bill of 1890. In public places after 1893 he was repeatedly hailed as the next candidate, but as the silver issue rose it appeared that there might be great difficulty in adapting his record to the new problem. He had favored bimetallism and free coinage in so many debates that the East, where lay the strongholds of the party, distrusted his soundness on the currency question. Yet if he abandoned free silver it was doubtful if he could hold the West. For months his friends, steered by Hanna, who spent his own money freely, endeavored to keep the tariff in the foreground, while the candidate preserved a discreet and exasperating silence upon the dominant issue of free silver.

The most important rivals of McKinley for the nomination were Harrison and Reed, but neither of these possessed a manager as shrewd and resourceful as Hanna. McKinley was nominated on the first ballot at St. Louis, with Garrett P. Hobart, of New Jersey, a corporation lawyer who believed in the gold standard, as his associate.

The nature of the Republican platform had been in debate throughout the spring of 1896. The organization was reluctant to take up the silver issue and the predetermined candidate was uncertain upon it. In the Platform Committee there was a contest involving the opportunists, who wanted to continue the policy of evasion; the Westerners, who felt that silver meant more to them than the party; and the representatives of the populous commercial East, who were devoted to the gold standard. Bimetallists had progressed in their education until most of them saw that bimetallism must be international if it could be at all. Various committeemen later assumed the credit for the plank that was finally adopted. After castigating the Democrats for producing the panic and renewing the pledge for protection, the party denounced the debasement of currency or credit. It opposed the free coinage of silver, asserted that all money must be kept at a "parity with gold," and pledged itself to work for an international agreement for bimetallism.

The fight for free silver was carried by the silver state delegations to the floor of the convention, where it was defeated by a vote of 818½ to 105½. At this point, led by Senators from Colorado and Utah, thirty-four members withdrew from the convention in protest. Even the Prohibition party had already been broken by the new issue. The humorous weekly, *Life*, spoke seriously when it declared that "The two great parties in the country at this writing are the Gold party and the Silver party. The old parties are in temporary eclipse." Few were satisfied with the Republican result, for while the platform pointed one way and the candidate's career pointed the other on free silver, the real interest of the party, protection, aroused no enthusiasm.

No Democrat was the predetermined candidate of his party when it met at Chicago in July, 1896. Cleveland, least of all, was not given even the scanty notice of a commendatory plank. He stood alone as no other President had done, at issue with the Republicans on their major policy, yet without followers in his own organization. Slow, patient, courageous, stubborn, he had twice held his party to its promise, and he had refused to be carried away by the transitory demand of the West for dangerous finance. He had guided the National Administration through eight years of expansion and reorganization, and had been a devoted servant of civil service reform. In May, 1896, he had aggravated his offenses in the eyes of the politicians by issuing new rules that extended the classified service to include some 31,000 new employees, making a total of 86,000 out of 178,000 federal employees. He passed out of party politics at least two years before his term expired, and in 1897 he took up his final abode in Princeton. From Princeton he wrote and spoke for eleven years, and before he died in 1908 the animosities of 1896 were forgotten, and he looked large in the American mind as a statesman whose independence and sincerity were beyond reproach.

Forces beyond the control of politicians carried the Democrats toward an alliance with Populism and free silver. As two minority parties they had felt in 1892 a tendency to fuse against the Republicans. By conviction they were both obliged to fight the party of Hanna and McKinley, in which the forces of business, finance, and manufacture were assembled in the joint cause of protection and the gold standard. It was convenient to make this fight in close alliance, the more so because the Populist doctrine of free silver had permeated the Democratic organization in the West and South. In the conventions of 1896 more than thirty States, as Nebraska had done in 1894, asked for immediate free coinage, and a majority of the Democratic delegates were pledged to this before they came to Chicago. They gained control of the convention on the first vote, determined contests in their own favor, and offered a plank demanding " the free and unlimited coinage of both silver and gold at the present legal ratio of sixteen to one without waiting for the aid or consent of any other nation."

The debate on the silver plank was long and bitter, although its passage was certain. It was closed by the leader of the Nebraska delegation, William Jennings Bryan, who had been a former Congress-

man, and who later said, " An opportunity to close
such a debate had never come to me before, and I
doubt if as good an opportunity had ever come to
any other person during this generation." He took
advantage of the moment, in a tired convention that
had been wrangling in bitterness for several days, that
had deserted the old politicians, and that had no
candidate. He was only thirty-six years old, his face
was unfamiliar, and his name had rarely been heard
outside his State, but he had been preaching free
silver with religious intensity and oratorical skill.
His speech had grown through repeated speaking,
and reached its climax as he pleaded for free silver :
" If they dare to come out in the open field and defend the gold standard as a good thing, we will fight
them to the uttermost. Having behind us the producing masses of this nation and the world, supported
by the commercial interests, the laboring interests,
and the toilers everywhere, we will answer their
demand for the gold standard by saying to them :
You shall not press down upon the brow of labor
this crown of thorns ; you shall not crucify mankind
upon a cross of gold." Swept off its feet by the enthusiasm for silver, and having no other candidate
in view, the convention nominated Bryan on the fifth
ballot, selecting Arthur Sewall, of Maine, as his com-
panion.

The Populists met in St. Louis on July 22. " If
we fuse, we are sunk," complained one of the most
devoted leaders; " if we don't fuse, all the silver
men will leave us for the more powerful Democrats."
Fusion controlled the convention, voting down the

" Middle-of-the-Road " group that adhered to independence. Bryan was nominated, although Sewall
was rejected for Thomas E. Watson, of Georgia.
The organization of the People's Party continued
after 1896, but its vitality was gone forever.

The campaign of 1896 was an orgy of education,
emotion, and panic. McKinley was driven by the
opposition to defend the gold standard with increasing intensity. Protection ceased to arouse interest
and other issues were forgotten. The Bryan party
attracted to itself the silver wings of the Republicans
and Prohibitionists, and absorbed the Populists. The
gold Democrats, after several weeks of indecision
as to tactics, became bolters, held a convention at
Indianapolis in September, and nominated John M.
Palmer and Simon Buckner. To this ticket, Cleveland and his Cabinet gave their support. Up and
down the land Bryan traveled, preaching his new gos-
pel, which millions regarded as " the first great protest of the American people against monopoly — the
first great struggle of the masses in our country
against the privileged classes." " Probably no man
in civil life," said the *Nation* at the end of the fight,
" has succeeded in inspiring so much terror without
taking life."

As chairman of the National Committee, Marcus
A. Hanna directed the Republican campaign. He
encouraged the belief that Bryan was waging a
" campaign against the Ten Commandments." He
drew his sinews of war from the manufacturers, who
were used to such demands, and from a wide range
of panic-stricken contributors who feared repudia-

tion. Insurance companies and national banks were assessed and paid with alacrity. The funds went into the broadest campaign of education that the United States had seen.

In contrast to the activity of Bryan, McKinley stayed at home through the summer, and delegations from afar were brought up to his veranda at Canton, Ohio. To these he spoke briefly and with dignity, gaining an assurance that grew with the campaign. His arguments were taken over the country by a horde of speakers whom Hanna organized, who reached and educated every voter whose mind was open on the silver question. In the closing days of the campaign panic struck the conservative classes and produced for Hanna campaign funds such as had never been seen, and cries of corruption met the charges of repudiation.

An English visitor in New York wrote on the Sunday before election: "Of course nothing can be done till Wednesday. All America is aflame with excitement — and New York itself is at fever heat. I have never seen such a sight as yesterday. The whole city was a mass of flags and innumerable Republican and Democratic insignia — with the streets thronged with over two million people. The whole business quarter made a gigantic parade that took seven hours in its passage — and the business men alone amounted to over 100,000. Every one — as, indeed, not only America, but Great Britain and all Europe — is now looking eagerly for the final word on Tuesday night. The larger issues are now clearer: not merely that the Bryanite fifty-cent dollar (instead of the standard hundred-cent) would have far-reaching disastrous effects, but that the whole struggle is one of the anarchic and destructive against the organic and constructive forces."

The vote was taken in forty-five States, Utah having been admitted early in 1896, and no election had evoked a larger proportion of the possible vote. Bryan received 6,500,000 votes, nearly a million more than any elected President had ever received, but he ran 600,000 votes behind McKinley. The Republican list included every State north of Virginia and Tennessee, and east of the Missouri River, except Missouri and South Dakota. The solid South was confronted by a solid North and East, while the West was divided. McKinley received 271 electoral votes; Bryan, 176.

Education played a large part in the result, and economic opinion believes that the better cause prevailed. But cool analysis had less effect than emotion and self-interest at the time. The lowest point of depression had been reached during 1894, while the harvests of 1895 and 1896 were larger and more profitable than had been known for several years. Free silver was a hard-times movement that weakened in the face of better crops. "Give us good times," said Reed to Richard Watson Gilder, "and all will come out right." Inflation was not to be desired by the citizen who had in hand the funds to pay his debts. When he became solvent he could understand the theories of sound finance. It is probable that nature as well as gold was a potent aid to Hanna in procuring the result.

William McKinley was advertised as the "Advance Agent of Prosperity," and before he was inaugurated in March, 1897, prosperity was in sight. His election had destroyed all fear that the currency would be upset by legislative act, while the liquidation after the panic of 1893 had nearly run its course. Business was reviving, crops were improving, and the luckless farmers of the Western plains had abandoned their farms or learned how to use them. After 1896 the financial danger was not silver but gold inflation. In that year great mines were opened in Alaska, drawing heavy immigration to the valley of the Yukon and, a little later, to the beach at Nome. Other discoveries increased the gold output and flooded the world with the more precious metal. By 1900 prices were rising instead of falling, and public interest was turned upon the high cost of living rather than the low prices of the previous period. The average annual output of gold for the fifteen years ending in 1896 was $132,000,000. For the fifteen years beginning in 1896, it was $337,000,000. The election of McKinley was in name a victory for the Republican party, but was in reality one for sound money. The organization upon which he stood was an amalgamation of creditors and manufacturers, reënforced by gold-standard men of all parties. Without the aid of the last element he could hardly have been elected, on this or any other issue. When he took office the Republican party had control in both houses of Congress, had been elected on a money issue, but had a permanent organization based upon the tariff propaganda. Be-

besides stimulating diplomatic correspondence (*q.v.*, in Foreign Relations Reports), led to the writing of W. F. Reddaway, *The Monroe Doctrine* (1898), which is still one of the most judicious discussions of the topic. J. B. Henderson, *American Diplomatic Questions* (1901), is useful also.

CHAPTER XV

THE mission of Populism did not end when free silver had been driven like a wedge into all the parties. Its more fundamental reforms outlasted both the hard times and the recovery from them. Although obscured by the shadow of the larger controversy, the reforms had been stated with conviction. The Populist party was not permitted to bring the reformation that it promised, but it stimulated within the parties in power a " counter-reformation," that was already under way. This counter-reformation was largely within the Republican ranks because that party dominated in every branch of the National Government for fourteen years after 1897, but it was essentially non-partisan. It derived its advocates from the generation that had been educated since the Civil War, and many of its leaders bore the imprint of democratic higher education. It derived its materials from historical, economic, and sociological study of the forces of American society.

Practical politics in America was at its lowest level in the thirty years after the Civil War. The United States was politically fatigued after the years of contest and turned eagerly to the business speculations that opened in every direction. Offices were left to those who chose to run them, while public scrutiny of public acts was materially reduced. The men in charge, unwatched in their business, used it often for personal advantage, and were aided in this by the character of both the electoral machinery and the electorate. A multitude of offices had to be kept filled in every State and city by voters who could know little of the candidates and who accepted the recommendation implied in the party name. Control of the nominations meant control of the elections, and was within reach of those who were persistent in attending caucuses and conventions and were not too scrupulous in manipulating them. The laws against bribery at the polls did not touch corruption at the primaries. The cities, rapidly growing through manufactures and immigration, were full of voters who could be trained to support the "bosses" who befriended them.

The American "boss" made his appearance in the cities about 1870. His power was based upon his personal influence with voters of the lower and more numerous class. Gaining control of party machinery he dictated nominations and policies, and used the government, as the exposures of the Tweed Ring showed, to enrich his friends and to perpetuate his power. Caring little for party principle, he made a close alliance with the new business that continually needed new laws, — building laws, transportation laws, terminal rights, or franchises. From these allies came the funds for managing elections, and, too often, for direct bribery, although this last was necessary only rarely.

Exposures of the evil of boss government were frequent after 1870, and in most cities occasional revolts of outraged citizens overturned the machines, but in the long run the citizen was no match for the professional politician. In the unequal contest city government became steadily worse in America at a time when European city government was rapidly improving. States, too, were afflicted with machine politics, and before 1890 it appeared that the dominant national party derived its most valuable support from organized business that profited by the partnership.

A minority of Americans fought continually for better and cleaner government as the evils of boss rule became more visible. One of them, Bishop Potter, of New York, gained wide hearing through a sermon preached at the centennial of the Constitution, in 1887, in which he turned from the usual patriotic congratulation to discuss actual government. The keenest interest in the subject was aroused by the *American Commonwealth* of James Bryce.

Not since Alexis de Tocqueville published his *Democracy in America*, in 1835, had any foreign observer made an equally intimate study of American life, until James Bryce, a young English historian, began a series of visits to the United States in the early seventies. For nearly twenty years Bryce repeated his visits, living at home a full life in his Oxford professorate, in the House of Commons, and in the Ministry. In America he knew every one worth knowing, and he saw the remoter regions of the West as well as the older society of the East. In

1888 he brought out the result of his studies in two volumes that were filled with admiration for the United States and with disheartening observation upon its practices. One of its chapters cut so close that its victim brought suit for libel, but American opinion accepted the book as a friendly picture and regarded attacks upon it as further evidence of its inherent truth. Probably no book in a generation so profoundly influenced American thought and so specifically directed the course of American reform. It became a textbook at once, teaching the truth that corruption and misgovernment were non-partisan, and until the Populists took them up the movements for reform were non-partisan as well.

The power of the boss lay largely in the structure of American governmental machinery, and though some preached the need for a reform in spirit, others saw that only mechanical improvements could accomplish results. A corruptible electorate, such as had long confused British and American politics, was one defect most easily improved. The prevailing system for conducting elections made it easy for the purchaser of votes to see that he got value for his money. The State provided the polling-place, but the candidate or the party provided the printed ballot. Party agents distributed these at the polls, and the voters who received them could be watched until the votes were cast. Intimidation of employees or direct bribery were easy and common, while secret deals were not unknown. The loyal party voter deposited the ballots provided for him; the boss could have these arranged to suit his needs. It was commonly supposed that in 1888, through an agreement between the Democratic and Republican bosses of New York, Hill and Platt, many Republicans were made to vote for Hill as Governor, while Democrats voted for Harrison as President.

A secret ballot was so reasonable a reform that once it had been suggested it spread rapidly over the United States. In 1888 Massachusetts adopted a system based upon the Australian Ballot Law, while New York advertised its value in the same year when Governor Hill vetoed a bill to establish it. Before the next presidential election came in 1892, open bribery or intimidation of voters was rapidly becoming a thing of the past, for thirty-three States had adopted the Australian ballot, provided by public authority and voted in secrecy. "Quay and Platt and Clarkson may find in this fact a fresh explanation of President Harrison's willingness to divest himself of their services," wrote Godkin in a caustic paragraph in 1892.

The Australian ballot enabled the honest citizen to vote in secrecy and safety, but it failed to touch the fact that the nominations were still outside the law. "To find the honest men," Bryce wrote, "and having found them, to put them in office and keep them there, is the great problem of American politics." So long as a boss could direct the nomination he could tolerate an honest election. The movement to legalize the party primaries was just beginning when the ballot reform was accomplished. The most extreme of the primary reformers saw the need for a preliminary election conducted within each party, but under all the safeguards of law, to the end that the voters might themselves determine their candidates. Direct primaries were discussed by the younger men, who were often ambitious, but helpless because of the rigor with which the bosses selected their own candidates. In 1897 a young ex-Congressman, Robert M. LaFollette, worked out a complete system of local and national primaries, and found wide and sympathetic hearing for it. The movement had to face the bitter opposition of the machine politicians because it struck directly at their power, but it progressed slowly. In 1901 it won in Minnesota; a little later it won in Wisconsin; and in the next ten years it became a central feature in reform platforms.

The reforms of the primary and the ballot were designed to improve the quality of public officers, and were supplemented by a demand for direct legislation which would check up the result. In Switzerland a scheme had been devised by which the people, by petition, could initiate new laws or obtain a vote upon existing laws. The idea of submitting special measures to popular vote, or referendum, was old in the United States, for in this way state constitutions and constitutional amendments were habitually adopted, and matters of city charters, loans and franchises often determined. The initiative, however, was new, and appealed to the reformer who resented the refusal of the legislature to pass desired laws as well as the unwillingness to pass worthy ones. The Populists, in 1892, recommended that the system of direct legislation be investigated, and they favored its adoption in 1896. A journal for the promotion of the reform appeared in 1894. In 1898 the first State, South Dakota, adopted the principle of initiative and referendum in a constitutional amendment. To those who attacked the device as only mechanical it was answered: "Direct legislation is not a panacea for all national ills. In fact it is not a panacea at all. It is merely a spoon with which the panacea can be administered. Specific legislation is the panacea for political ills."

The West was more ready than the East to break from existing practice and take up the new reforms. It had always been the liberal section of the United States. Between 1800 and 1830 it had led in the enlargement of the franchise and in the removal of qualifications of wealth and religion. It now approached the one remaining qualification of sex. With the admission of Wyoming in 1890, full woman suffrage appeared among the States. Colorado adopted an amendment establishing it in 1893. Utah, in the words of the women, "completing the trinity of true Republics at the summit of the Rockies," became the third suffrage State in January, 1896, while Idaho adopted woman suffrage in the same year. It was fifteen years before a fifth State was added to the list, but the women's movement was advancing in all directions. A General Federation of Women's Clubs was organized in 1890 as a clearing-house for the activities of the women, and through organizations like the Consumers' League, the movement fell into line with the general course of reform. A clearer vision of the defects in governmental machinery and of the needs of society was spreading rapidly. Hull House, opened in 1889 by Jane Addams, had a host of imitators in the cities, and enabled social workers to study the results of industrial progress upon the laboring class.

The new reforms, mechanical and otherwise, established themselves about 1890, and were taken up by the Populist party between 1892 and 1896. Neither great party noticed the reforms before 1896, but in each party the younger workers saw their point. As non-partisan movements they gained adherents before the Populist party died out, and were pressed more and more seriously upon reluctant organizations. As a whole they were an attempt to make government more truly representative of the voters, and to take the control of affairs from the hands of men who might and often did use them for private aggrandizement. They were overshadowed in 1896 by the paramount issue of free silver, and were deferred in their fulfilment for a decade by accidents which drove them from the public mind. The Spanish War, reviving prosperity, and the renewal of tariff legislation, did not check the activities of the reformers, but did divert the attention of the public.

William McKinley was inaugurated on March 4, 1897. He had served in five Congresses and had been three times governor of Ohio. He "knew the legislative body thoroughly, its composition, its methods, its habits of thought," said John Hay. "He had the profoundest respect for its authority and an inflexible belief in the ultimate rectitude of its purposes." He was not likely to embarrass business

through bluntness or inexperience. He had risen
through a kindly disposition, a recognition of the
political value of tact, and an unusual skill as a
moderator of variant opinions. He believed that his
function was to represent the popular will as rapidly
as it expressed itself, differing fundamentally in this
from Cleveland, who thought himself bound to act
in the interest of the people as he saw it. His Cabinet reflected the interests that secured his election.

The trend of issues had made the Republican
party, by 1897, the party of organized business.
For twelve years the alliance had grown steadily
closer. Marcus A. Hanna was its spokesman. The
burlesque of his sincere and kindly face, drawn by a
caricaturist, Davenport, for Eastern papers, created
for the popular eye the type of commercialized magnate, but it did him great injustice. Self-respecting
and direct, he believed it to be the first function of
government to protect property, and that property
should organize for this purpose. Without malevo-
lence, he conducted business for the sake of its
profits, and regarded government as an adjunct to it.
He possessed great capacity for winning popularity,
and after his entry into public life in 1897 gained
reputation as an effective speaker. He destroyed,
before his death, much of the offensive notoriety that
had been thrust upon him during the campaign of
1896, but he remained the best representative of the
generation that believed government to be only a
business asset. He did not enter the Cabinet of
McKinley, but was appointed Senator from Ohio
when John Sherman vacated his seat.

The pledge of the Republicans for international bimetallism created a need for a financial Secretary of State, and John Sherman, though old and infirm, was persuaded to undertake the office. The routine of the department was assigned to an assistant secretary, William R. Day, an old friend of the President. A magnate of the match trust, Russell A. Alger, of Michigan, received the War Department. The president of the First National Bank of Chicago, Lyman J. Gage, received the Treasury. The other secretaries, too, were men of solidity, generally self-made, and likely to inspire confidence in the world of business.

The new Senators who appeared at this time represented the same alliance of trade and politics. Hanna, in Ohio, and Thomas C. Platt, president of the United States Express Company, in New York, were the most striking instances. In Pennsylvania Quay was able to nominate his colleague in spite of the opposition of his old associate, John Wanamaker, and selected Boies Penrose. Only with the aid of the silver Senators could a Republican majority be procured in the Senate. This made currency legislation impossible, but the managers hoped that there would be a majority for a protective tariff when Congress met in special session, two weeks after the inauguration.

Preparations for a revision of the tariff had been made long before Cleveland left office. Reed was certain to be reëlected as Speaker by a large majority. Nelson Dingley, of Maine, was equally certain to be chairman of the Committee on Ways and Means, and began to hold tariff hearings early in 1897. A

rampant spirit for protection was revealed as the
manufacturers stated their wishes to the committee.
It was often told how the low rates of the Wilson
Bill had caused the panic of 1893, and a New York
maker of "Oriental rugs" created amusement by
asking to be protected from the competition, not of
the Orient, but of the German manufacturers. Since
1890 the strength of the Republican organization had
been directed toward this revision, and the leaders
had held back the silver issue lest it should derange
their plans. Now, though returned to power only on
the issue of the currency, they held themselves empowered to act as though the tariff had been dominant in 1896. The call stated the need for tariff
legislation, and Reed held the House to its task by
refusing to appoint the committees without which
other business could not be undertaken.

The Dingley Bill passed the House of Representatives after a perfunctory debate which every one
regarded as only preliminary to the real struggle
in Senate and Conference Committee. In the Senate it became a new measure at the hands of the
Finance Committee, whose secretary, S. N. D. North,
was also secretary of the Wool Manufacturers' Association. Revenue was everywhere subordinated to
protection, until the Chief of the Bureau of Statistics,
Worthington C. Ford, declared that the act would
prolong the deficit which it was designed to cure. On
its final passage, the Democratic Senator, McEnery,
of Louisiana, left his party to vote for protection to
sugar. He was welcomed home in August, in spite
of his "treason," by a reception committee with

four hundred vice-presidents. The silver Senators, headed by Jones, of Nevada, were induced to support the bill. They had procured the Sherman Silver Bill in 1890 by the same tactics, and now, holding the balance of power, secured a group of amendments for themselves, covering hides, wool, and ore. The measure passed the Senate early in July and became a law July 24, 1897. Senator William B. Allison, of Iowa, was largely responsible for its final passage, although the law continued to bear the name of its forgotten originator, Dingley.

The Republican party was in no condition in 1897 to become the vehicle of the non-partisan reforms that the Populists advocated and that many young Republicans had taken up. The interest in tariff legislation drove everything else from the national organization, while returning prosperity destroyed the mental attitude in which reforms had flourished. Political introspection was less easy in 1897 and 1898 than it had been in the years of confusion and enforced economy since 1890. The civil service and ballot reforms had been started on the upward course, but party machines continued in control of each great organization.

The conduct of the Senate discouraged many of the reformers in the spring of 1897. Cleveland had left in its hands a treaty of arbitration with Great Britain, but no action had been taken upon it when he left office. Arbitration had been a common international tool between Great Britain and the United States. Boundaries, fisheries, and claims had repeatedly been submitted to courts or commissions of

varying structure, and even the claims affecting the
honor of Great Britain had been settled by arbitration at Geneva. After the Venezuela excitement
friends of peace gathered in a convention at Lake
Mohonk to discuss the extension of the method of
arbitration. When Great Britain had accepted the
principle in the case of Venezuela, Cleveland entered into a general arbitration treaty, which was
signed at Washington in February, 1897. Public
opinion received it cordially, but the Senate was slow
to take it up. Late in the spring it was ratified with
amendments that destroyed its force and showed the
reluctance of Senators to accept the principle of
arbitration. International peace was thus postponed,
while the rising insurrection in Cuba drove it as well
as general reform from the center of public interest.

BIBLIOGRAPHICAL NOTE

The *American Commonwealth* of James Bryce (1888) is the
starting-point for the study of political conditions of the nineties, and is to be reinforced by W. Wilson, *Congressional
Government* (1885), T. Roosevelt, *Essays on Practical Politics*
(1888), and P. L. Ford, *The Honorable Peter Stirling* (1894).
Among the personal narratives the most useful are T. Roosevelt, *Fifty Years of My Life* (1913); R. M. LaFollette, *A Personal Narrative of Political Experiences* (1913; also published
serially in the *American Magazine*, 1911, as "Autobiography");
Tom L. Johnson's *My Story* (1911; edited by E. J. Hauser);
C. Lloyd, *Henry Demarest Lloyd* (2 vols., 1912); *Autobiography
of Thomas Collier Platt* (1910; edited by L. J. Lang, and
highly unreliable); and Jane Addams, *Twenty Years of Hull
House* (1910). Much light is thrown upon the mechanics of
tariff legislation by I. M. Tarbell, *The Tariff in Our Times*
(1911), and by the lobby investigations conducted by committees of Congress in 1913, and by the campaign fund investiga-

tions conducted by similar committees in 1912. The progress of the Australian ballot reform must be traced through the periodicals, as it has no good history. E. C. Meyer, *Nominating Systems: Direct Primaries versus Conventions in the United States* (1902), is standard in its field, as are E. P. Oberholtzer, *The Referendum in America* (1893), and E. C. Stanton, S. B. Anthony, and M. J. Gage, *History of Woman Suffrage, 1848–1900* (4 vols., 1881–1902). The Annual Reports of the Lake Mohonk Conferences on International Arbitration are a useful aid in tracing the principles of arbitration.

CHAPTER XVI

THE SPANISH WAR

CUBA broke out in one of her numerous insurrections in 1895. The island had been nominally quiet since the close of the Ten Years' War, in 1878, but had always been an object of American interest. More than once it had entered into American diplomacy to bring out reiterations of different phases of the Monroe Doctrine. Its purchase by the United States had been desired to extend the slave area, or to control the Caribbean, or to enlarge the fruit and sugar plantation area. The free trade in sugar, which the McKinley Bill had allowed, ended in 1894, and almost immediately thereafter the native population demanded independence.

The revolt of 1895 was defended and justified by a recital of the faults of Spanish colonial government. Caste and monopoly played a large part in Cuban life. The Spanish-born held the offices, enjoyed the profits, and owned or managed the commercial privileges. The western end of the island, most thickly settled and most under the influence of Spain, gave least support to the uprising, but in the east, where the Cubans and negroes raised and ground cane, or grazed their herds, discontent at the system of favoritism and race discrimination was an important political force. Here the insurgents soon gained a

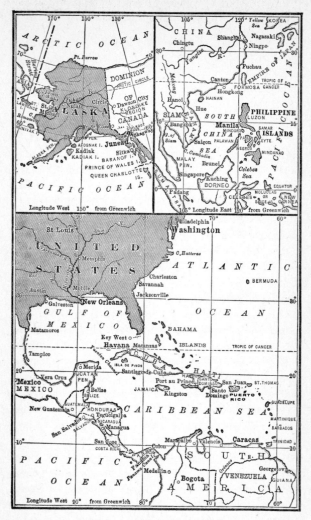

**ALASKA, THE PHILIPPINES, AND THE SEAT OF THE
SPANISH WAR**

foothold in the provinces of Santiago, Puerto Prin-
cipe, and Santa Clara. From the jungle or the mountains they sent bands of guerrillas against the sugar
mills and plantations of the ruling class, and when
pursued their troops hid their weapons and became, os-
tensibly, peaceful farmers. A revolutionary government, sitting safely in New York, directed the revolt,
raised money by playing on the American love of
freedom, and sent cargoes of arms, munitions, and
volunteers to the seat of war. Avoiding pitched battles and living off the country, the patriot forces compelled Spain to put some 200,000 troops in Cuba
and to garrison every place that she retained.

Through 1895 and 1896 the war dragged on with
no prospect of victory for the authorities and with
growing interest on the part of the United States.
Public sympathy was with the Cubans, and news
from the front was so much desired that enterprising
papers sent their correspondents to the scene of action. The reports of these, almost without exception,
magnified the character and promise of the native
leaders and attacked the policy of the Spanish forces
of repression.

The insurgents began, in 1895, a policy of terror,
destroying the cane in the fields of loyalists and
burning their sugar mills. To protect the loyalists
and repress the rebels the Queen Regent sent General Valeriano Weyler to the island in 1896, with
orders to end the war. Weyler replied to devasta-
tion with concentration. Unable to separate the loyal
natives from the disloyal, or to prevent the latter
from aiding the rebels, he gathered the suspected

population into huge concentration camps, fortified his towns and villages with sentinels and barbed-wire fences, and endeavored to depopulate the area outside his lines. American public opinion, unused for a generation to the sight of war, was shocked by the suffering in the camps and was aroused in moral protest. Sympathy with the insurgents grew in 1896 and 1897, as exaggerated tales of hardship and brutality were circulated by the "yellow" newspapers. The evidence was one-sided and incomplete, and often dishonest, but it was effective in steering a rising public opinion toward ultimate intervention.

The nearness of the contest brought the trouble to the United States Government through the enforcement of the neutrality laws. There was no public war, and Spain was thus unable to seize or examine American vessels until they entered actual Cuban waters. It was easy to run the Spanish blockade and take supplies to the rebel forces, which was a permissible trade. It was easy, too, to organize and send out filibustering parties, which were highly illegal, and which the United States tried to stop. Out of seventy-one known attempts, the United States broke up thirty-three, while other Powers, including Spain, caught only eleven. Enough landed to be a material aid to the natives and to embitter Spain in her criticism of the United States. Cleveland issued proclamations against the unfriendly acts of citizens, and enforced the law as well as he could in a population and with juries sympathizing with the law-breakers. Even in Congress he found little sympathy in his attempt to maintain a sincere neutrality.

Congress felt the popular sympathy with the Cubans and responded to it, as well as to the demands of Americans with investments in Cuba. In the spring of 1896 both houses joined in a resolution favoring the recognition of Cuban belligerency. This Cleveland ignored. In December, 1896, the Senate Committee on Foreign Relations reported a resolution for the recognition of Cuban independence, and individual members of Congress often read from the newspapers accounts of horror, and made impassioned speeches for recognition and intervention. But Cleveland kept his control over the situation until he left office, as Grant had done during the Ten Years' War and the excitement over the Virginius affair. He left the determination of the time and manner of ultimate intervention to his successor.

Among the planks of the Republican platform of 1896 was one asserting the duty of the United States to " use its influence and good offices to restore peace and give independence to Cuba," but there is no evidence that President McKinley contemplated a forcible intervention when he organized his Cabinet. John Sherman had, as Senator, spoken freely in sympathy with Cuba. As Secretary of State he recalled Hannis Taylor from Madrid and sent out General Stewart L. Woodford, with instructions looking toward a peaceful mediation. Not until the autumn of 1897 was it possible to press the Cuban matter, for Spain suffered two changes of Ministry and the murder of a Prime Minister. But by the

end of September Spain had been notified that Mc-
Kinley hoped to be able to give positive assurances
of peace to Congress when it met in December.

A Liberal Government, headed by Sagasta, took
office in Spain in October, 1897. It declined mediation by the United States, retorting that if the
United States were to enforce the law of neutrality
the war would soon cease. It recalled Weyler, however, sent out a new and milder governor-general,
modified the *reconcentrado* orders that had so enraged the United States, and issued, on November
25, a proclamation establishing a sort of home
rule, or autonomy, for Cuba. In the winter of 1897
the Spanish Government was endeavoring to give
no excuse for American intervention, and at the
same time, by moderate means, to restore peace
in Cuba. The Spanish population of Cuba opposed
autonomy and made the establishment of autonomous
governments a farce. In January there were riots in
Havana among the loyal subjects. Outside the Spanish lines the rebels laughed at autonomy, for they
were determined to have independence or nothing.
Woodford, in touch with the Spanish Government,
believed that in the long run the Spanish people
would let the Queen Regent go beyond autonomy
to independence, and that with patience Cuba might
be relieved of Spanish control.

There was no positive news for Congress in December, 1897, but by February the conditions in
Cuba had become the most interesting current problem. The New York *Journal* obtained and published
a private letter written by the Spanish Minister,

De Lome, in which McKinley was characterized as a temporizing politician. The Minister had no sooner been recalled than the Maine, a warship that had been detached from the North Atlantic Squadron, and sent to Cuba to safeguard American citizens there, was destroyed by an explosion in the harbor of Havana, on February 15, 1898. There was no evidence connecting the destruction of the Maine with any person, but unscrupulous newspapers made capital out of it, using the catch-phrase, " Remember the Maine," to inflame a public mind already aroused by sympathy and indignation. After February, only a determined courage could have withstood the demand for intervention and a Spanish war.

The negotiations with Spain continued rapidly in the two months after the loss of the Maine. McKinley avoided an arbitral inquiry into the accident, urged by Spain, but pressed increasingly for an end of concentration, for relief for the suffering population, and for full self-government. He did not ask independence for Cuba, and every demand that he made was assented to by Spain. Notwithstanding this, on April 11, 1898, he sent the Cuban correspondence to Congress, urged an intervention, and turned the control of the situation over to a body that had for two years been clamoring for forcible interference. Nine days later Congress resolved, " That the people of the Island of Cuba are, and of right ought to be, free and independent." On April 21 the Spanish War began.

The administrative branches of the Government

had made some preparations for war before the declaration. The navy was small but modern. It dated from the early eighties, when Congress was roused to a realization that the old Civil War navy was obsolete and began to authorize the construction of modern fighting ships. The " White Squadron" took shape in the years after 1893. Only two armored cruisers were in commission when Harrison left office, but the number increased rapidly until McKinley had available for use the second-class battleships Maine and Texas, the armored cruiser Brooklyn, and the first-class battleships Iowa, Indiana, Massachusetts, and Oregon. From the beginning of the McKinley Administration these, as well as the lesser vessels of all grades, were diligently drilled and organized. The new Assistant Secretary of the Navy, Theodore Roosevelt, had foreseen and hoped for war. He spent the contingent funds on target practice, and had the naval machine at its highest efficiency when the Maine was lost. On March 9, 1898, Congress, in a few hours, put $50,000,000 at the disposal of the President for national defense, and the navy spent its share of this for new vessels, transports, and equipment. The vessels in the Orient were mobilized at Hongkong under the command of Commodore George Dewey ; the Oregon, on station in the Pacific, was ordered home by the long route around the Horn ; the ships in the Atlantic were assembled off the Chesapeake. Part of the latter were organized as a flying squadron, for patrol, under Commodore Winfield Scott Schley, while toward the end of March Captain William T. Sampson was promoted over the heads of many ranking officers and given command of the whole North Atlantic Squadron, including the fleet of Schley.

Congress debated a new army bill while the navy was being prepared for war. Not until April 22 did it permit the enlargement of the little regular army of 25,000. Until war had begun the volunteers, of whom some 216,000 were taken into the service, could not be called out or made ready for the field. Some preparations were made within the War Department, but the little staff of clerks, used to the small routine of the peace basis, and having no plan of enlargement or mobilization worked out, made little headway. The navy was ready to strike the day war was declared, but the army had yet to be planned, recruited, clothed, drilled, and transported to the front. The men of the navy knew their duty and were ready for it; in the army thousands of civilians had to blunder through the duties of strange offices. William J. Bryan accepted the colonelcy in a Nebraska regiment. Theodore Roosevelt resigned his office in the Navy Department to raise a regiment of volunteer cavalry. Politicians struggled for commissions for themselves and friends. Civil War veterans fought for reappointment, and enough soldiers of the Confederacy put on the blue uniforms, or sent their sons, to show that the breach had been healed between the North and South. It was an enthusiastic rather than an effective army that was brought together in the two months after the war began.

Cuba, the cause of the war and its objective, was the center of the scheme of strategy. The navy was called upon to protect the Atlantic seaboard from the fleet of Spain, which was reputed to be superior to that of the United States. It had also to maintain a blockade of Cuba and prevent the landing of reinforcements until the army could be prepared to invade the island. Dewey's fleet in the Pacific was ordered to destroy the Spanish naval force in the Philippine Islands, and moved immediately upon Manila when Great Britain issued her proclamation of neutrality and made it impossible to remain longer in her waters at Hongkong.

On the morning of May 1 Dewey led his squadron past the forts, over the submerged mines, and up the channel of Manila Bay. The Spanish forces in the islands, already contending with a native insurrection, were helpless before evening, having lost the whole fleet. Dewey was left in a position to take the city when he chose, and sent home word to that effect. He waited in the harbor until an army of occupation had been got ready, hurried to the transports at San Francisco, and sent out under General Wesley Merritt. He brought the native leader Aguinaldo back to the islands, whence he had been expelled, to foment insurrection. The first American reinforcements arrived at Manila by the end of June. On August 13 they took the city.

Before the news of the surprising victory at Manila reached the United States there was nervousness along the Atlantic Coast because of the uncertain plans of the main Spanish fleet, which had left the Cape Verde Islands, under Admiral Cervera, on April 29, and which might appear off New York or Boston at any time. The naval strategists knew it must be headed for the West Indies, but seaboard Congressmen begged excitedly for protection, and the sensational newspapers pictured the coast in ruins after bombardment.

To Sampson and Schley was assigned the task of guarding the coast, keeping up the blockade, and finding Cervera's fleet before it reached a harbor in American waters. San Juan, Santiago de Cuba, Cienfuegos, and Havana were the only probable destinations. Sampson watched the north side of Cuba and Porto Rico, while Schley and the flying squadron moved to Key West, and on May 19 started around the west end of Cuba to patrol the southern shore. On that same day, entirely unobserved, Cervera slipped into the port of Santiago, at the eastern extremity of Cuba. When the rumor of his arrival reached Sampson at Key West, Schley was already well on his way and firm in his belief that Cervera was heading for Cienfuegos.

The flying squadron, impeded by its colliers and its tenders, moved deliberately around Cuba to Cienfuegos, outside of whose harbor it remained for two days. Here Sampson's orders to proceed immediately to Santiago reached it. On May 26 the fleet was off the entrance to Santiago Harbor, and in this vicinity it stayed for two more days. Schley could get no news that Cervera was here; he feared that his coal would give out and that heavy seas would prevent his getting what coal he had out of his colliers. He decided, in spite of orders, to go back to Key West; he started a retrograde movement, reconsidered it, and was again on blockade when, early on Sunday morning, May 29, he discovered the Spanish fleet at anchor in the channel, where it had been for the last nine days.

The blockade of Santiago was strengthened on June 1 by the arrival of Sampson, who had rushed thither on hearing that Schley had decided to leave the post. The two fleets were merged, and Schley, outranked by Sampson, became a passenger on his flagship Brooklyn. By day, the warships, ranged in a great half-circle, watched the narrow outlet of the harbor. By night they took turns standing close in, with searchlights playing on the entrance. For five weeks they kept this up, not entering the harbor because of their positive orders not to risk the loss of any fighting units, and waited for the arrival of an army to coöperate with them against the land defenses of Santiago.

Sampson asked for military aid early in June, and on June 7 the War Department ordered the army that had been mobilized at Tampa to go to his assistance. General Nelson A. Miles, in command of the army, was not allowed to head the expedition, but was kept at home while General William R. Shafter directed the field work. At Tampa there was almost hopeless confusion. The single track railway that supplied the camp was unable to move promptly either men or munitions, the Quartermaster's Department sent down whole trainloads of supplies without bills of lading, and when the troops were at last on board the fleet of transports they were kept in the river for a week before they were allowed to start for Santiago. Sixteen thousand men, mostly regulars, with nearly one thousand officers and two hundred war correspondents, sailed on June 14, and were in conference with Sampson six days later.

A misunderstanding as to strategy arose in this conference. Sampson left it believing that the army would land and move directly along the shore against the batteries that covered the entrance to the harbor. Shafter, however, though he issued no general order to that effect, was determined to march inland upon the city of Santiago itself. On June 22 and 23 the army was landed by the navy, for it had neither boats nor lighters of its own. The first troops, climbing ashore at the railway pier at Daiquiri, marched west along the coast to Siboney, and then plunged inland, each regiment for itself, along the narrow jungle trail leading to Santiago. Shafter himself, corpulent and sick, followed as he could. Before he established his control over the army on land the head of the column had engaged the enemy at Las Guasimas, nine miles from Santiago, on June 24. The First Volunteer Cavalry, under the command of Colonel Leonard M. Wood, with Theodore Roosevelt as lieutenant-colonel, had marched most of the night in order to be in the first fighting. After a sharp engagement the Spanish retired and the American advance upon Santiago continued in a more orderly fashion.

The narrow trail between Siboney, on the shore, and Santiago, was some twelve miles long. There were dense forests on both sides. Along this the

American army stretched itself at the end of June. There were few ambulances or wagons, and they could not have been used if they had been more numerous. Rations for the front were packed on mules or horses. The troops, hurried to the tropics in the heavy, dark, winter clothing of the regular army, suffered from heat, rain, and irregular rations. Before them the San Juan River crossed the trail at right angles. Beyond this were low hills carrying the fortifications, trenches, and wire fences of Santiago, behind which the Spanish force could fight with every advantage in its favor. Some five miles to the right of the line of advance was the Spanish left, in a blockhouse at El Caney. On the night before July 1, the American army moved on a concerted plan against the whole Spanish line.

Lawton, with a right wing, moved against El Caney, with the idea of demolishing it and crumpling up the Spanish left. The main column followed the trail, crossed the San Juan River, and stormed the hills beyond. The fight lasted all day on July 1, leaving the American forces to sleep in the Spanish trenches, and to re-face them the next day. There was more fighting on July 2 and 3, after which Santiago was besieged by land, as it had been by sea since June 1.

Cervera watched the invading army with growing desperation. He knew the inefficiency of his fleet, that it had left Spain unprepared because public opinion demanded immediate action, that its guns were lacking and its morale low, that if it stayed at anchor in the harbor it would be taken by the army, and that if it went to sea it would be annihilated by Sampson. His only chance was to rush out, scatter in flight, and trust to luck. On Sunday, July 3, he led his ships out of the harbor in single file, turned west against the Brooklyn, which guarded the American left, and endeavored to escape.

Sampson had already issued orders for battle in case Cervera should come out. He had himself started with his flagship, the New York, for a conference with Shafter, and was some seven miles east of the entrance to the harbor when the fleet appeared and the battle began. He turned at once to the long chase that pursued the Spanish vessels along the Cuban shore. The Brooklyn, at which Cervera had headed, instead of closing, circled to the right, and nearly rammed her neighbor, the Texas, before she regained her place at the head of the pursuit. Schley was the ranking officer in the battle, but no one needed or heeded the orders that he signaled to the other ships. Before sundown the Spanish fleet was completely destroyed.

The land and naval battles at Santiago brought the Spanish War to an end. For several weeks the army kept up the investment, with health and morale steadily deteriorating. On July 17 the Spanish army at Santiago was surrendered. On July 27 an invasion of Porto Rico under General Miles took place, and on August 12 the preliminaries of peace were signed on behalf of Spain by the French Minister at Washington. Manila fell the next day, and the war closed with the American army in possession of the most valuable of Spain's remaining colonies.

The Spanish and American peace commissioners met in Paris in October to fix a basis for settlement. An American demand that Cuba should be set free, without debt, and left to the tutelage of the United States, and that Porto Rico should become an American possession, was formulated early in the autumn. There was less certainty about the retention of the Philippines, for here the desire for expansion was checked by a conservative opposition to the adoption of foreign colonies. The evil effects of imperialism were already being pictured by those who had opposed the war. The difficulties of returning the islands to Spain were greater than those involved in their retention, and McKinley finally determined that the cession must include the Philippine Archipelago, and the island of Guam in the Ladrones. The chief of the American commissioners was William R. Day, who had become Secretary of State early in the war, and who was succeeded in that post by John Hay. Under his direction the Treaty of Paris was signed December 10, 1898.

The war and the conquest of the Philippines hastened another though peaceful expansion. The Hawaiian Islands had been a matter of interest to the United States since the American missionaries had begun to work there in the thirties. A growing, American, sugar-raising population had long hoped for annexation and had carried out a successful revolution shortly before 1893. Harrison had concluded a treaty of annexation with the provisional government, but Cleveland had refused to approve it. On July 7, 1898, however, the Newlands Resolution

The Spanish-American War (1901) ; H. H. Sargent, *The Campaign of Santiago de Cuba* (3 vols., 1907) ; J. Wheeler, *The Santiago Campaign* (1899) ; J. D. Miley, *In Cuba with Shafter* (1899) ; and T. Roosevelt, *The Rough Riders* (1899). The navy may be followed in J. D. Long, *The New American Navy* (2 vols., 1903) ; E. S. Maclay, *History of the United States Navy* (3 vols., 1901, the third volume containing allegations that precipitated the Schley-Sampson controversy); G. E. Graham, *Schley and Santiago* (1902) ; W. S. Schley, *Forty-five Years under the Flag* (1904); W. A. M. Goode, *With Sampson through the War* (1899). The public documents of the war are easily accessible, especially in the Annual Reports for 1898 of the Secretaries of War and Navy, and in the Foreign Relations volume for that year. The controversies after the war illuminated many details, particularly the Schley Inquiry (57th Congress, 1st Session, House Document, no. 485, Serial nos. 4370, 4371), and the Miles-Eagan Inquiry (56th Congress, 1st Session, Senate Document, no. 270, Serial nos. 3870–3872).

CHAPTER XVII

THEODORE ROOSEVELT

Out of the humiliating debates upon the war, on the capacity of Alger and Shafter, on the management of the commissary and the field hospitals, on the failure of Sampson and Shafter to coöperate, on the tactics and the alleged weakness of Schley, and on the diplomatic sincerity of McKinley, only one name caught the public ear. The only career that placed a soldier in line for political promotion was that of Theodore Roosevelt, who was still under forty years of age, although he had lived a keen, aggressive, and public life for nearly twenty years. Just out of Harvard in 1880, Roosevelt entered the rough and tumble of New York politics. He was a reform legislator when Cleveland was governor, and an opponent of the nomination of Blaine in 1884. He did not fight the ticket or turn Mugwump, for he had already formed a political philosophy, that only those who stayed within the party could be efficient in reform; but he dropped out of the ranks and took up ranch life in the West. Harrison made him a Civil Service Commissioner and supported him in a stern administration of the merit system. Before he left this office in 1895, to become Police Commissioner of New York City, the breezy and vigorous assaults of Roosevelt upon political corruption had already marked him as a reformer of a new type, who remained an active politician and a party man without losing his interest in reform. As police commissioner he gained new fame and more admirers. In 1897 he took the post of Assistant Secretary of the Navy and prepared for war. He had already found time to write many books on the West, reform, naval history, and out-door life. He resigned his post in April, 1898, on the eve of war, raised a regiment of volunteers, which the public speedily named the "Rough Riders," kept his men in the center of the stage while there was fighting, risked and violated all theories of dis-cipline to attack the sanitary policy of the Adminis-tration in the autumn, and in October received the nomination of his party for Governor of New York, over the ill-concealed opposition of Thomas Collier Platt.

During the campaign of 1898 Roosevelt carried his candidacy to the voter in every part of the State. He spoke from rear platforms day after day. Rough Riders, in uniform, accompanied his party and rein-forced his appeal to mixed motives of good gov-ernment and patriotic fervor. He was elected in November, and on the same day the Republican con-trol of Congress was assured. It was made possible for the party to fulfill the last of the obligations laid upon it by the election of 1896.

A currency act, passed in March, 1900, was the result of Republican success. It established the gold dollar by law as the standard of value, legalized the gold reserve at $150,000,000, and made it the duty of the Treasury to keep at a parity with gold the $313,000,000 of Civil War greenbacks, the $550,000,000 of silver and silver certificates, the $75,000,000 of Sherman Act treasury notes, as well as the national bank notes, which aggregated $300,000,000 in 1900. The law left the currency far from satisfactory in that it made it dependent upon redemption, and hence liable to sudden changes in value, but it silenced the fear of free-silver coinage.

In the spring of 1900 Congress was forced to consider the basis of colonial government. Governments similar to those of the Territories were provided for Hawaii and Porto Rico, but a troublesome revolt prevented such treatment of the Philippine Islands. There had been a native insurrection in these islands before the Spanish War began, and the aid of the rebels had made it easier for the United States to overthrow the power of Spain. Instead of receiving a pledge of independence, as Cuba did, the islands became a territorial possession of the United States. In February, 1899, under the native leader, Emilio Aguinaldo, insurrection broke out against the United States and received the sympathy of large numbers of Americans. The spectacle of the United States subduing a spirit of independence in the Philippines aroused and stimulated the movement of anti-imperialism that had fought against the acquisition of the islands. The incompatibility of republican institutions and foreign colonies, the demoralizing influence of ruling on the ruling class, the lesson of the fall of Rome, were held up before the public. Carl Schurz was one of the leaders in the protest, and his followers included many whose names were already well known in the advocacy of tariff and civil service reform. In 1901 the Supreme Court upheld the constitutionality of expansion and imperial control. The people had already decided in their favor in 1900.

There was no contest for either nomination in the campaign of 1900. Bryan had established his right to the leadership that had come to him by chance in 1896. Although conservative Democrats still distrusted him, their voices were drowned by the popular approval of his honesty and humanity. " Four years ago," said Altgeld, in the Democratic Convention at Kansas City, "we quit trimming, we quit using language that has a double meaning. . . . We went forth armed with that strength that comes from candor and sincerity and we fought the greatest campaign ever waged on the American continent. . . . [For] the first time in the history of this Republic the Democracy of America have risen up in favor of one man." On a platform that repeated the currency demands of 1896 and denounced imperialism, Bryan was unanimously renominated, with Adlai E. Stevenson for the Vice-Presidency.

The emphatic denunciation of imperialism brought to Bryan and Stevenson the support of a group of independents, — the "hold-your-nose-and-vote" group, as the Republican press called them, — who were strong for the gold standard, but believed that currency was less fundamental than imperialism. The Republican party had accepted and approved the war and the benevolent intentions of the United

States, and had renominated McKinley at Philadelphia, without a dissenting voice. Vice-President Hobart had died in office, or the original ticket might have been continued. As a substitute, rumor had attacked the name of Governor Roosevelt, while Senator Platt, preferring not to have him reëlected Governor of New York, had encouraged his boom for the Vice-Presidency. Repeatedly, in the spring of 1900, Roosevelt declared that he would not seek or accept the Vice-Presidency. Hanna and McKinley did not desire him on the ticket, but at the convention the delegates broke down all resistance and forced him to accept the nomination.

The policy of dignity, which McKinley had assumed in 1896, was continued by him in 1900, but the vice-presidential candidate proved the equal of Bryan as a campaigner. In hundreds of speeches, reaching nearly every State, they carried their personality to the voters. The two issues, imperialism and free silver, divided the voters along different lines, but the Administration had an economic basis for support in the recovery of business on every hand. The Republicans took credit for the general and abundant prosperity, and their cartoonists emphasized the idea of the "full dinner pail" as a reason for continued support. A smaller percentage of citizens voted than in 1896, for the issue was less clear than it had been then. Many who were discontented with both candidates voted with the Prohibitionists or Socialists. The Republican ticket was elected, with 292 electoral votes, as against 155 received by Bryan and Stevenson. A continuance of the Republican control of Congress was assured at the same time.

William McKinley was the first President after Grant to receive a second consecutive term. He made few changes in his Cabinet in 1901. Elihu Root remained in the War Department, for the sake of which he had refused to consider the Vice-Presidency, and strove for order in the Philippines, in Cuba, and in the United States Army itself. John Hay, as Secretary of State, continued his correspondence with the Powers over the Chinese revolt, without a break.

Only Seward and John Quincy Adams can rival John Hay as successful American Ministers of Foreign Affairs. Born in the Middle West in 1838, Hay served in Lincoln's household as a private secretary throughout the Civil War. He held minor appointments after this and alternated diplomatic experience with literary production. The monumental *Life of Abraham Lincoln* was partly his work. His graceful verse gained for him a wide reading. His anonymous novel, *The Breadwinners*, was an important document in the early labor movement. McKinley sent him to London as Ambassador in 1897, following the tradition that only the best in the United States may go to the Court of St. James, and had recalled him to be Secretary of State in the fall of 1898. The Boxer outbreak in China in 1900 gave the first opening to the new diplomacy of the United States, broadened out of its insularity by the Spanish War and interested in the attainment of international ideas. Hay led in the adjustment which settled the Chinese claims, opened the door of China to the commerce of the world, and prevented her dismemberment. He was still engaged in this correspondence when President McKinley was murdered by an anarchist, and Theodore Roosevelt became President of the United States, September 14, 1901.

In the hurried inaugural ceremony held in the Buffalo residence in which McKinley died, Roosevelt declared his intention to continue the term as his predecessor had begun it. He insisted that all the members of the Cabinet should remain with him, as they did for considerable periods. He took up the work where it had been dropped, and for some months it was not apparent that a change had been made from a party administration to a personal administration. The suave and cordial tolerance of McKinley was succeeded by the aggressive certainty of his successor. Through John Hay's skillful hand this new tone made a deeper impression on the politics of the world than had that of any President since Washington gave forth the doctrine of neutrality.

Cuba was a pending problem. The American army, under General Leonard Wood, had cleaned up the island. The medical service had learned to isolate the mosquito, and had expelled the scourge of yellow fever. The natives formed a constitution which became effective on May 20, 1902. On this day the United States withdrew from the new Republic, leaving it to manage its own affairs, subject only to a pledge that it would forever maintain its independence, that it would incur no debt without providing the means for settling it, and that the United States might lawfully intervene to protect its independence or maintain responsible government. In the winter of 1901–02 Roosevelt urged Congress to adopt a policy of commercial reciprocity with Cuba. He was supported in this by opinion in Cuba, and by officials of the American Sugar Trust, but was opposed in the Senate by a combination of beet-sugar Republicans and cane-sugar Democrats. The measure failed in 1902, creating bad feeling between President and Congress, but a treaty of modified reciprocity was ratified in 1903.

In 1902 the United States became the first suitor to test the efficacy of the new court of arbitration at The Hague. In 1898 the Czar of Russia had invited the countries represented at St. Petersburg to join in a conference upon disarmament. His motives were questioned and derided, but the conference met the next summer at Huis ten Bosch, the summer palace of the Queen of the Netherlands, at The Hague. Here the plan of disarmament proved futile, but a great treaty for the settlement of international disputes was accepted by the countries present. It seemed probable that the Hague Court, thus created, would die of neglect, but President Roosevelt, appealed to by an advocate of peace, produced a trifling case and submitted it to arbitration. The Pious Fund dispute, with Mexico and the United States as suitors, involved the control of church funds in California. The suit was won by the United States, but derived its chief importance from being the first Hague settlement.

The pledge of the United States for Cuban independence had hardly been fulfilled when another Latin Republic became involved in trouble. Venezuela, torn by war, had incurred obligations to European creditors, and had defaulted in the payments upon them. In December, 1902, Great Britain and Germany announced a blockade of the Venezuelan ports in retaliation, and they were soon joined by other Powers with similar claims. Disclaiming intent to protect Venezuela in defaulting, Roosevelt urged the European claimants to abandon force for arbitration. Under his leadership joint commissions were finally established, and in 1903 the legal technicalities involved were sent to The Hague. The episode involved a new interpretation of the Monroe Doctrine, making it clear that unless the United States wished to protect the South American Republics in the evasion of their debts it must assume some responsibility for the honest settlement of them.

The boundary of Alaska next became a subject for arbitration. Since the valley of the Yukon had attracted its first great migration in the summer of 1897 the mining-camps had steadily increased in importance. Many of these were on the Canadian side of the meridian of 141°, and all were reached either by the river steamers or the trails from the south. The most important ports of entry were Dyea and Skaguay, at the head of the Lynn Canal, a long fiord projecting some ninety miles into the continent. From these ports the prospector plunged inland, climbed the Chilkoot or the Chilkat Pass, and followed one of several overland trails to the Upper Yukon.

The importance given to Dyea and Skaguay re-

vived the question of their ownership and with this
the boundary of Alaska. When Seward bought
Alaska for the United States in 1867 he received it
with the boundaries agreed upon at St. Petersburg
between England and Russia in 1825. These followed the meridian of 141° from Mount St. Elias to
the Arctic Ocean, and followed the irregularities of
the shore-line southeast from that mountain to the
Pacific at 54° 40', North Latitude. The narrow coast
strip was described as following the windings (*sinu-
osités*) of the shore, bounded by the shore mountains
if possible, but in no case to be more than thirty miles
wide. The narrow Lynn Canal pierces the thirty-
mile strip, and the dispute turned chiefly upon interpretation : whether the canal should be regarded as a
sinuosité of the shore, around which the boundary
must go, or as a stream which it might properly
cross.

For thirty years after 1867 the British and Canadian government maps treated the Lynn Canal and
other similar fiords as American, but it became convenient for Canada, after 1897, to urge that the boundary should cross the canal and leave Dyea and
Skaguay on British soil. A Canadian and American
Joint High Commission, meeting in 1898, had been
unable to adjust the controversy. In 1903 it was
submitted to a tribunal, three to a side, which sat in
London. It was doubtful whether the three American adjudicators, Root, Lodge, and Turner, were all
" jurists of repute," as the treaty provided, but the
arguments of the American counsel convinced Lord
Chief Justice Alverstone, one of the British adjudi-

cators, and his vote, added to the American three, gave a verdict that sustained most of the claims of the United States.

In Cuba and Venezuela, at The Hague, and in the Alaskan matter, Roosevelt and Hay showed at once a firmness and a reasonableness that attracted European attention to American diplomacy as never before. The subject of American diplomacy became a common study in American universities. England and Germany appeared to be desirous of conciliating the United States. The German Emperor bought a steam yacht in the United States, sent his brother, Prince Henry of Prussia, to attend the launching, and sent as Ambassador a German nobleman who had long been a personal friend of the President. The reputation for firmness was enhanced, but that for fairness was lessened by the next episode, which involved the Colombian State of Panama.

The dangerous voyage of the Oregon in 1898 completed the conviction of the United States that an isthmian canal must be constructed, and that the Clayton-Bulwer Treaty was no longer adequate. The activity of De Lesseps and his French company at Panama had raised the question about 1880, but nothing had been done to weaken the treaty that obstructed American construction and control until Hay undertook a negotiation under the direction of McKinley in the fall of 1899. Congress was in the midst of a debate over a Nicaragua canal scheme when it was announced that on February 5, 1900, Hay and Lord Pauncefote had signed a treaty opening the canal to American construction, but providing for its neutralization. The treaty forbade the fortification of the canal or its use as an instrument of war. It was killed by amendment in the Senate, but on November 18, 1901, Lord Pauncefote signed a second treaty, by which Great Britain waived all her old rights save that of equal treatment for all users of the canal, and left the future waterway to the discretion of the United States. With the way thus opened, — for the Senate promptly confirmed this treaty, — a new study of routes and methods was hurried to completion.

An Isthmian Commission, created by the United States in 1899, was ready to report upon a route when the second Hay-Pauncefote Treaty was concluded. The practicable routes had been reduced in number to two, at Panama, and through Nicaragua. The former was under the control of the French company, which placed so high a price upon its concession that the commission recommended the Nicaragua route as, on the whole, more available. In Congress there was a strong predisposition in favor of this same route, but during 1902 this was weakened. Senator Hanna preferred the Panama route and worked effectively for it. The French Panama Company, frightened by the popularity of the Nicaragua route, reduced its price. The earthquake and volcanic eruption on the Island of Martinique reminded the world that Nicaragua was nearer the zone of active volcanic life, and hence more exposed to danger, than Panama. In June Congress empowered the President to select the route and build a canal at once.

Negotiations with Colombia for the right to build at Panama dragged on through 1902 and 1903. Weakened by continuous revolution, that Republic realized that the isthmian right of way was its most valuable asset. Only after prolonged discussion did its Government authorize its Minister at Washington to sign a treaty reserving Colombian sovereignty over the strip, but giving to the United States the canal concession in return for $10,000,000 in cash and an annuity of $250,000. This treaty was signed in Washington in January, 1903, and was received as a triumph for the diplomacy of Hay and Roosevelt. It was ratified in March by the Senate, in spite of a last filibuster by the friends of Nicaragua, but the Colombian Congress rejected the treaty and adjourned.

By the autumn of 1903 Roosevelt had determined upon the route at Panama, the French company had become eager to sell, and the Colombians living on the Isthmus were anxious to have the negotiations ended and the digging begun. In October the President wrote to an intimate friend hoping that there might be a revolt of the Isthmus against Colombia, though disclaiming any intent to provoke one. The friend made the wish public over his own name, but before it appeared in print the revolt had taken place. It was known in advance to the State Department, which telegraphed on November 3, 1903, asking when it was to be precipitated. It took place later on this day, the independence of the Republic of Panama was proclaimed, the United States prevented Colombia from repressing it by force, recognized the new Republic by cable, and on November 18 signed at Washington a treaty with Panama granting the canal concession. " I took Panama," boasted President Roosevelt some years later, when critics denounced his policy as a robbery of a weak neighbor.

The construction of a canal proceeded rapidly, once the diplomatic entanglements had been brushed away. The incidental problems of sanitation, labor, supplies, and engineering were solved promptly and effectively. Congress poured money into the enterprise without restraint, the first boats were passed through the locks in 1914, and in 1915 the formal opening of the canal was celebrated by a naval procession at the Isthmus and an Exposition at San Francisco.

Vigor and certainty of purpose marked the conduct of domestic affairs as well as foreign, but the necessity for the concurrence in these by Congress made the former results less striking than the latter. The appointments of President Roosevelt were such as might be expected from one who had himself devoted six years to the Civil Service Commission. Few of them met with opposition from the reform element. In the South he became involved with local public opinion, especially in the cases of a negro postmistress at Indianola, Mississippi, and the negro collector of the port of Charleston, in which he maintained that although federal appointments ought generally to go to persons acceptable in their districts, the door of opportunity must not be shut against the negro. Within a few weeks of his inauguration he precipitated a severe discussion upon the status of the negro by entertaining Booker T. Washington at the White House. He disciplined Republican leaders in the South who endeavored to exclude negroes from the party organization and to build up a " lily-white " Republican machine.

The administrative duties of the United States expanded rapidly after the Spanish War. The extension of scientific functions beginning in the eighties continued until the volume of work forced the creation of new offices. Federal civil employees numbered 107,000 in 1880, 166,000 in 1890, 256,000 in 1900, and 384,000 in 1910. Among the newer scientific activities was included that of the reclamation of the arid or semi-arid lands of the Southwest.

The region between the Missouri River and the Sierra Nevada had been regarded as uninhabitable since the days of Pike. Known as the " American Desert," it figured in the atlases as a place of sand and aridity, and became the home chosen for the Indian tribes between 1825 and 1840. Under the influence of migration to Oregon and California the real character of the Far West became known, but not until the continental railways were finished did many inhabitants enter it. In 1889 and 1890 the " Omnibus " States were admitted, embracing all the northwest half of the old desert. Utah followed in 1896. Arizona and New Mexico and Oklahoma developed rapidly after 1890 and were all demanding statehood in 1902.

The advance of population into the Far West revealed the existence of large areas in which an

abundant agriculture could be produced through irrigation. Private means were inadequate for this
and the land laws discouraged it. A demand for
federal reclamation appeared in the eighties. In
1889 a survey of available sites for reservoirs was
made by government engineers, and in 1902 Roosevelt coöperated with the Far-Western Congressmen
in securing the passage of the Newlands Reclamation Act. By this bill the proceeds of land sales in
the arid States became a fund to be used by the reclamation service for the construction of great public irrigation works. In the succeeding years dams,
tunnels, and ditches were undertaken that were
rivaled in magnitude only by the railroad tunnels
at New York and the excavations at Panama.

The aggressive assurance with which the Roosevelt Administration handled the problems of diplomacy and administration created for the President
a wide and unusual popularity, which was strongest
in the West. Many critics, also, were created, who
distrusted personal influence when injected into
government, and who doubted the solidity of Roosevelt's judgment. Personal altercations, in which the
President was often the aggressor, were numerous.
Among professional politicians dislike was mingled
with fear because the President had established personal relations immediately with their constituents.
Under President McKinley the state delegations in
Congress had controlled the appointive federal offices
of their States, and had been secure in their personal
standing; under Roosevelt their control of appointments was less secure. When matters of legislation

CHAPTER XVIII

BIG BUSINESS

THE panic of 1893 ended the first period of the trust problem. The preceding years had been years of formation and experiment. They had been accompanied by an increasing popular distaste for combinations of capital and a growing activity in the organization of labor. The Sherman Law of 1890 had temporarily quieted the anti-trust movement, while economic depression had checked the extravagance of speculation that had been prevalent everywhere. During the years of depression attention was shifted to tariff and currency, but a new era began with the recurrence of prosperity about 1897.

The industrial revival was marked by an extension of the scope of industry, as every similar period had been. After the panic of 1837 the railroad had appeared among the important new activities of American society. Improvements in manufacturing technique followed the panic of 1857. After 1873 the varied applications of electricity to industry and communication gave a new direction to investment. After 1893, with every preceding activity stimulated and extended, there came the first successful construction of a trackless engine — the motor-car — and the rebuilding of the physical plants of cities, railways, and suburban residences. The recovery of confidence came after 1896, and before the end of the century speculation was at full blast.

The drift toward monopoly was marked. The trusts had already shown their profitable character. Concentration had been made possible by the development of communication in the eighties, and grew now on a larger scale than the eighties had imagined. Within the field of transportation the promoters reorganized the railroads after the panic, reduced their number, and gathered their control into the hands of a few men.

The railway system by 1900, with 198,000 miles of track, was directed by a few powerful groups of roads. In the East the New York Central and Pennsylvania systems were dominant. In the West the continental railways formed the basis of new organizations. The keenest interest gathered round the reconstruction of the Union Pacific by Edward H. Harriman, who reorganized its finances after 1897. The Union Pacific had been forced into combination by its location and its neighbors. Running from Omaha to Ogden it was dependent for through traffic upon the Central Pacific that ran from Ogden to San Francisco. When the latter came under the control of the California capitalists who owned the Southern Pacific lines, the Union Pacific was driven to build or buy outlets of its own, and extended into Oregon and Texas as the result. Jay Gould had begun the consolidation in the eighties and Harriman continued it after the panic of 1893. He rebuilt the main line and improved the value and

May 9, 1901. Only the speculators suffered by the panic, but public attention was drawn by it to the gigantic size of the combinations which held arbitrary control over nearly half the United States.

Minor consolidations followed these in 1902 and 1903, but none aroused so much fear as the Northern Securities Company of New Jersey, the holding company in whose hands Hill and Morgan determined to put the control of their lines. The fate of any single company could be determined by the ownership of not over fifty-one per cent of its stock. If this was owned by another corporation, a similar proportion of the stock of the latter would control the whole. The holding company was a machine whereby capital could control property several times its bulk. The Governors of the Northwest States, alarmed at the monopolization of their railways, protested and started suits. It was claimed that this sort of merging of railroads was, after all, a conspiracy in restraint of trade. In March, 1902, President Roosevelt instructed his Attorney-General, Philander C. Knox, to test the Sherman Act of 1890, and bring suit under it for the dissolution of the Northern Securities Company. For several years after 1897 foreign affairs and big business had been dominant in the American mind, which had admired their bigness and activity, but now the social consequences of big business aroused the fears of the nation. In 1903 Congress passed the Elkins Law, forbidding railroads to give rebates to favored customers, and an Expedition Law, to make the wheels of justice move more rapidly when prosecutions under the

Sherman and Interstate Commerce Laws were under way.

Industrial consolidation, like that of the railways, began again in 1897, and many of the new corporations assumed a type that marked an evolution for the trust. In the earlier period the aim of the trust had been to eliminate competition by gathering under a single control the whole of a given business. Oil, sugar, steel, whiskey, and tobacco were notable instances in which extreme consolidation had been reached. Competition changed its character as consolidation increased. It ceased to mean a struggle between rivals in the same trade, and came to mean a struggle between successive processes of manufacture. The mine-owner struggled for his profits with the smelter who used his ore. The smelter struggled with the steel manufacturer in the same way. Control of single industries left untouched this newer competition, but an integration of great groups of related processes promised to avoid it.

In 1901 the greatest of the integrated trusts, the United States Steel Corporation, was created. The iron and steel industry had been expanding since the Bessemer and other commercial processes for the manufacture of steel had made it available for railway, bridge, and architectural construction. Andrew Carnegie, with his Pittsburg mills, was the most successful producer. His partnership controlled by 1901 about twenty-five per cent of the output of finished steel. He already included many related and successive processes, but now he allowed his works to be merged with those of his rivals into a large com-

pany. The resulting United States Steel Corporation
owned and operated the ore deposits and the mines,
the necessary coal fields, the local railways and freight
steamers, the smelters and the blast furnaces, the
rolling mills and the factories in which iron and steel
were manufactured into a multitude of shapes for
sale. With a New Jersey charter it was capital-
ized at $1,100,000,000, and drew attention to the
industrial phase of the trust problem much as Harriman, Hill, and Morgan had drawn it to the railroads.

Promotion of new trusts, with billions of aggregated capital, was the order of the day from 1897 to
1902. The fear of monopoly was speedily aroused,
and in 1898 Congress created an Industrial Commission, whose nineteen volumes of reports contain
the facts upon which the history of the trusts must
be based. In the fall of 1899 there met in Chicago a
great conference on the trusts, where business men,
economists, and politicians discussed the economic
and social possibilities of the movement. A willingness to hear and perhaps to rely on the judgment
of experts was shown in the discussions over the
trusts. It marked a change in the American attitude
toward government. By 1902 the demand for a solution of the trust problem was heard repeatedly, but
there was little agreement as to whether the trusts
were good or bad, or whether they should be abolished, regulated, or owned outright by the Government. It was not even certain what powers the United
States possessed to regulate general industry, but a
group of Supreme Court cases suggested that the

power could be found. In the Trans-Missouri Freight
Case (1897), the Supreme Court declared that the
Sherman Law applied to railway conspiracies, and
in the Addystone Pipe Case (1898), a decision
against an industrial combination, written by Circuit
Judge William H. Taft, was upheld by the court of
last appeal. The Northern Securities Case, started
in 1902, was pushed to a successful end in 1904,
when it became apparent that legal control could be
exercised if Congress so desired.

Labor followed the course of industry and transportation, becoming stronger and better united, and
showing a keen jealousy of centralized control. The
years of trust promotion were years of notable strikes
and of episodes which drew attention to the social
results of industrial concentration. Sometimes the
trust had labor at a disadvantage, as was shown in
the strike against the Steel Corporation by the Amal-
gamated Association in 1901. In 1892 this union had
conducted a great strike against the Carnegie Works
and had lost public sympathy and the strike. Its men
had committed open violence, and an anarchistic sym-
pathizer had tried to murder Carnegie's representative
at Homestead, Henry C. Frick. In 1901 the strike
affected the unionized mills of the Steel Corporation,
but that trust had only to close down the mills involved and transfer pending contracts to other mills,
remote and non-unionized. The strike collapsed because of the superior organization of the trust.

More important than the steel strike in its effect
upon the public was the strike of the miners in the
anthracite coal fields of Pennsylvania. In 1900 these

workers were organized by the United Mine Workers of America, under the leadership of John Mitchell. They gained concessions in a strike in this year, partly because the strike threatened to disturb political conditions and embarrass the Republican national ticket. The mine-owners, most of whom were Republicans, were persuaded by Hanna and others to end the quarrel.

In the spring of 1902 the strike broke out again, turning largely upon the question of the formal recognition of the union. All through the summer John Mitchell held his followers together, gaining an unusual degree of public sympathy for his cause. In the autumn, with both sides obstinate, a third party, the public, took an interest in the strike. The prospect of a coalless winter alarmed political leaders and citizens in general. It was felt that public interest was superior to the claims of either contestant, but there was neither law nor recognized machinery through which the public could protect itself. At this stage, in October, 1902, President Roosevelt secretly reached the intention " to send in the United States Army to take possession of the coal fields" if necessary. He called the operators and Mitchell to a conference at the White House, spoke to them as a citizen upon their duty to serve the public, and with rising public opinion behind him and supporting him, forced the owners to consent to an arbitration of the points at issue. The men returned to work, pleased with the President, to whose interference they and the public owed industrial peace.

In 1903 another miners' union, the Western Federation of Miners, conducted a great strike in the mines of Cripple Creek. Public opinion in Colorado knew no middle class. The miners and the operators represented the two chief interests of the section. Hard feeling and violence accompanied the strike. The malicious murder of non-union men added to the bitterness, which the presence of the militia and a series of arbitrary arrests could not allay. The strike was complicated by the presence among the workers of a strong element of Socialists, whose ends were political as well as economic. The leaders of the Federation, Moyer and Haywood, were Socialists, and for them the strike was only a beginning of political revolution. The strike lasted until the outraged citizens of Cripple Creek formed a vigilance committee and deported the chief agitators to Kansas.

Socialism played an increasing part in labor discussions after 1897. A Socialist Labor party had presented a ticket and received a few votes in 1892 and 1896, but socialism had not taken a strong hold on the American imagination. The swelling immigration that followed the new prosperity brought new life to socialism. In 1900 a Social Democratic party polled 94,000 votes for Eugene V. Debs for President. In 1904, with the same candidate, it received 402,000 votes. Society was reorganizing amid the industrial changes, while the discontented classes were growing more coherent and constructive.

President Roosevelt met the changes in transportation, industry, and labor with vigor. He invoked the Sherman Law against the Northern Securities Company. He brought suits against certain of the trusts which he stigmatized as the "bad trusts." Not all concentration, he urged, was undesirable. Capital, like labor, had its rights, but it must obey the law. Partly through his efforts Congress created in 1903 a new administrative department of Commerce and Labor. George B. Cortelyou became the first Secretary of this department. Through its Bureaus of Corporations and of Labor there was new activity in the investigation of the facts of the industrial movement.

The vigor with which the President directed foreign relations, interfered in big business, and espoused the cause of labor produced a breach between him and many of the regular leaders of the party. Through two campaigns Marcus A. Hanna had worked on the theory that the Republican party was the party of business, and had attracted to its support all who believed this or had something to make out of it. Many of these Republicans could not understand what Roosevelt was trying to do, and maintained an opposition, silent or open, to his policies.

The popularity of Hanna was used by many Republicans to offset the popularity of Roosevelt. Before 1896 Hanna had taken little part in public politics. Entering the Senate in 1897, he developed great influence. By 1900 he began to speak in public with directness and effect, and to undo the work of the cartoonists who had misrepresented his character. He interfered to bring peace in the anthracite regions in 1900, became interested in the labor problem on its own account, and discovered that he was popular.

He was essentially a direct and honest man, who had had no reason to doubt that it was the chief end of government to conserve business. As he came into touch with public affairs he broadened, saw new responsibilities for capital, and had a new understanding of the wants of labor. The only personality that even threatened to rival that of Roosevelt in 1904 was that of " Uncle Mark " Hanna.

Roosevelt had been made Vice-President to get rid of him in New York. The single life that stood between him and the White House was removed by an assassin, and as a President by accident he desired to establish himself and secure a nomination on his own account in 1904. By the summer of 1902 he appreciated the growing interest in the problems of capital and labor. A speaking tour in 1902 gave him a chance to demand a " square deal " for all, and the control of the trusts. From some sections of the West came the suggestion that the way to approach the trusts was through the tariff.

The Dingley Tariff was unpopular with the Republican farmers of the Northwest, and for some years they tolerated it in silence as a test of party loyalty. In 1902 a liberal faction, controlled by Governor Albert B. Cummins, captured the Iowa convention and demanded a revision of the more extreme schedules. The belief that the tariff was the "mother of trusts" was spreading, and the Iowa idea gained wide acceptance. In Congress, in the session of 1902, the Republican organization had shown the stubbornness with which any opening in the tariff wall would be opposed.

Cuba was set free in the spring of 1902, her government having been formed under the guidance of the United States. The duty to aid the young Republic, and in particular to mitigate the severities of the Dingley Tariff impressed the President, who used all his influence to get such legislation from Congress. He failed signally, raising only a new issue by his attempt to coerce Congress. His speeches in the summer showed a willingness to revise the tariff, while his interference in the coal strike in the autumn showed his willingness to oppose the ends of capital. How far he would go in breaking with the leaders of his party was unknown, but their disposition to "stand pat" and do nothing with the tariff was marked before the end of 1902.

In 1902 it became a habit of Republican state conventions to demand the renomination of Roosevelt in 1904. Whatever his effect upon the party leaders, the rank and file liked him and believed in him, while his personal popularity among Democrats led many to think his strength greater than it was. His candidacy was formal and authorized, but his opponents hoped that Hanna might be induced to try to defeat him. In 1903 the Ohio convention, with the consent of Hanna, approved the candidacy of Roosevelt, and early in 1904 the death of Hanna removed the last hope of Roosevelt's Republican opponents. The delegates went to a national convention in Chicago, for which the procedure had all been arranged at the White House, where it had been determined that Elihu Root should be temporary chairman, and that Joseph G. Cannon, the Speaker, should be permanent chairman. Through these the convention registered the renomination of Roosevelt and selected Charles W. Fairbanks, of Indiana, as Vice-President.

In the Democratic party the forces that had dominated in 1896 and 1900 had lost control. William Jennings Bryan, after two defeats, was not a candidate in 1904. He had become a lay preacher on political subjects, lecturing and speaking constantly in all parts of the United States, and reinforcing his political views in the columns of his weekly *Commoner*, which he founded after his defeat in 1900. Roosevelt had adopted many of his fundamental themes, but Bryan retained an increasing popularity as did the President, and, like the latter, had relations of doubtful cordiality with the leaders of his own party. The Cleveland wing of the Democrats still believed Bryan to be dangerous and unsound upon financial matters, and some of them made overtures to Cleveland to be a candidate for a third term himself. His emphatic refusal to reënter politics compelled the conservatives to find a new candidate. Judge Alton B. Parker, of New York, was their choice. The owner of the most notorious of the sensational newspapers, William Randolph Hearst, offered himself. Several other candidates were presented to the Democratic Convention at Chicago, but Parker received the nomination, over the bitter opposition of Bryan. When a doubt arose as to his status on the silver issue, Judge Parker telegraphed to the convention that he regarded " the gold standard as firmly and irrevocably established." Bryan supported the ticket, Parker and Henry G. Davis of West Virginia, but without enthusiasm.

There was no issue that clearly divided the parties in the campaign of 1904. Roosevelt asked for an indorsement of his Administration and for approval of his general theory of a " square deal," but it was obvious that his party associates were less enthusiastic for reform than he, and that only his great personal popularity prevented some of them from withdrawing their support. The Bryan Democrats were drawn more toward Roosevelt than toward their own party candidate. It was clear that Parker represented, on the whole, the weight of conservatism, while Roosevelt embodied the spirit of progress, and that neither was typical of his party. Parker was driven by the progressive Democrats to insist upon a regulation of the trusts ; Roosevelt acquiesced in the desire of the " stand-pat " Republicans and refrained from advocating a lowering of the tariff.

The result of the election was proof of the public confidence in Roosevelt. He carried every State outside the South, and Missouri and Maryland besides. His popular vote was over 7,500,000, while his plurality over Parker was more than 2,500,000. In the last week of the canvass Parker charged that the trusts were supporting Roosevelt, and that the reform demands were only a pose. He pointed out that the Chairman of the Republican National Committee, who had succeeded Hanna, George B. Cortelyou, had been Secretary of Commerce and Labor, and thus in a position to examine the books of corporations. He hinted at a political blackmail of the trusts, and many of the papers that supported him were outspoken in their charges. An indignant denial of blackmail appeared over the President's signature the Saturday before election. Later investigation proved that many of the great corporations had, as usual, contributed to the campaign fund, and that Roosevelt had urged the railroad magnate, Harriman, to contribute toward the campaign in New York.

As soon as the results of the election were known, Roosevelt answered a question that was on the lips of many. His three and a half years constituted his first term. He was now elected for a second term, and he characterized as a " wise custom " the limiting of a President to two terms. " Under no circumstances will I be a candidate for or accept another nomination," he declared.

BIBLIOGRAPHICAL NOTE

The history of the recent trust movement may be followed in the writings upon the United States Steel Corporation by E. S. Meade and H. L. Wilgus. There is a detailed and gossipy *Inside History of the Carnegie Steel Company* (1903), by J. H. Bridge. W. F. Willoughby has made searching analyses of Concentration and Integration, which may be found in the *Yale Review*, vol. VII, and the *Quarterly Journal of Economics*, vol. XVI. The prosecution of the Northern Securities Company brought out many typical facts of railroad consolidation, and is best described in B. H. Meyer, *A History of the Northern Securities Case* (in University of Wisconsin Bulletin, no. 142). More general material upon these topics may be found in E. R. Johnson, *American Railway Transportation* (1903, etc.) ; F. A. Cleveland and F. W. Powell, *Railway Promotion and Capitalization in the United States* (1909, with an admirable bibliography); Poore's *Railroad Manual;* and the files of the *Com-

CHAPTER XIX

THE "MUCK-RAKERS"

BEFORE Roosevelt was inaugurated for his second term, the national " revival," in which he and Bryan and other preachers of civic virtue had played the speaking parts, was sweeping over the country. The menace of the trusts was seen and exaggerated as railways, corporations, and labor availed themselves of the means of coöperation. The connection between the great financial interests and politics was believed to be dangerous to public welfare. All the mechanical reforms for the recovery of government by the people, that had been originated between 1889 and 1897, were revived once more, and there was added to confidence in them a widespread belief in the existence of a malevolent, plundering class.

It was not enough that the trust movement should be explained as an unavoidable development from modern communication. It was believed to constitute more than an economic evolution. The public was prone to place an ethical responsibility upon an individual or groups of individuals, and there came a series of revelations or exposures that appeared, in part, to fix the blame. All the old uprisings against boss-rule were revivified, and capitalistic control was placed upon the Index.

Miss Ida M. Tarbell, an historical student who

had gained an audience through popular and discriminating lives of Napoleon and Lincoln, published a history of the Standard Oil Company in *McClure's Magazine* during 1903. She showed conclusively the connection between transportation and monopoly in the oil industry, revealing the mastery of the tools of transportation, by rebates, by control of tank cars, or by pipe lines, that had enabled John D. Rockefeller to establish his great trust. She showed also the unlovely methods of competition, long common to all business, but magnified by their use in the hands of a monopoly to establish itself. "What we are witnessing," wrote Washington Gladden a little later, "is a new apocalypse, an uncovering of the iniquity of the land. . . . We have found that no society can march hellward faster than a democracy under the banner of unbridled individualism."

Three years before Miss Tarbell displayed the tendency of the trusts, President Hadley, of Yale, had suggested that social ostracism, or social stigma, might be made an efficient tool for reform. Other writers used the tool. Lincoln Steffens, in a series of articles on "The Shame of the Cities," exposed the connection between graft and politics. Thomas Lawson, with spectacular exaggeration, laid the troubles of society at the feet of "Frenzied Finance." *Collier's Weekly* undertook to reveal the worthlessness and fraud in the trade in patent medicines. Many of the exposers encroached upon the fields of fiction in their work, while books of avowed fiction exploited the conditions they portrayed. *Coniston*, by

Winston Churchill, was based upon the control of a State by a railroad boss. Upton Sinclair wrote *The Jungle* to expose the meat-packers.

A new journalism aided and was aided by the zeal to expose and the greed of the public for literature of exposure. In the later nineties city journalism was reorganized under the influence of the "yellow" papers, and sensational news was made a profitable commodity as never before. The range of the daily paper was, however, limited by a few hundred miles, and its influence could not become national. A new periodical literature, resembling the old literary monthlies, but using many timely and journalistic articles, sprang into life and gained national circulation and influence. S. S. McClure was one of its pioneers. *Everybody's*, the *Cosmopolitan*, *Munsey's*, the *American*, and weeklies like *Collier's*, the *Outlook*, and the *Independent* were among the journals that helped to spread the conclusions and advocate reforms. Besides these a horde of imitators fattened for a time upon exposure.

Journalism had a large part in directing the American revival, and private investigators furnished many of the facts. Public suits marked an attempt to act upon the facts and remedy them. In Missouri Joseph W. Folk conducted a series of prosecutions against grafters in St. Louis that elevated him in a few months to the head of his party and the governorship of his State. The Bureau of Corporations, attached to the new Department of Commerce and Labor in 1903, made a series of reports the most notable of which showed that the charges against the

Standard Oil Company for extorting rebates, and against the meat-packers for unsanitary conditions, were founded upon fact.

The most notable public exposure of indiscretion and wrongdoing in high finance occurred in New York. Here, during 1905, a quarrel over the management of the Equitable Life Insurance Company led to a legislative investigation by a so-called Armstrong Committee. One of the attorneys employed by the committee, Charles E. Hughes, soon became the spirit of the examination. One by one he called insurance officers to the witness stand, and drew from their reluctant lips the story of their relation to banking, to speculative finance, and to politics. He revealed the existence of a group among the bankers not unlike a money trust. He proved that for at least three national campaigns the insurance companies, like other corporations, had given heavy subsidies to the campaign funds, sometimes of both but always of the Republican party.

Whenever an investigator rose above the level and established his reputation for honesty and competence, the aroused public seized upon him for use in politics. In September, 1906, the Democrats of New York nominated the most successful of the sensational journalists, Hearst, for governor. On the same day the Republican Convention, in which no delegate had been instructed for him, nominated Hughes as governor of New York, because public opinion in the party would take no other candidate. Hughes was elected in 1906 and again in 1908, in spite of the hostility of Republican party leaders. His administrations were prophetic of the new spirit that was entering politics.

Many of the problems raised by the investigations were old and presented only a need for an honest enforcement of the law against lawbreakers. Others were simple and prescribed their own methods of treatment. The evil of corporation contributions to campaign funds was met in 1907 by a law forbidding national banks to contribute to any election, or any corporations to contribute to a presidential or congressional election. In 1906 the gift of free railroad passes upon interstate railroads was prohibited by law. The presidential candidates in 1908 pledged themselves to publicity in the matter of contributions, while the complaints of poverty-stricken campaign managers in 1908 and 1912 indicated that the laws were generally obeyed. Still other problems raised large questions of scientific investigation and legislation.

The reaction from the carelessness revealed by the investigation of the meat-packers stimulated a pure-food movement that had had its advocates for many years. With the concentration of food manufacture and the increase in the consumption of "package products," the consumer had given up the preparation of his own food and thrown himself upon the dealer. The numerous domestic industries typical of the American family in 1880 had been sorted out. The sewing had gone to the sweat shop and the factory, the baking had gone to the public baker, the laundry was going, the killing and preservation of meat and the preparation of canned vegetables and fruits were nearly gone. Population followed the industries to work in the factories. Country life lost much of its variety and interest, while the congested masses in the cities were made dependent for their health and strength upon private initiative. Rigorous bills for the inspection of meats at the slaughter houses, and for the proper labeling of manufactured foods and medicines, were carried through Congress in 1906 on the strength of the popular revulsion against the manufacturers. Hereafter the Department of Agriculture stood between the people and their food. James Wilson, of Iowa, had been Secretary since 1897 and remained in the office until 1913. He and his subordinates, notably Dr. Harvey Wiley, in charge of the pure-food work, administered the law amid the proddings of consumers and the protests of manufacturers. With much complaint, but with little difficulty because of the consolidation of control, business adjusted itself to the new requirements and labels in the next few years.

The anti-railroad movement reminded the public that the Interstate Commerce Law of 1887 was an imperfect statute. It had always done less than its framers had intended. Judicial interpretation had limited its scope. The commission did not have power to fix a rate or to compel in the railroads the uniformity of bookkeeping without which no scientific rates could be established. After Roosevelt had directed his speeches of 1903 and 1904 to the subject, Congress responded to the public interest thus aroused with a flood of projected railroad bills. One of these passed the House of Representatives in 1905, but was held up in the Senate while a new investigation of interstate commerce, the most exhaustive since the Cullom investigation of 1885, was undertaken. In 1906 the Hepburn Railway Bill was passed. In its chief provisions it gave the Interstate Commerce Commission power to fix rates and to prescribe uniform bookkeeping, and it forbade railways to issue free passes or to own the freight they carried. The long railroad debate was made notable by the speeches of a new Senator, Robert M. LaFollette, of Wisconsin, who had fought his way to the governorship on this issue and gone through a prolonged fight with the railroads of his own State. He insisted that public rate-making could not succeed without a preliminary physical valuation of the roads that would show the extent of their real capitalization. He talked, often, to empty chairs in the Senate, but he prophesied that the people had a new interest in their affairs, and that many of the seats, vacant because of the indifference of their owners, would soon be filled with Senators of a new type. In vacations he spoke to public audiences on the same subject, reading his "roll-call," and telling the people how their representatives voted for or against commercial privilege. With its enlarged powers the Interstate Commerce Commission made rapid headway against rebates and discrimination.

The popular revival was well advanced by 1905, but was becoming more sensational every month. Led on by an expectant public, the magazines manufactured exposures to supply the market, and hysteria often took the place of investigation. The real needs of reform were in danger of being lost in a flood of denunciation. In the spring of 1906 President Roosevelt spoke out to check the indiscriminate abuse. He drew his topic from Bunyan's "Man with the Muck-Rake," pointed out that blame and exposure had run its course, and demanded that enforcement of the law be taken up, and that efforts be turned from destruction to construction. He had done much himself to "arouse the slumbering conscience of the nation," and turned now to direct it toward a permanent advantage.

The trend of criticism injured the party under whose administration corporate abuse had grown up. The personal popularity of Roosevelt, and his associates, Root, Taft, Knox, and Hughes, saved the party from defeat. In 1906 the congressional campaign was fought on the basis of holding on to prosperity, enforcing the law against all violators, and strengthening the hands of government. Roosevelt wrote the substance of the platform, and his party gained control of its sixth consecutive Congress since 1896. The canvass over, Roosevelt departed from an old precedent, left the territory of the United States, and visited the Isthmus of Panama to inspect the work on the canal.

Six months after the signing of the Panama Treaty in 1903 the United States took possession of the Canal Zone and began to dig. It had to learn lessons of both management and tropical engineering. One by one its chief engineers deserted the enterprise. The choice between a sea-level and a lock canal divided the experts. The legislation by Congress was inadequate. In the spring of 1906 Roosevelt, with the approval of Taft, who had been recalled from the Philippines to be Secretary of War, determined to build a lock canal. The President tramped over the workings in November, 1906, and sent an illustrated message about them to Congress on his return. In 1907 Major George W. Goethals was detailed from the army to be benevolent despot and engineer of the Canal Zone. Inspired and encouraged by repeated visits from Taft, the work now made rapid progress toward completion. Sir Frederick Treves, the great English surgeon, visited the canal in 1908, and found there not only gigantic engineering works, but a triumph for the preventive medicine of Colonel William C. Gorgas, chief of the sanitary officers.

The attention of the world, directed toward the United States since 1898, was held by the canal and by a continuation of a vigorous and open diplomacy. In February, 1904, Russia and Japan, unable to agree upon the conduct of the former in Manchuria, had gone to war. Hostilities had continued until Russian prestige was shattered and Japanese finance was wavering. In June, 1905, the United States directed identical notes to the belligerents, offering a friendly mediation. The invitation was accepted, and during the summer of 1905 the envoys of Russia and Japan met in Portsmouth, New Hampshire, to conclude a treaty of peace. In 1906 the Nobel Committee awarded to Roosevelt the annual prize for services to peace.

Relations with all the world were friendly between 1905 and 1909. Great Britain contributed to the

cordiality by sending to the United States as her
ambassador the best-fitted of her subjects, James
Bryce. Under his tactful management the next five
years were a period of unprecedented friendship. The
South American republics, always sensitive about the
headship of the United States, were brought to kind-
lier feelings. There had been two congresses of all
the Americas, one in 1889, at the instigation of
Blaine, the next in Mexico in 1901. In 1906 the
American republics convened at Rio de Janeiro in
July. Secretary of State Elihu Root made a plea
for friendship before this congress. From Rio he went
to other capitals of South America, achieving notable
triumphs in his public speeches.

The Pan-American Conference at Rio was an
American preliminary to a larger meeting in which
the United States played an important part in 1907.
During 1904 Roosevelt had agreed to start a movement for a second conference at The Hague. He took
up the negotiation during the Russo-Japanese War,
deferred it at the instance of the Czar, and then
stood aside to let the latter issue the formal invitation. The American delegation at the Second Hague
Conference was led by Joseph H. Choate, leader of
the American Bar and former ambassador to Great
Britain. It forced the discussion throughout the session, tried in vain to produce an agreement to abol-
ish the right of capture of enemy property on the
high seas in time of war, and helped to strengthen
the permanent court of arbitration. In January,
1906, the United States had sat in conference at
Algeciras, over the affairs of Morocco. It had medi-

ated in the Oriental war. It had strengthened its position at home. It was no longer true that the United States was entirely disinterested in the affairs of Europe, for it had become a world power.

A visible emblem of power was afforded to the world in 1907. Since the Treaty of Portsmouth there had been friction with Japan over the treatment of Japanese subjects on the Pacific Coast, and alarmists had drawn pictures of a possible war. Late in 1907 the President announced a practice voyage for the whole effective navy that would carry it around South America and into the Pacific. In December he reviewed the fleet, and saw it off from Hampton Roads. From the Pacific it was ordered round the world, visited Japan and China, and was received with keen interest everywhere. It came home early in 1909, having made a record for holding together without breakdown or accident.

While the fleet was going round the world and business was adjusting itself to the new constructive laws, an old problem was formally ended. The tribal sovereignty, which had made the Indians a problem, was terminated. The Dawes Act of 1887 had substituted severalty for tribal landholdings among the Indians. Out of the first cessions which followed the act Oklahoma Territory had been made in 1890. This had developed more rapidly than any previous Territory because of the railroads that crossed it in every direction. By 1900 it demanded statehood. In 1906 it was enabled, and during 1907 it was admitted, with the longest and most radical of state constitutions. Fear of the activities of corporate wealth and distrust of the agents of government were written into nearly every article.

In the spring of 1908 nearly all of the forty-six governors met with President Roosevelt in the White House and registered another problem upon which agitation and revelation had led to public reflection. The coal strikes of 1900 and 1902 had drawn attention to the possible relation of government to the coal supply of the people. The beginnings of reclamation in 1902 had revealed the fact that public reclamation was impeded by large private and corporate water rights. The natural resources of the country were seen to be following the course of all business and settling into the control of great corporations. The waste of coal and timber and water and land itself was unreasonable. The denudation of the hills led to terrible floods along the rivers. The future was being darkened by the organized selfishness of the present. A movement for conservation grew out of the conference of governors, but Congress for the present would not encourage it.

In popular education, in initiation of new administrative policies, and in the passage of constructive laws efforts were being made to adjust government to the needs of modern industry and to safeguard society. The business interests affected by the changes obstructed the process when they could, and were intensified in their opposition by the series of prosecutions brought by Attorney-General Knox, and his successor Charles J. Bonaparte, under the Sherman Law. At no time in the earlier history of this law had there been a strong disposition to test its merit, and no one of the notorious trusts had been attacked before the Northern Securities case. In later years it was turned against the Standard Oil Company, the beef-packers, the Tobacco Trust, the Sugar Trust, and the United States Steel Corporation, while railways and smaller corporations, in great number, were prosecuted. The enforcement of the law aroused blind opposition among many of the victims, and stimulated queries as to whether or not any attempt to limit the size of business was sound public policy. The debate upon regulation, as against prohibition of trusts and monopolies, ran on with no sign of victory for either side of the argument. Personal hostility against the Administration for applying the law gave color to the last two years of Roosevelt's Administration.

By 1907 there had been ten years of the prosperity that had begun with the election of McKinley. Finance had developed with industry and trade. The needs of corporations dealing in millions and hundreds of millions of capital had induced the consolidation of banks and the concentration of financial power in the hands of a small group of men. The holding companies were great aids in the furtherance of this concentration. J. Pierpont Morgan and John D. Rockefeller were best known as representative of the inner circle. Their speculations and investments were embarrassed by the weakening of public confidence. It was certain there would come a time when the whole surplus capital of the United States would be invested in permanent improvements. Such periods had followed eras of boom in 1837, 1857, and

1873. It was too probable that some accident occurring in the period of liquidation would create a panic. Suspicion had been directed against the controlling agents of business by the revelations of 1902–07. It was exaggerated by sensational journalism. It reached a climax in the fall of 1907 when a group of banks, reputed strong, failed through dishonesty and speculative management. The failure of the Mercantile National Bank and the suspension of the Knickerbocker Trust Company in New York brought the crisis on October 22, 1907. The loss to the public was lessened by resolute and sympathetic coöperation among the clearing-houses, Morgan, Rockefeller, and the United States Treasury, but a period of enforced economy was begun for all.

The managers of big business attributed the panic to "Theodore the Meddler." They claimed that business was sound and honest, and the upheaval was caused by the agitation of demagogues. The President, they asserted, had destroyed confidence by his attack on the commercial class. Federal prosecutions, new laws, and the enforcement of inquisitorial pure-food regulations had made it impossible for business to live. "Let us alone," they cried.

They convinced only themselves, a small minority of the people of the United States. Since 1902 the people as a body, regardless of the great parties, had opened their eyes to the trend of business and had decided that public authority must be summoned to the defense of democracy. The independent vote broke away from each party in increasingly numerous cases. The old American view that democracy meant unrestrained individualism had given way to the newer view that democratic opportunity was dependent upon the restriction of monopoly. The ostensible leaders, from the President down, were only the mouths that spoke the new language. Without them the same condition would have existed in large degree. The attack of the financial interests and Wall Street upon the President only convinced the people that the Roosevelt policies were, on the whole, their policies, and that individual interest and party machinery must give way to their attainment.

BIBLIOGRAPHICAL NOTE

The periodicals and special articles alluded to in this chapter constitute the best sources as yet available for the period. There were numerous investigations by committees of Congress that furnished facts in their reports. Certain of the departments of government, notably the Bureau of Corporations and the Department of Agriculture, were active in the publication of facts. Thoughtful surveys of society in the United States may be found in E. A. Ross, *Changing America* (1912); H. Croly, *The Promise of American Life* (1909); A. B. Hart, *National Ideals Historically Traced* (in *The American Nation*, vol. 26, 1907). The autobiography of R. M. LaFollette is of considerable value. A great number of books upon America by foreign visitors bring out special viewpoints. Among these are F. Klein, *In the Land of the Strenuous Life* (1905); A. Bennett, *Your United States* (1912) ; W. Archer, *America To-Day* (1899); Anon., *As a Chinaman Saw Us* (1904); and James Bryce has revised and brought down to date his *American Commonwealth*.

CHAPTER XX

NEW NATIONALISM

THE process of adjusting national administration and laws, to meet the needs of life and business that knew no state lines, had been begun during the Roosevelt period. For its completion it was necessary that a successor be found, convinced of the Roosevelt policies and able to carry them out. Three Republicans of this type were often mentioned for the Presidency in 1908. Elihu Root had been the legal mainstay of three administrations, and had received the public commendation of Roosevelt often and without restraint. His availability for the elective office was, however, weakened by his prominence as a corporation lawyer, which would be urged against him in a campaign. William H. Taft, Secretary of War, had a wider popularity than Root; had, as federal judge, long been identified with the enforcement of law, and had been used repeatedly as the spokesman of the President. He knew the colonies as no other American knew them, and was in touch with every detail of the Panama Canal. Neither he nor Root had won a leadership in competitive politics as had the third candidate, Charles E. Hughes, who, as Governor of New York, had shown his capacity to fight professional politicians on their own ground.

In 1907, President Roosevelt announced his preference for Judge Taft, and fought off, as he had often done, suggestions that he accept another term himself. He controlled the Republican convention at Chicago, where his candidate was nominated on the first ballot. A Republican Representative from New York, James S. Sherman, was nominated for the Vice-Presidency, and the party leaders were driven to a platform of enthusiastic indorsement of the Roosevelt policies.

The Democratic party, meeting at Denver in 1908, was again under the control of the radical element, and nominated William J. Bryan for the third time. The career of Roosevelt had modified the emphasis of the Bryan reforms. " Any Republican who, after following Roosevelt, should object to Bryan as a radical, would simply be laughed at consumedly," said one of the weeklies. In the ensuing campaign both candidates professed ends that were nearly identical, and their advocates were forced to explain whether the Roosevelt policies would have a better chance under Bryan or Taft. There was no clear issue, and in each party there was a powerful minority that wanted neither of the candidates. The election of Taft had been discounted throughout the campaign, but it was accompanied by a demonstration of independent voting that revealed the weakness of party ties. Four Democratic governors were elected in States that were carried by the Republican national ticket.

The Administration of President Taft was greeted with cordial good will by the progressive elements in both parties. His courage and sincerity had never been questioned. Roosevelt was unlimited in his praise. His judicial training made impossible for him types of political activity that had made. enemies for his predecessor among many conservatives, yet his devotion to policies of administrative reform was beyond dispute. He immediately fulfilled one pledge of the Republican platform by summoning Congress to meet on March 15, 1909, to revise the tariff, and on this subject he had for several years avowed a desire that revision should be downward, to remove all trace of special tariff privilege.

The movement for tariff reform had begun in the Middle West about 1902, and had spread with the feeling against the trusts. Roosevelt had indicated a sympathy with it in 1902 and 1903, and had fought Congress for tariff modification in the interest of Cuban reciprocity. But most of the party leaders had opposed tampering with the protective system. Speaker Cannon was an avowed protectionist and defended the attitude of the stand-pat tariff advocates. After 1904 the President had ceased to discuss the tariff, confining himself to other schemes for reform. He left the problem of revision to his successor.

The tariff of 1909 bore the names of Sereno E. Payne, of New York, chairman of the House Committee of Ways and Means, and Nelson W. Aldrich, chairman of the Senate Committee on Finance. As it passed the House it embodied numerous reductions from the Dingley rates. In the Senate it was reframed and became an instrument of even greater protection than the existing law. It was debated in a stronger glare of public interest than any other tariff, and its details were explained and fought by a group of Republicans who refused to accept the control of the inner circle of the party, and who were determined that the revision should be downward and sincere. They did less to affect the bill, however, than President Taft, who forced the conference committee to accept a few reductions in the rates, notably on hides and lumber, and to include a provision for levying an income tax on corporations. A constitutional amendment, authorizing a general income tax, was a part of the agreement. The bill became a law in August, 1909. " The bill, in its final form," said the *Outlook*, which inclined toward free trade, "is by far the most enlightened protectionist measure ever enacted in the history of the country." " I think that the present tariff," wrote Roosevelt, who had returned to private life, "is better than the last, and considerably better than the one before the last."

Whatever its relation to earlier tariffs the Payne-Aldrich Act was distasteful to the country, which had since 1897 become critical of the methods of tariff legislation. Seven Republican Senators and twenty Representatives voted against it on its final passage. These represented the Middle West and the new generation, and returned home to find their constituents generally with them in denouncing the measure as an instrument of privilege. Some of them had broken with President Taft during the debate, and the breach was deepened when the latter spoke in the West, at Winona, Minnesota, and defended the act as a compliance with the party pledge. It became apparent that the new President was unable to procure party legislation and to maintain at the same time an appearance of harmony in the party. Roosevelt had dissatisfied but had overriden the conservative wing; Taft failed to satisfy the most progressive wing and failed to silence them.

In the autumn of 1909 began a series of administrative misunderstandings that greatly embarrassed the Taft Administration. A prospective minister to China was dismissed abruptly before he left the United States, on account of a supposed indiscretion. In the Department of Agriculture there was dissension between the Secretary, James Wilson, and the chemist engaged in the enforcement of the Pure Food Law, Harvey W. Wiley. The chief of the forestry service, Gifford Pinchot, quarreled openly with the Secretary of the Interior, Richard A. Ballinger, and raised the question of the future of the policy of conservation.

The work of the forestry and reclamation services was at the center of the scheme for conservation of natural resources that had grown out of Roosevelt's conference with the governors in 1908. A subordinate of the forestry service attacked the Secretary of the Interior in 1909, charging favoritism and lack of interest in conservation. He was dismissed in September, upon order of President Taft, whereupon *Collier's Weekly* undertook an attack upon the President as an enemy of conservation, receiving the moral support of many of the progressives who disliked the tariff act. In January, 1910, the growing controversy led the President to dismiss Pinchot from the service, for insubordination, and Congress to erect a joint committee to investigate the Pinchot-Ballinger dispute.

The Ballinger committee ultimately vindicated the Secretary of the Interior, but the testimony taken brought out a fundamental difference between the theory of Taft, that the President could act only in accordance with the law, and that of Roosevelt, that he could do whatever was not forbidden by law. Although Taft stood by his subordinate, claiming that he and Ballinger were both active in conservation, a large section of the public believed that the aggressive movement for reform had lost momentum. What Roosevelt thought of it was impossible to learn, since he had gone to Africa in 1909, and remained outside the sphere of American politics until the summer of 1910.

The progressive Republicans revolted in 1909 and 1910 against the domination of the "stand-pat" group, and received the name "Insurgents." Senators LaFollette and Cummins, both of whom desired to be President, were the avowed leaders. In the House of Representatives, in March, 1910, the Insurgents coöperated with the Democratic minority, defeated a ruling of Speaker Cannon, and modified the House rules in order to curtail the autocracy of the presiding officer. They asked the country to believe that Taft had ceased to be progressive and had become the ally of the stand-pat interests. The split in the Republican party enabled the Democrats to carry the country in 1910, and to obtain a large majority in the House of Representatives. Champ Clark, of Missouri, and Oscar Underwood, of Ala-

bama, both aspirants for the Democratic presidential nomination, became, respectively, Speaker and
chairman of the Committee on Ways and Means in the
new House. No one man controlled or led either party
by his personality as Theodore Roosevelt had done;
the rivalry of lesser leaders destroyed the harmony
of both parties, and neither party even approached
unanimity in regard to the great policies of the future. In January, 1911, the Insurgent Republicans organized a Progressive Republican League
for the purpose of capturing the nomination in
1912 for one of their number, presumably Senator
LaFollette.

The Taft policies differed from those of his predecessor chiefly in the method of their advocacy.
Like Roosevelt, Taft had trouble in getting them
enacted, and unlike Roosevelt, he failed to magnet-
ize the people and carry them with him. He procured, however, funds for the creation of a board of
tariff experts to aid in future revisions of schedules,
and for a commerce court, to handle appeals in interstate commerce cases. The income tax amendment
secured his support. He used his influence to prevent the seating of William Lorimer, a Senator
elected from Illinois under conditions of grave scandal. The Interstate Commerce Law was revised and
strengthened in 1910. An enabling act for Arizona
and New Mexico was passed in 1910, under which
both of these Territories became States in 1912. He
continued the series of anti-trust suits begun under
Roosevelt, and procured decisions ordering the dissolution of the Southern Pacific merger, the Stand-

ard Oil Company, and the Tobacco Trust, and the penalizing of many others.

In the field of administration President Taft showed an instinct for orderly and economical government. He urged upon Congress the adoption of a budget system for expenditures, and employed a body of experts to aid in reducing the cost and inefficiency of the executive departments. He extended the civil service until in 1912 only 56,000 of the 334,000 federal employees were still outside the classified service.

The foreign negotiations of the Taft Administration were most distinguished in respect to Latin-American trade, to arbitration, to neutrality, and to reciprocity. With the Latin-Americas he continued the policy of friendly support, through Philander C. Knox, his Secretary of State. The critics of this policy stigmatized it as "dollar diplomacy," but Taft and Knox defended it as leading these republics through sound finance to stable government. A protracted revolution in Mexico led to the expulsion of President Porfirio Diaz in 1911, and was followed by counter-revolutions in 1912. Throughout the disturbance Taft maintained a rigid neutrality, and induced Congress to permit him to prohibit the export of arms for sale to the belligerents. This constituted an advance upon the customary practice of neutrals, who are permitted under international law to sell munitions of war to either belligerent.

In 1908, Roosevelt had signed general arbitration treaties with Great Britain and other countries, containing the usual reservations of cases involving

honor or national existence. In 1911, Taft signed
yet broader treaties with Great Britain and France,
providing for the arbitration of all justiciable disputes, and for a commission to determine whether
disputed cases were justiciable or not. The Senate
declined to ratify these agreements.

Canadian reciprocity was a part of Taft's tariff
program. In 1911, he called Congress in special
session to approve an agreement for a modification
of the Payne-Aldrich rates with Canada. The Democratic majority in the House of Representatives supported this measure, as did enough of the regular
Republicans to insure its passage. But the Insurgents opposed it as likely to injure the interests of
the farmer. In September, 1911, Canada rejected
the whole measure after a general election in which
a fear of annexation by the United States was an
important motive.

The Taft policies failed to thrill the party or the
people. They were less spectacular than the evils
which the muck-rakers had portrayed. They were
constructive and detailed, and aroused as opponents
many who had joined in the general clamor for reform. They interested the party leaders little, for
these were more concerned with their own personal
fates, and were not overshadowed by the President
as they had been for eight preceding years. They
were all conceived in the spirit of a lawyer and judge,
and were passed in an alliance with the wing of the
Republican party that was most impervious to the
new reforms, and were hence open to the attack that
they were in spirit and intent reactionary.

In June, 1910, with the Republican schism well advanced, Theodore Roosevelt returned to the United States. A few weeks later he made a speaking trip in the West, and at Osawatomie, Kansas, he laid down a platform of reform that he called "New Nationalism." This was in substance an evolution from the history of forty years. It assumed the fact of the development of business and society along national lines, and demanded that the Government meet the new problems. It believed that constitutional power already existed for most of the needed functions of government, and demanded that where the power was lacking it should be obtained by constitutional amendment. The platform was received with equally violent commendation and attack. Many Progressives hailed it as an exposition of their faith. Conservatives were prone to call it socialistic or revolutionary. It restored Roosevelt to a position of consequence in public affairs, and emphasized the fact that Taft had developed no power of popular leadership comparable to that of his friend and predecessor. It gave the Progressives hope that Roosevelt, debarred from the Presidency by his pledge and by the unwritten third-term tradition, would aid them in forcing the Republican party to nominate a Progressive in 1912.

The concrete principles of the Progressive group embraced a series of policies looking toward the destruction of ring-controlled politics. They demanded and generally concurred in the initiative and referendum, the direct primary, and the direct election of delegates to national conventions, and the direct election of United States Senators. Many of them believed in a new doctrine, the recall, which was to be applied to administrative officials, to judges, and even to judicial decisions. Woman suffrage was commonly acceptable to them.

The cause of woman suffrage had made great progress since Idaho became, in 1896, the fourth suffrage State. A modified form of suffrage in local or school elections had been allowed in many States. A new period of agitation for unrestricted woman suffrage had begun in England about 1906, and had been given advertisement by the deliberate violations of law and order by the militant suffragettes. The agitation, though not the excess, had spread to the United States. In 1910, Washington, and in 1911, California, had become woman suffrage States. By 1914, the total was raised to twelve by the addition of Arizona, Kansas, Oregon, Illinois,[1] Nevada, and Montana.

In the winter of 1911–12, the prospect of Republican success in the next national campaign was slight. The Democrats had gained the House in 1910, and they, with the aid of Progressive Republican votes, had passed and sent up to the President several tariff bills, reducing the rates, schedule by schedule. Every one of these had been vetoed, each veto tending to convince the Progressives that Taft was conservative, if not stand-pat in his sentiments. The Progressive Republicans were pledged to work against the renomination of Taft, and were unlikely

[1] In Illinois the right was somewhat restricted, yet included the voting for presidential electors and for local officials.

to support him vigorously, if renominated. Many regular Republicans believed he could not be re-elected. The section of the party that desired a Progressive President became larger than the group that believed in LaFollette, and demands that Roosevelt return were heard from many sources.

In February, 1912, an appeal signed by seven Republican governors, all of whom dwelt in States now likely to go Democratic, urged Roosevelt to withdraw his pledge and become a candidate for the nomination. The demand was concurred in by admirers who believed that only he could bring about the new nationalism, by Progressives who distrusted LaFollette's capacity to win, and by Republicans who wanted to win at any price and saw only defeat through Taft. On February 24, Roosevelt announced his willingness to accept the nomination, explained that his previous refusal to accept another term had meant another consecutive term, and entered upon a canvass for delegates to the Republican National Convention.

The campaign before the primaries was made difficult because in most States the Republican machinery was in the hands of politicians who disliked Roosevelt, whether they cared for Taft or not. It began too late for the voters to overturn the state and national committees, or to register through the existing party machinery their new desire. It brought out the defects in methods of nomination which direct primaries were expected to remedy, and in some States public opinion was strong enough to compel a hasty passage of primary laws to permit the overturn of the convention system. The LaFollette candidacy was deprived of most of its supporters, through the superior popularity of Roosevelt.

When the convention met at Chicago on June 18, 1912, there were some 411 Roosevelt delegates among the 1078, and more than 250 more who, though instructed for Taft, were contested by Roosevelt delegations. When the national committee overruled the claims of these, Roosevelt denounced their action as "naked theft." He had definitely allied himself with the wing of the party that opposed Taft. When the convention, presided over by Elihu Root, and supported by nearly all the men whom Roosevelt had brought into public prominence, finally renominated Taft and Sherman, Roosevelt asserted that no honest man could vote for a ticket based upon dishonor. The Roosevelt Republicans did not bolt the convention, but when it adjourned they held a mass convention of their own, were addressed by their candidate, and went home to organize a new Progressive party.

The Democratic counsels were affected by the break-up of the Republican party and the success of its conservative wing at Chicago. They met at Baltimore the next week, with Bryan present and active, but not himself a candidate. They had to choose among Clark, the Speaker, Underwood, the chairman of the Committee on Ways and Means, and Governors Harmon, of Ohio, Marshall, of Indiana, and Woodrow Wilson, of New Jersey.

The last of these had risen into national politics since 1910. He had long been known as a brilliant essayist and historian. He was of Virginian birth, and had left the presidency of Princeton University to become Democratic candidate for Governor of New Jersey in 1910. He had shown as governor great capacity to lead his party in the direction of the progressive reforms. He differed in these less from Roosevelt and LaFollette than he or they did from the reactionaries in their own parties. " The President is at liberty, both in law and conscience," he had written long ago, " to be as big a man as he can. His capacity will set the limit. . . . He has no means of compelling Congress except through public opinion." Unembarrassed by previous attachment to any faction of the Democratic party, with a clear record against special privilege and corporation influence in politics, and supported obstinately by Bryan and the young men who had urged his candidacy, Woodrow Wilson was nominated on the forty-sixth ballot, with Governor Thomas Marshall for Vice-President. The conservative nomination by the Republicans had thrown the Democrats into the hands of their radical wing.

The Progressives held a convention in Chicago on August 5, and nominated Theodore Roosevelt and Governor Hiram Johnson, of California. Their platform included every important reform seriously urged, and was built around the idea of social justice and human rights. They denied that either of the old parties was fitted to carry on the work of progress. In the campaign their candidates and speakers revealed the vigor and the bitterness of the former Insurgents.

The schism threw the election into the hands of the Democrats, who retained the House, gained the Senate, and elected Wilson, though the latter received fewer votes than Bryan had received in each of his three attempts. The struggle was one of personalities, since few openly attacked the avowed aim of progressive legislation. The popularity of Roosevelt detached many Democratic votes from Wilson, but his unpopularity among Republicans who feared him and Progressive Republicans who resented his return to politics, drove to Wilson votes that would otherwise have gone to Taft. Taft received only eight electoral votes in November, and ran far behind both his rivals in the popular count. More than four million votes were polled by the new third party in an independent movement that was without precedent. The Socialist vote for Debs rose from 420,000 in 1908 to 895,000 in 1912.

The last year of the administration of President Taft was overshadowed by the party war, and reduced in effectiveness by the Democratic control of the House. The prosecutions of the trusts were continued, a parcel post was established as a postal savings bank had been, the income tax amendment became part of the Constitution, and an amendment for the direct election of Senators made progress.

When Woodrow Wilson succeeded to the Presidency he formed a cabinet headed by William J. Bryan as Secretary of State, and including only Democrats of progressive antecedents. He called Congress in April, 1913, to revise the tariff once more, and overturned a precedent of a century by

delivering to it his message in person. With almost
no breathing space for eighteen months, he kept
Congress at its task of fulfilling his party's pledges
as he interpreted them.

Tariff, currency, and trust control were the main
topics upon which the Democrats had avowed positive convictions, and upon which the great mass of
progressive citizens, regardless of party affiliation,
demanded legislation. One by one these were taken
up, the President revealing powers of coercive leadership hitherto unseen in his office. Only the fact
that non-partisan opinion was generally with him
made possible the mass of constructive legislation
that was placed upon the books. The tariff, which
became a law on October 3, 1913, was a revision
whose downward tendency was beyond dispute. The
Federal Reserve Act, revising the banking laws in
the interest of flexibility and decentralization, was
signed on December 23 of the same year. In January, 1914, President Wilson laid before Congress
his plan of trust control, advocating a commission
with powers over trade coördinate with those of the
Interstate Commerce Commission, and an elaboration of the anti-trust laws to deal with unfair practices and interlocking directorates. The Federal
Trade Commission and Clayton Anti-Trust bills fulfilled these recommendations in the autumn of 1914.
The Panama Canal Act of 1912 had meanwhile
been revised so as to eliminate a preference in rates
to American vessels which the President believed to
be in violation of the guaranty of equal treatment
pledged in the Hay-Pauncefote Treaty. With a more

portentous list of constructive laws than had been
passed by any Congress since 1890, the Democratic
majority allowed an adjournment on October 24,
1914, and its members went home to sound their
constituents upon the state of the Union.

The passage of economic laws had called for tact
and force upon the part of the President, whose
party, like the Republican party, was without a clear
vision of its policy and included many reactionaries.
Added embarrassments were found in the continuance of civil strife in Mexico. Here, shortly before
the inauguration of President Wilson, there had
been another revolution, followed by the elevation
by the army of General Victoriano Huerta to the
Presidency. The followers of the deposed Madero
went into revolt at once, and the new Government
was refused recognition by the United States on the
ground that it was not a Government *de facto*, and
that its title was smirched with blood. Patiently and
stubbornly the United States held to its refusal to
recognize the results of conspiracy in Mexico. In
April, 1914, Vera Cruz was occupied by American
forces in retaliation for acts of insult on the part of
the Huerta régime, and in July the steady pressure
of "watchful waiting" brought about the resignation of the dictator. The Constitutionalists, succeeding him, quarreled shortly among themselves, but
the danger from Mexico appeared to be lessening as
the year advanced.

From Europe came other embarrassments in August. Here, the policy of national armament which
had been adopted i the middle of the nineteenth

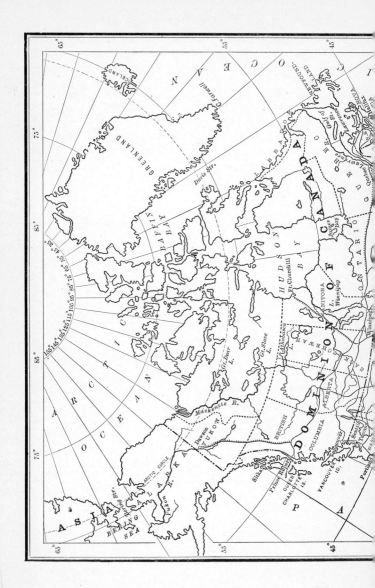

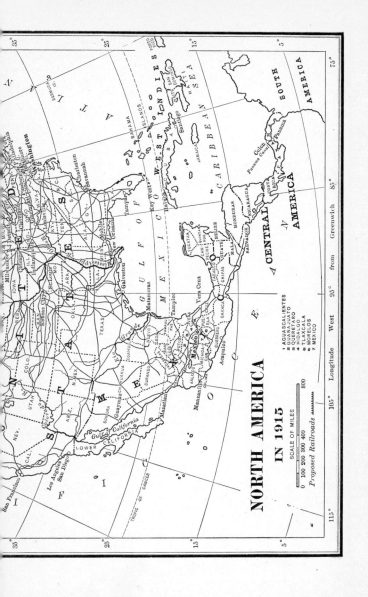

NORTH AMERICA
IN 1915

SCALE OF MILES
0 100 200 300 400   800
Proposed Railroads ══════

1 AGUASCALIENTES
2 GUANAJUATO
3 QUERETARO
4 HIDALGO
5 TLAXCALA
6 MORELOS
7 MEXICO

Longitude   West   from   Greenwich

century, reached its logical outcome in a great war which was precipitated by Austria in an attack upon Servia. Russia immediately came to the aid of her Slavonic kinsmen, and upon her Germany declared war on August 1. In a few more days Great Britain and France had joined Russia against the German-Austrian alliance, and most of Europe was at war. To bring home the thousands of American tourists whom the war had reduced to suffering was the first work of the administration. The American ministers in Europe became the custodians of the affairs of the belligerents in every enemy country, and with the aid of all the belligerent nations Americans were carried home. After this came the problems of neutrality and American business. Suffering, due to the stoppage of the export trade, particularly that of cotton, brought wide depression throughout the United States. A new law for the transfer of foreign-built vessels to American registry, and another for federal insurance against war risks, were hurriedly passed, and the question of a public-owned line of merchant ships was discussed. All these problems were distracting the attention of the United States when Congress brought to an end its prolonged labors, and adjourned.

The congressional election of 1914 was profoundly affected by the European war. Early in the year it appeared that conservative opposition to the Democratic program was growing, and that the Democratic majority was likely to be cut down. The Progressive party appeared to be weakening, and the control of the Republican party was settling back among those

Republicans against whom the Insurgents had made their protest. But President Wilson's precise neutrality won the confidence of all parties, and although conservatives like Cannon, of Illinois, and Penrose, of Pennsylvania, won over Democrats and Progressives alike in a few cases, he retained for the Sixty-fourth Congress a working majority in the House and an enlarged majority in the Senate. His election in 1912 had been, in part, due to the dispersion of Republican strength caused by the Progressive schism; in 1914, the influence of the Progressives was negligible and the Democrats retained their power in the face of the whole Republican attack.

BIBLIOGRAPHICAL NOTE

Between 1909 and 1914, the *Outlook*, to which Theodore Roosevelt had been an occasional contributor, and which had been a strong supporter of Republican policies since 1898, was the regular organ through which Mr. Roosevelt addressed the public, over his signature as Contributing Editor. In a similar way William J. Bryan reached his followers through the *Commoner* (1900–), and Robert M. LaFollette through his *LaFollette's Weekly* (1909–). *Collier's Weekly* became a center of the adverse criticism of President Taft. All of these, as well as the more general periodicals, are indispensable sources for the period, but are so highly partisan as to need constant correction for prejudice. The election of 1908 is treated in Stanwood's *History of the Presidency from 1897 to 1909*, while that of 1912 is excellently described in the *New International Year Book* for 1912. The theories of the new nationalism are in T. Roosevelt, *The New Nationalism* (1910).

INDEX

The Riverside Press

CAMBRIDGE . MASSACHUSETTS

U . S . A